PERSPECTIVES ON POVERTY IN INDIA

PERSPECTIVES ON POVERTY IN INDIA

Stylized Facts from Survey Data

THE WORLD BANK
Washington, D.C.

ISBN: 978-0-8213-8689-7
eISBN: 978-0-8213-8728-3
DOI: 10.1596/978-0-8213-8689-7

Library of Congress Cataloging-in-Publication Data have been requested.

Cover design: Naylor Design

Contents

Figures

Maps

Tables

Acknowledgments

This book was prepared by a team led by Peter Lanjouw and Rinku Murgai (principal coauthors), under the overall guidance of Ernesto May, N. Roberto Zagha, and Miria Pigato. Core team members include Tara Vishwanath and Nobuo Yoshida, on poverty map estimation and analysis; Ericka Rascon, on poverty map analysis and inequality; Jishnu Das and Puja Vasudeva Dutta, on nonincome dimensions of poverty; and Maitreyi Das and Soumya Kapoor, on social exclusion. Pinaki Joddar provided research assistance. Administrative support was provided by Shiny Jaison, Rita Soni, and Jyoti Sriram. This report has been prepared alongside a parallel World Bank report on poverty and social exclusion in India led by Maitreyi Das. The two reports have a few common team members and often drew on common material.

We gratefully acknowledge financial support from the United Kingdom Department for International Development World Bank trust fund to carry out background research. Background papers prepared for the book include works by the following: Gaurav Datt and Martin Ravallion, on the relationship between poverty reduction and growth; Angus Deaton (Professor, Princeton University), on price trends in India and their implications for measuring poverty; Himanshu (Assistant Professor, Jawaharlal Nehru University), on nonfarm employment; Amaresh Dubey (Professor, Jawaharlal Nehru University), on estimates of poverty and inequality from the 2004–05 India Human Development Survey; Benjamin Crost (University of California, Berkeley), Alain de Janvry (Professor, University of California, Berkeley), and Elisabeth Sadoulet (Professor, University of California, Berkeley), on income disparities in India; Stefan Dercon (Professor, University of Oxford) and Sonya Krutikova (University of Oxford), on welfare dynamics, using International Crops Research Institute for the Semi-Arid Tropics data; Devesh Kapur (Director, Center for the Advanced Study of India, University of Pennsylvania) and Jeffrey Witsoe (Visiting Scholar, Center for the Advanced Study of India, University of Pennsylvania), on a case study of migration from rural Bihar; and Maitreyi Das, Gillett Hall (Visiting Professor,

Georgetown University), Soumya Kapoor, and Denis Nikitin (independent consultant), on tribal issues.

We thank peer reviewers Abhijit Sen (Member, Planning Commission, and Professor, Jawaharlal Nehru University), Nicholas Stern (IG Patel Chair and Director, LSE Asia Research Centre), and Salman Zaidi (World Bank), and participants at Ministry of Finance, Planning Commission, and World Bank seminars for their comments. The team received valuable guidance from Stephen Howes (Professor, Australian National University).

The report has been discussed with the Government of India but does not necessarily bear their approval for all its contents, especially where the Bank has stated its judgment, opinion, or policy recommendations.

Abbreviations

ASER	Annual State of Education Report
CBD	community-based development
CDD	community-driven development
DHS	Demographic and Health Surveys
DISE	District Information System for Education
GDP	gross domestic product
GE	General Entropy class
GIC	growth incidence curves
HCR	head-count rate
MUS	Muslims
NAS	National Accounts Statistics
NCAER	National Council of Applied Economic Research
NCERT	National Council on Educational Research and Training
NCEUS	National Commission on Enterprises in the Unorganized Sector
NFHS	National Family Health Surveys
NNMB	National Nutrition Monitoring Bureau
NSDP	net state domestic product
NSS	National Sample Surveys
OBC	other backward caste

PESA   Panchayat (Extension to Scheduled Areas) Act

PPP   purchasing power parity

SC   scheduled castes

SPG   squared poverty gap index

ST   scheduled tribes

Executive Summary

This report's objective is to develop the evidence base for policy making in relation to poverty reduction. It produces a diagnosis of the broad nature of the poverty problem and its trends in India, focusing on both consumption poverty and human development outcomes. It also includes attention in greater depth to three pathways important to inclusive growth and poverty reduction—harnessing the potential of urban growth to stimulate rural-based poverty reduction, rural diversification away from agriculture, and tackling social exclusion.

India has maintained steady progress in reducing poverty as measured by consumption. Using the Government of India's official poverty lines, in 2004–05, 28 percent of people in rural areas and 26 percent of people in urban areas lived below the poverty line, down from 47 percent and 42 percent, respectively, in 1983. Improvements in the last two decades represent a continuation of a long-term secular decline of both urban and rural poverty under way in India since the 1970s. At this pace, acceleration of progress against poverty since economic reforms began in earnest in the early 1990s is suggested, but it is too early to say that that is a (statistically) robust new trend.

Data issues cloud our assessment of whether the growth process has become more or less pro-poor in the postreform period. Poverty has declined and growth has tended to reduce poverty, including in the postreform period. However, the data present no robust case for saying that the responsiveness of poverty to growth has either increased or decreased since the early 1990s. The main source of data uncertainty is the large and growing gap in mean consumption per person found by the household surveys and by the national accounts. With the available evidence, it seems likely that the surveys are missing the growth in top-end incomes and, therefore, do a better job of measuring poverty than inequality or aggregate growth. High premium should be placed on better understanding and resolving the sources of discrepancy between India's national surveys and the national accounts.

New drivers of poverty reduction—urban growth and nonfarm growth—have emerged since the 1990s. Historical evidence in India from the 1970s to the early 1990s has shown agricultural growth to be a major factor in reducing poverty. Indeed, for decades, poverty reduction in India has been synonymous with rural and, in particular, agricultural growth. But since the 1990s agriculture has lagged other sectors, shrinking in its contribution to less than half of rural GDP. That poverty reduction has continued apace despite a slowdown in agriculture points to the emergence of new drivers of poverty reduction. This report draws on survey evidence to identify two—urban growth and nonfarm growth.

Since the 1990s, urban growth has reduced urban poverty as before, but evidence is now appearing of a much stronger link from urban growth to rural poverty as well. With nearly three-quarters of India's poor residing in rural areas, any driver that does not affect the rural poor is unlikely to make a significant dent in Indian poverty. This report shows that urban growth, which has increasingly outpaced growth in rural areas, has helped to reduce poverty for urban residents directly. In addition, evidence appears of a much stronger link from urban economic growth to rural (and therefore overall) poverty reduction. Stronger links with rural poverty are due to a more integrated economy. Urban areas are a demand hub for rural producers, as well as a source of employment for the rural labor force. They are aiding the transformation of the rural economy out of agriculture. In urban areas, it is small and medium-size towns, rather than large cities, that appear to demonstrate the strongest urban-rural growth links. Urban growth also stimulates rural-urban migration. But although some increase in such migration has occurred over time, migration levels in India remain relatively low compared to other countries.

The process of rural transformation out of agriculture toward the nonfarm sector is assuming a greater role in reducing Indian poverty. Between 1993–94 and 2004–05, rural nonfarm employment has grown about four times as fast as farm employment, and more rural jobs have been created off-farm than on. The fact that even the lowest-paid nonfarm jobs—casual wage employment—on average, pay considerably more than those in agriculture (the wage premium is about 45 percent) suggests that the growth of the nonfarm sector is likely to have been poverty reducing. Nonfarm employment also reduces rural poverty indirectly by driving up agricultural wages. Agricultural wage growth in the 1990s slowed; the analysis shows that in the absence of labor market tightening due to the nonfarm sector, agricultural wage growth would have been slower still.

Continued debate about the appropriate sectoral focus for poverty reduction efforts is warranted. Agriculture is still the employer of too many of India's poor (and especially the female and elderly poor) to be ignored, but urban growth and nonfarm rural employment deserve greater attention. The rural nonfarm sector as a sustainable source of poverty reduction will need close scrutiny—the quality of nonfarm employment has been falling in a trend toward growing "casualization" of the sector. Within the urban sector, large cities may well continue to drive India's growth. But as small and medium-size towns are home to 80 percent of India's urban poor, and given the strong links between such towns and rural areas, it is necessary to make sure that any barriers to small-town growth, or biases in policy stances that prevent small towns from realizing their potential, are eliminated. One place to look for such biases is in access to basic infrastructure services.

In contrast to consumption poverty, India's record on improving basic health and education indicators is mixed. Although some outcomes are improving, others remain stubborn and are worse for, but not confined to, the poor. Child undernutrition, in particular, remains extremely high, and improvements have been only half what would be expected given India's pace of GDP growth. In education, literacy rates are improving, and children are much more likely to be attending school. The most rapid improvements in school attendance are occurring among girls and children from poor households and in rural areas and relatively educationally backward states. But learning outcomes among Indian school children are very low, relative to their curriculum, and inequality in learning levels is high.

Inequality is on the rise and may be higher than often thought. Consumption inequality has fallen over the longer term in India but is now on the increase. Rural growth switched from being pro-poor (largely benefiting the poorer) between 1983 and 1993–94, to benefiting income groups equally between 1993–94 and 2004–05. In urban areas, over the same period, growth went from being distributed equally, to favoring the rich—that is, the gap between the rich and the poor widened. And the gap between rural and urban areas also widened. The resulting moderate increase in inequality revealed in the survey data likely understates the increase in inequality as a result of underreporting of consumption at the top end.

Some types of inequality, but not all, are harmful for poverty reduction. Everything else being equal, a rise in inequality will dampen the poverty-reducing impact of an increase in mean incomes. But everything else is not equal, and some growth accelerations may not be possible without an increase in inequality. The recent experience of India might fall into such a category, as increasing returns to education are an important factor driving the rise in inequality. The growing importance of education fits exactly with a story of accelerating urban growth and a growing nonfarm sector, as the less the economy is dominated by agriculture, the more important education is. National accounts data also point to growing disparities between states, although the household survey data do not reveal similar patterns. Even so, other sources of inequality may be more structural in nature and may hold back participation of some groups in the development process.

Structural inequalities by caste, tribe, and gender are present and visible. Scheduled tribes are being left behind. Structural inequalities take different shapes in different parts of India. Overall, however, although multiple welfare indicators for scheduled castes and scheduled tribes are improving, the gap between them and the general population is large and persistent. Scheduled tribes today (2004–05) experience levels of poverty seen in the general population 20 years earlier (1983), while scheduled castes lag 10 years behind the general population. Female disadvantage in India continues, despite high rates of growth, and women die both in infancy and in motherhood, with poorer outcomes for women from scheduled castes and tribes. Economic and social outcomes for women are underpinned by low levels of security within and outside their home. Caste remains a potent indicator of labor market outcomes and social status, but positive signs of dynamism are also appearing within the caste hierarchy. Indicators that India's educational expansion is leaving scheduled tribes behind, especially at the secondary school and higher levels, are worrying. Scheduled tribes show the least improvement in intergenerational mobility in education and also display the worst indicators of child nutrition and mortality. Scheduled tribes appear to be at risk of becoming locked out of sharing in India's growth and prosperity.

Improving human development outcomes for the poor remains a key challenge for India. It is central to improving their income-earning opportunities and welfare. Given the recent record, it is simply not the case that continued rapid economic growth will automatically translate to commensurate improvements on human development outcomes. Our analysis of structural inequalities would, for instance, suggest a redoubling of efforts to retain scheduled tribe children in school past the primary level. At the same time, some problems, such as undernutrition and poor learning outcomes, are endemic and alarming and are not confined to the poor. That suggests that improving human development outcomes is not merely, or even primarily, an issue of better targeting of existing programs and services to the poor. Larger, and systemic, challenges of service delivery remain.

Overview

India's Poverty Challenge

India is a country of continental proportions, and poverty is a multidimensional phenomenon. Not surprisingly, the debate over poverty in India—its extent, trends, causes, and cure—is complex and controversial.

Fortunately, India also has a much higher quality and more substantial evidence base than most other countries for understanding poverty. Questions of poverty in India have engaged a large community of researchers over the years. But in recent decades, because difficult measurement issues have arisen, a disproportionate amount of attention has been devoted to assessments of the extent of poverty and the rate of poverty decline. Much less is known about how the rapidly changing economic landscape has altered the underlying profile of poverty—and how that affects the consequent search for its causes and cure. This report seeks to fill that gap.

We work with two objectives. The first is to produce a diagnosis of the broad nature of the poverty problem and its trends in India, relying primarily on household survey data. We focus on both consumption poverty and human development outcomes.[1] Second, we attempt a more detailed treatment of a subset of issues that have been identified as particularly important for achieving inclusive growth, a central objective of the Government's Eleventh Five-Year Plan. Sustained and rapid growth is a central component of any poverty reduction strategy. But the fact that the responsiveness of poverty reduction to economic growth has been uneven over time and across regions leads us to analyze potential pathways to make growth more inclusive. It is clearly not feasible to aim for an exhaustive treatment of all the myriad pathways that are likely to be of relevance in India. Instead, the focus in this second objective is on three key themes revealed in the diagnostic section to be important.

First, since the early 1990s, urban growth has emerged as a much more important driver of poverty reduction than in the past. Our analysis of urban poverty examines the specific nature and dimensions of urban poverty, focusing in particular on the role of small and medium-size conurbations in India, both as the urban subsector in which urban poverty is overwhelmingly concentrated and as a subsector that could potentially stimulate *rural-based* poverty reduction. Second, in rural areas we focus on the nature of transformation out of agriculture to the nonfarm economy. Stagnation in agriculture has been accompanied by dynamism in the nonfarm sector, but debate is vigorous about whether the growth seen has been a symptom of agrarian distress or a source of poverty reduction. Finally, alongside the accelerating economic growth and the highly visible transformation that is occurring in India's major cities, inequality is on the rise, raising concern that economic growth in India has bypassed significant segments of the population. The third theme, social exclusion, asks whether despite the dramatic growth, historically grounded inequalities along lines of caste, tribe, and gender have persisted.

It is not possible to tackle every poverty-related issue in a single report, and this report does not attempt to do so. It does not focus on the international (for example, the impact of globalization on poverty), class (the divide between landlords and tenants, for example), or sectoral dimensions (export industry and different manufacturing sectors, for example). The choice of focus must be made, and in this report, we select themes of clear importance for which a combination of data availability and analytical tractability offers some prospect of new insights.

The government has launched many initiatives that have a bearing on poverty, for example, in areas of rural infrastructure (Bharat Nirman), employment (National Rural Employment Guarantee Act), education (Sarva Shiksha Abhiyan), rural health (National Rural Health Mission), and urban infrastructure (National Urban Renewal Mission). Indeed, the task of poverty reduction is one on which almost every policy instrument of government has a bearing. The report does not focus on how specific government programs are working or how the current poverty situation reflects specific policy measures taken in the past. Its objective is to develop the evidence base for policy making in relation to poverty reduction. While the focus of the report is resolutely on descriptive analysis rather than on the articulation of policy recommendations, certain general policy directions and questions do emerge. They are summarized at the end of this overview.

The poverty reduction challenge facing India needs to be defined broadly. Our analysis argues against a narrow definition of the poverty reduction challenge confronting India. As discussed in chapter 1 and summarized in figure 1 below, little difference is evident in consumption levels between the poor and a large section of the middle class, especially in rural areas. The median rural person in India lives

Figure 1 India's Middle-Class Lives Barely or Not Far above India's Poverty Line, and Below International Poverty Lines, Especially in Rural Areas

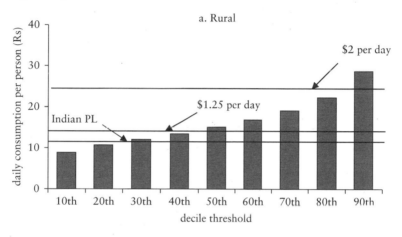

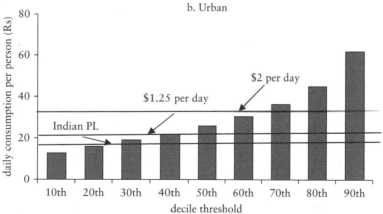

Source: Authors' estimates from NSS 2004–05 Schedule 1.0.

Note: Consumption estimates are in all-India rural or urban rupees and are corrected for cost-of-living differences between states using the official poverty lines. International poverty lines were converted to rupees using 2005 purchasing power parity rates of 11.4 Rs/$ in rural areas and 17.24 Rs/$ in urban areas.

on Rs 15 per day (with a purchasing power parity, or PPP, of $1.30), spending only Rs 3 each day more than a person on the official Indian rural poverty line. India's poverty line is very low by international standards, and 80 percent of the rural population lives below the median developing-country poverty line of Rs 22 (PPP $2) a day.[2] Qualitative surveys show that most Indians think of themselves as poor. Moreover, when the definition of poverty is expanded to include other dimensions of well-being, such as access to education, health care, and basic infrastructure, then poverty clearly continues to afflict more than half of India's population. Inequality is on the rise, raising concerns that India's history of social stratification may be excluding groups from the development process. For all these reasons, although a large portion of the report is devoted to analysis of households falling below India's official poverty line, the report also examines how outcomes are changing for the officially nonpoor.

The report is structured around three themes: consumption poverty and growth, human development, and inequality and social exclusion. Chapters 1 to 3 of the report analyze trends in consumption poverty in India and the links between it and the pattern of economic growth. Chapter 1 focuses on trends and patterns of poverty. Chapters 2 and 3 focus on two new drivers of poverty reduction in India: urban growth and rural nonfarm employment. Chapter 4 turns to the nonincome dimensions of poverty. It analyzes trends in relation to education and health, including nutrition. Chapter 5 examines and attempts to understand India's rising inequality. The final chapter examines disadvantaged groups, with a focus on women, scheduled castes, and scheduled tribes. This overview follows the same approach.

Poverty on the Decline

India has continued to record steady progress in reducing consumption poverty. Focusing on the experience of the last 20 years and using the official poverty lines, in 2004–05, 28 percent of people in rural areas and 26 percent of people in urban areas lived below the poverty line, down from 47 percent and 42 percent, respectively, in 1983 (figure 2). With population growth, however, it has proved difficult to reduce the number of poor at a comparably rapid pace. So despite India's success in bringing down its poverty rate, more than 300 million people remained in poverty in 2004–05.

Figure 2 Evolution of Poverty since the Early 1980s

Population below poverty line

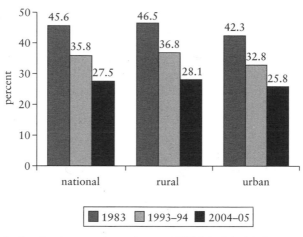

Source: Authors' estimates using unit-record NSS Schedule 1.0 data.
Note: Data based on uniform recall period consumption aggregates and official Planning Commission poverty lines.

Improvements in the last two decades represent a continuation of a long-term secular decline of both urban and rural poverty under way in India since the 1970s (figure 3). At this pace, accelerated progress against poverty since economic reforms began in earnest in the early 1990s is suggested, but it is too early to say that it is a (statistically) robust new trend.

Definitive views on the pace of poverty decline are hostage to data uncertainties. India's official poverty lines have been criticized on multiple counts and are in urgent need of an overhaul. The recent report of an expert group constituted by the Planning Commission (GoI 2009), which addresses the price index problems that currently plague comparability over time as well as comparisons between urban and rural areas, is a welcome step in that direction. Revision of official poverty lines and price indexes after due deliberation of the expert group's recommendations will help put poverty measurement on a sounder footing. The growing divergence shown in figure 4, between mean consumption per person from the National Sample Survey (NSS) and the private consumption component of the national accounts statistics (NAS), also per person, further confounds efforts to be definitive. In levels, aggregate household consumption implied by the NSS is barely half that of the household component of the NAS. Such a gap is unusually large by international standards. It is

Figure 3 Evolution of Poverty, 1951–2006

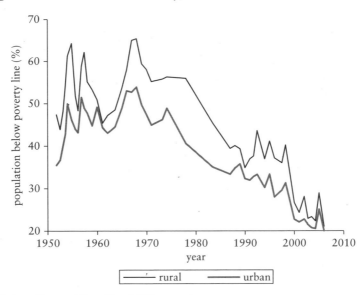

Source: Datt and Ravallion 2009.

Note: Data based on Datt-Ravallion poverty lines and annual rounds of NSS consumption data, except between 1978 and 1988 for which only four rounds of NSS data are available.

also notable that the NSS series does not reflect the large gains in mean consumption indicated by the NAS from the early 1990s on. Although the measurement issues cloud efforts to quantify the rate of poverty decline or to determine whether poverty reduction has accelerated over time, little doubt remains that poverty levels today are lower than they were in the past.

High premium should be placed on understanding the sources of discrepancy between the National Sample Survey and National Accounts Statistics estimates of consumption. Discrepancies such as these will also have implications for poverty and inequality measurement.[3] The extent of bias in poverty estimates depends on how much of the discrepancy is attributed to the NSS or the NAS. Choosing between the NSS and NAS is not easy and is well beyond the scope of this report. With the available evidence it is likely that surveys do a better job of measuring poverty than inequality. Getting to the bottom of, and resolving, sources of differences should be a priority for India's statistical system.

Growth has tended to reduce poverty. But problems with data cloud our assessment of whether the growth process has become

Figure 4 NSS and NAS Consumptions Are Diverging

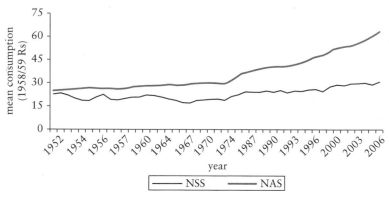

Source: Datt and Ravallion 2009.

more or less pro-poor in the postreform period. Per capita income growth has clearly picked up: per capita GDP grew by only about 1 percent in the 1960s and 1970s, at about 3 percent in the 1980s, and at about 4 percent to 5 percent after 1992. The evidence that growth has tended to reduce poverty, including in the postreform period, is also clear. However, the evidence on whether the responsiveness of poverty to growth increased or decreased in the postreform period is inconclusive. The answer depends crucially on whether one is talking about growth in mean household consumption, as measured in the surveys, or growth based on the national accounts. As it is, we do not see in the data a robust case for saying that the poverty elasticity has either risen or fallen.

The pattern of growth matters for the pace of poverty reduction. Agricultural growth, long considered the key driver of poverty reduction in India, has slowed. It appears that, in its effect on poverty reduction, the acceleration of nonagricultural growth has only been able to offset the reduction in agricultural growth, roughly speaking. (Note the rapid reduction in poverty shown in figure 1 for the 1970s refers to a period when aggregate growth was low but the Green Revolution was under way in agriculture.) Of course, if the growing discrepancy between the National Sample Surveys and the National Accounts Statistics shown in figure 4 is due to an underestimation by NSS of consumption among the poor as well as the rich, then the rate of poverty reduction after the 1990s might well be significantly underestimated. But on balance, the evidence points to the NSS underestimating the incomes of the rich rather than those of the poor.

Calorie poverty has not declined. Although consumption poverty has steadily declined in India, the number of people who actually consume calories above the minimum level associated with the poverty line—2,400 and 2,100 kilocalories per day in rural and urban areas, respectively—has not risen (figure 5). As of 2004–05, as many as 80 percent of rural households were estimated to be "calorie poor."

A possible explanation for this paradox is a shift in food preferences and reduced caloric requirements. Declining poverty, based on consumption expenditures, implies that India's households could buy more calories. The Indian poverty line was originally anchored in the amount that would enable minimum calorie needs to be met, if a household so chose. So why aren't households devoting incremental consumption spending to additional calories? There is tentative support for two reasons: First, some evidence is seen of a shift in food preferences from cheaper sources of calories toward more expensive foods. That is likely to be due to changes in incomes and relative food prices, as well as nonincome factors (such as exposure to new foods, imitation of consumption patterns of the wealthy, the influence of advertising, and changes induced by public policy). Second, calorie requirements may be less as a result of improvements in the public health environment. A number of developments over the last two decades also imply a decline in activity levels, particularly in rural areas, including greater mechanization of agricultural activities and domestic work, greater ownership of consumer durables, greater access to safe drinking water, and expansion of transportation networks.[4] In this regard, it is interesting to note that self-reported hunger has fallen. The share of individuals reporting inadequate food fell from 17.3 percent to 2.5 percent between 1983 and 2004–05 in rural areas.

Consistent with the decline in consumption poverty, communities also self-report improvements in well-being or declining perceived poverty. Improvements are seen not only in increases in incomes and purchasing power, but also in some education and health outcomes and an increase in personal freedom and choices (related to reduced dependence on patrons in rural areas and greater enterprise in urban areas).[5] In self-reported evaluations of well-being in the 2006 World Gallup Poll survey for India, half the respondents said that their life is "getting better." Only 12 percent felt that their lives have been getting worse over time (Srinivasan 2007).

Large differences in poverty levels persist across India's states and indeed are growing in urban areas. Figure 6 shows that rural areas of India's poorest states have poverty rates that are comparable to the highest anywhere in the developing world. In contrast, urban areas of Punjab and Himachal Pradesh have poverty rates that are

Figure 5 The Calorie-Income Puzzle: Declining
Calorie Consumption during a Period of Rising
Per Capita Expenditure

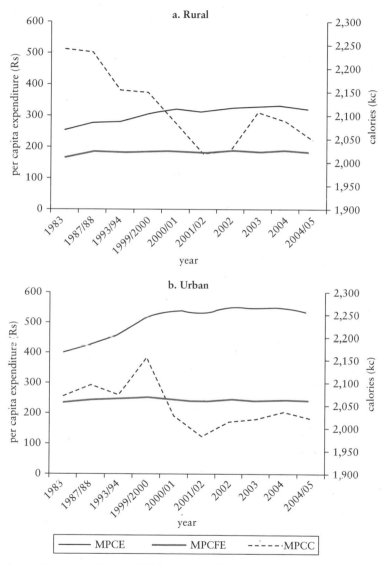

Source: Deaton and Drèze 2009, tables 1 and 2.
Note: MPCE = monthly per capita (total) expenditure; MPCFE = monthly per capita
food expenditure; MPCC = monthly per capita calorie consumption.

Figure 6 Poverty Rates in Indian States Span the Best in the Developing World to the Worst

percent

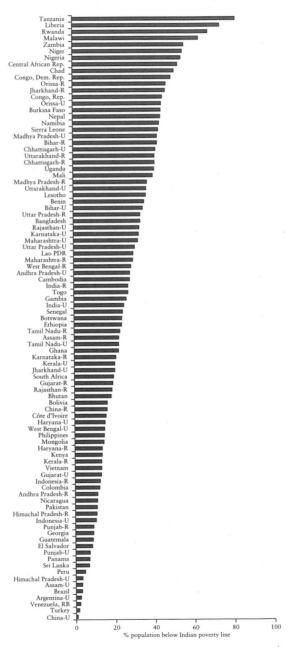

Source: Authors' estimates based on data from http://iresearch.worldbank .org/PovcalNet/.

Note: R = rural; U = urban.

similar to those found in countries such as Turkey or the richer Latin American countries. There is no clear pattern over time in the spread of rural poverty across India's states, but in urban areas the range of poverty rates across states has been increasing.

It is still the case that because poorer states in general are also the most populous, a large proportion of the poor are concentrated in the poorest states. Accelerating progress in the poorest states is important as they are also the states where fertility rates are particularly high.

City Size Matters: Urban Growth and Poverty

Urban growth not only reduces urban poverty, which is assuming increased importance in relative terms in India, but since 1991 it is also helping to bring down rural poverty. Urban poverty in India is becoming more important relative to rural poverty for two reasons. First, India's urban population is on the increase, especially since 1990. In the 40 years after 1950 the urban sector's share of India's population only rose from 17 percent to 26 percent, but in the 15 years after 1990 it is projected to have risen to 29 percent. Second, urban and rural poverty rates are converging, at least if official poverty lines are used (see figure 1). Even though the gap between urban and rural mean consumption levels is growing, urban inequality has increased, with the result that urban poverty reduction has been slower than that in rural areas (figure 7).

Urban growth obviously helps to reduce urban poverty directly, but since 1991 evidence has also appeared of a much stronger link from urban economic growth to rural (and therefore overall) poverty reduction (figure 8). That could be due in part to the more rapid rural-urban migration that urban growth now appears to be inducing—though migration levels in India remain low compared to those in other countries. Evidence is also seen that other horizontal links have strengthened: urban areas are a demand hub for rural producers, a place of employment for rural workers, and, increasingly, a source of domestic remittances. Indeed, the analysis of the nonfarm sector, discussed below, confirms that urban areas act as a stimulus for rural nonfarm growth.

Urban poverty reduction and urban growth have been most visible in large cities. The share of metropolises (cities with 1 million people or more) in India's urban population increased from just 19 percent in 1983 to 27 percent in 2004–05. During that period, poverty levels have halved in these large cities, from 29 percent in 1983 to 15 percent in 2004–05.

However, more than 70 percent of India's urban population lives in towns with a population of less than 1 million, and roughly

Figure 7 Even Though Urban and Rural Consumption
Levels Are Diverging, Rising Urban Inequality Explains
Why Urban and Rural Poverty Levels Are Converging

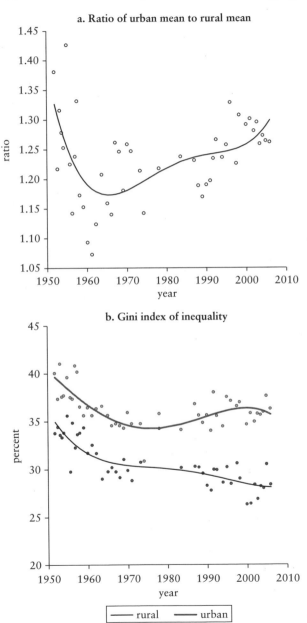

Source: Datt and Ravallion 2009.

Figure 8 Growing Poverty Impacts of Urban Economic
Growth

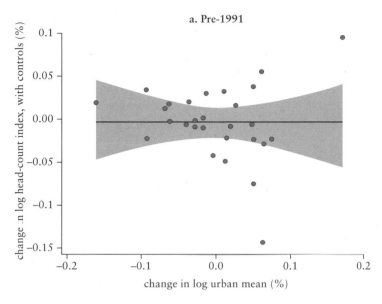

a. Pre-1991

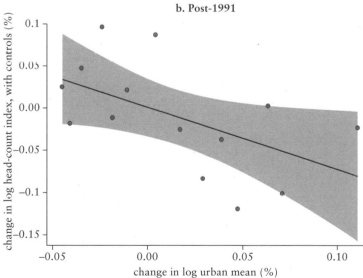

b. Post-1991

Source: Datt and Ravallion 2009.
Note: The shaded area shows 95 percent confidence intervals.

85 percent of the urban poor can be found in these smaller cities and towns. Poverty rates in small towns (population less than 50,000) are significantly higher than in medium-size towns (population 50,000 to 1 million), which again are significantly higher than the average for metropolises. Access to key services in small towns also lags behind the larger cities. Small and medium-size towns contain the bulk of India's urban population (about 70 percent) and, because they are poorer, an even larger proportion of India's urban poor (about 85 percent).

These smaller towns are poorer, but they have also experienced a 15-percentage-point reduction in their poverty levels. Poverty is falling in small towns and large cities alike, at roughly the same rate in absolute terms. Thus, smaller and larger towns are contributing to poverty reduction more or less in line with their population shares. Overall, only about 10 percent of aggregate urban poverty reduction is due to the increasing size of the more affluent metropolises. Since small and medium-size towns hold the bulk of India's urban population, they are responsible for the bulk of India's urban poverty reduction.

More remote urban centers also tend to be poorer. A recent "poverty mapping" exercise for three states—West Bengal, Orissa, and Andhra Pradesh—which combined NSS household survey data with census data to estimate poverty at a much more disaggregated level than previously possible, shows that the finding of smaller towns' having more poverty survives even when infrastructure access is controlled for. Distance from a large metropolis is also shown to be a significant determinant of urban poverty.

Not only would poverty reduction in these smaller conurbations target most of India's urban poor, but there is also evidence that it would have a larger spillover effect on rural poverty. We present evidence that poverty reduction in small towns has a larger spillover effect on rural poverty reduction than poverty reduction in large cities. Various mechanisms might explain the greater connection of small towns with rural areas. For example, small towns might offer greater scope for daily commuting from rural areas to town, rather than full migration; employment opportunities in small towns may be less skill and human capital intensive; and many small-town services and industries may be oriented around the support of agriculture in surrounding areas.

A Casual Transformation: Rural Nonfarm Employment

Rural areas are being slowly transformed by growth of the nonfarm sector. Traditionally, agricultural growth and rural growth have been regarded as synonymous. That has always been a simplification, but it is one that has become increasingly misleading. Chapter 3 focuses on the nonfarm sector, which now provides 30 percent of jobs in rural areas, up from 20 percent 20 years ago. In the last 10 years, nonfarm employment has been growing about four times as fast as farm employment, and more rural jobs have been created off-farm than on (figure 9).

While the number of people moving into nonfarm employment is growing, the quality of nonfarm employment is falling. Contrary to popular perception, more than two-thirds of nonfarm jobs are in the service sector. Construction is the fastest-growing rural nonfarm sector and now provides almost 20 percent of nonfarm employment, up from 10 percent only a decade ago. About 50 percent of participants in the nonfarm sector are self-employed, a ratio that has stayed fairly constant over time. The share of casual employment in total nonfarm employment has risen from 24 percent in 1983 to 29 percent in 2004. Growth in the formal sector has mainly been at the lower-paid end, and a dual wage structure is emerging in the regular employment category: well-paid regular employees have seen a growth in their average wage; poorly paid regular employees have seen little growth in their average wage and more growth in numbers. The effect is a trend toward the casualization of the nonfarm sector.

Figure 9 The Nonfarm Sector Is Now the Source of Most New Rural Jobs

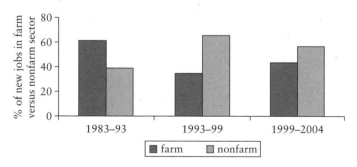

Source: Authors' estimates based on employment and unemployment surveys of respective NSS rounds.
Note: Employment defined on the basis of principal-cum-subsidiary (usual) status. Farm versus nonfarm assignment is based on workers' reported industry, occupation, and employment status. The numbers of farm and nonfarm workers are calculated using (a) estimated proportions from unit-level data and (b) total rural workforce as in Sundaram 2007.

Nonfarm growth reduces rural poverty. It is mainly young men who obtain nonfarm jobs. The poor are more likely to obtain casual than regular employment as they are more likely to be uneducated and socially disadvantaged, which are greater barriers to regular than to casual employment. Because casual nonfarm employment, though worth considerably less than regular employment, still pays considerably better than agriculture (the wage premium is about 45 percent; see figure 10), the rapid growth of casual employment in recent years is likely to have been poverty reducing.

A regression analysis of the impact of nonfarm employment, which also takes into account its indirect effects, tells a similar story. Chapter 3 presents evidence that nonfarm employment reduces poverty both directly and through upward pressure on the agricultural wage rate. The agricultural wage growth of the 1990s has slowed, but the analysis shows that without the labor market tightening due to the nonfarm sector, agricultural wage growth would have been slower still. All that said, nonfarm employment growth today is neither rapid nor inclusive enough to displace agriculture as a key determinant of rural poverty in India.

India's nonfarm growth, slow by international standards, is driven by urban growth, education levels, and state and local factors. Although India's nonfarm employment growth has increased,

Figure 10 The Increasing Premium of Casual Nonfarm Wages Compared with Agricultural Wages

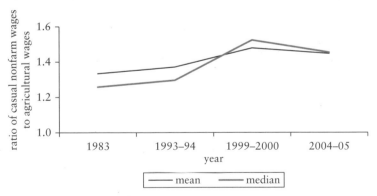

Source: Authors' estimates based on employment and unemployment surveys of respective NSS rounds.

Note: Employment defined on the basis of principal-cum-subsidiary (usual) status. Farm versus nonfarm assignment is based on workers' reported industry, occupation, and employment status. The numbers of farm and nonfarm workers are calculated using (a) estimated proportions from unit-level data and (b) total rural workforce as in Sundaram 2007. Mean and median daily wages are in Rs and are calculated for 19 major states of India.

it remains slow when compared to those in China and other success-ful Asian countries. Chapter 3 takes advantage of the variations in the nonfarm sector across the country to explore the determinants of its growth. The analysis finds that the expansion of the nonfarm sector in recent years has been more closely linked to urban than agricultural growth, thus confirming the previous chapter's findings of the importance of urban growth for poverty reduction in India. The nonfarm sector is also seen to be expanding more rapidly in areas of the country where education levels are higher. As might be expected, state and local factors are also important.

Beyond Consumption: Toward Health and Education for All, Haltingly

In contrast to the steady reduction in consumption poverty, India's record on improving human development indicators is mixed. In several dimensions problems remain stubborn, and though worse for the poor, they are not confined to the poor. Literacy rates are at par with Sub-Saharan African countries' and much behind those in China (see figure 11). In 1975, 32 percent of China's adult population had secondary education, versus just 16 percent of India's in 2004.

Viewed through the prism of nutrition and health outcomes, Indians are not doing well. In 2005–06, 43 percent of children (age less than five years) were underweight, 48 percent were stunted, and 20 percent were wasted (NFHS-III Report). More than half of adult

Figure 11 India's Educational Attainment Is below China 30 Years Ago

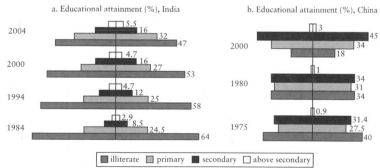

Source: Riboud, Savchenko, and Tan 2007.
Note: Educational attainment among the share of the population aged 15 and older. Illiterate includes both the illiterate and below-primary-educated populations.

women in India are anemic, and a third of all adults have low body-mass index. South Asians are among the shortest people in the world and attain adult height at a later age than people in other countries, a marker of childhood insults.

Contrasted with consumption poverty rates of 26 percent to 28 percent, it is clear that poor human development indicators are not a problem only of the poor, even though outcomes are substantially worse among the poor. The infant mortality rate among poor children is double that among rich children in rural and urban areas (figure 12). In 1998–99, only about two-thirds of poor children in urban areas were fully immunized, compared to nearly all children belonging to the richest quintile.

Variations in human development indicators across states are enormous. In general, southern states, especially Kerala and Tamil Nadu, have nutrition and human development outcomes comparable with those in developed countries, but states such as Bihar, Madhya Pradesh, Orissa, and Uttar Pradesh do poorly.[6]

Signs of improvement are appearing. But improvements in nutrition and some other key indicators have been extremely slow and remain cause for serious concern. India lies on the regression line linking basic health indicators (life expectancy) to income per capita (Deaton 2006). But progress lags that in countries such as Brazil and Mexico, and over time the pace of improvement has been slower since 1990 relative to periods of slower economic growth.

Figure 12 Health Outcomes Are Substantially Worse among the Poor

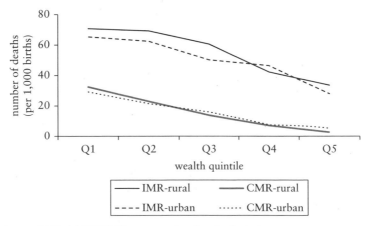

Source: 2005–06 NFHS III report and authors' calculations.

Note: CMR = child mortality rate; IMR = infant mortality rate; Q1–Q5 = asset index–based quintiles of population.

Key indicators such as child immunization have stagnated or worsened (table 1). Self-reported morbidity in India is high, taking a significant toll on productive capabilities. Basic sanitation remains a challenge, with two-quarters of rural households reporting no toilet facilities even in 2005–06, hampering improvements in health outcomes.

In the area of nutrition, as with consumption poverty, data inconsistencies make the detection of clear trends difficult. Data from the National Nutrition Monitoring Bureau (NNMB) suggest progress since the mid-1970s, whereas National Family Health Survey (NFHS) data suggest hardly any progress at all in combating malnutrition over the last decade. Even assuming that the more optimistic NNMB data are correct, the pace of this decline has been slow relative to India's pace of economic growth. Cross-country data suggest that the rate of decline of the proportion of underweight children tends to be about half the rate of growth of GDP per capita (Haddad et al. 2003). This would predict a decline of 38 percent between 1980 and 2005, compared to an actual decline of 29 percent. Similarly, the rate of growth of average adult height has been much slower than has been the case in several European countries in the past and in China in recent decades (Deaton and Drèze 2009).

The good news is that elementary school attendance has increased substantially in the last decade. Literacy, educational equity, and mobility in education across generations have improved as a result. Table 2 shows the rapid growth in school attendance. Today 80 percent of rural girls attend school, up from less than 60 percent

Table 1 Trends in Key Indicators of Health and Morbidity

	1992/93		1998/99		2005/06	
Indicators	Rural	Urban	Rural	Urban	Rural	Urban
Life expectancy at birth (years)	59.0	65.9	61.0	67.6	61.8	68.5
Infant mortality rate (%)	85.0	56.1	73.3	47.0	62.2	41.5
Child mortality rate (%)	119.4	74.6	103.7	63.1	92.0	51.7
Total fertility rate (%)	3.7	2.7	3.1	2.3	3.0	2.1
% children fully immunized	30.9	50.7	36.6	60.5	38.6	57.6

Sources: Life expectancy from SRS Bulletins; all other information from NFHS II and III reports.

Note: Total fertility rate for the 1- to 36-month period preceding the survey.

Table 2 Attendance Increased Substantially in the Past Decade, Particularly in Elementary Schools

percent

| Age group | 1993/94 | | | | 2004/05 | | | |
| | Rural | | Urban | | Rural | | Urban | |
	Male	*Female*	*Male*	*Female*	*Male*	*Female*	*Male*	*Female*
Age 5–29 years	45.4	30.5	47.7	34.9	53.2	43.6	54.1	51.9
Age 3–5 years	17.2	15.0	35.5	32.3	30.6	29.0	49.0	47.9
Age 6–14 years	74.5	58.2	87.0	82.4	86.9	79.5	91.0	89.5
Age 6–10 years	74.0	60.4	87.5	83.8	87.6	83.2	88.7	85.0
Age 11–14 years	75.3	54.5	86.4	80.6	85.8	74.1	88.4	86.9
Age 15–18 years	43.0	22.3	59.1	52.0	49.4	36.0	61.0	59.3
Age 19–29 years	8.0	2.4	16.8	9.9	8.6	3.9	17.4	12.3

Source: Authors' estimates based on NSS data.

Note: Table reports percentage of age group currently attending school.

in the early 1990s. More children are also in the age-appropriate grade than a decade ago. And school attendance gaps have narrowed, with the most rapid increases in attendance rates occurring among girls and children from poor households and in rural areas and relatively educationally backward states. As a result, the disparity in primary school attendance between boys and girls in rural and urban areas had largely been bridged by 2004–05. Disparities are more pronounced at higher age groups and levels of education, but even those have narrowed over time, especially in urban areas.

Literacy has risen in India from about 52 percent in 1991 to 75 percent in 2001 and is expected to rise more rapidly with the surge in schooling. Mobility in education has improved significantly across generations for all major social groups and wealth classes. In fact, in sharp contrast to its image of low social mobility, India appears to have average, or above average, mobility (defined as the lack of persistence in education attainment levels across generations) compared to estimates from studies of other countries (Jalan and Murgai 2008).

But children are learning little in school. Since the mid-1990s, several national and state-specific studies testing learning achievement of children at the terminal grades of primary school have been undertaken.[7] Differences in test content, test administration, and study sample render precise comparisons across studies and over time difficult. However, all studies agree overall learning levels are low. The National Council of Educational Research and Training (NCERT) national midterm achievement survey for Class V students found average scores of 48 percent and 60 percent on curriculum-based mathematical and language tests (NCERT 2009). The 2009 ASER (Annual Survey of Education Report) survey carried out by the nongovernmental organization Pratham showed that children typically know little, both relative to their curriculum and relative to what they need to know to function in society (figure 13). For example, 9 percent of children in grade 5 could not identify numbers up to 100, 44 percent could not read a short paragraph at grade 2 difficulty, and 29 percent were unable to divide or subtract. Smaller-scale, internationally comparable testing of students in secondary school (grade 9) in Orissa and Rajasthan supports the evidence that learning levels are low.

Inequalities in learning outcomes are very high. One dimension of inequality is large differences across states (NCERT 2009; Pandey, Goyal, and Sundararaman 2008). Another is inequality within states. At the secondary school level, the inequality in the distribution of mathematics test scores among ninth graders in Orissa and Rajasthan is second only to that in South Africa among

Figure 13 Children Learn Little Even after Spending 5 Years in School

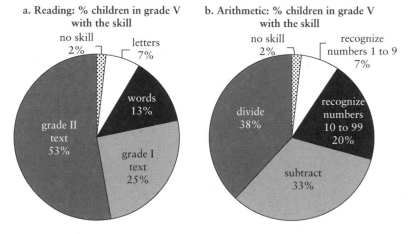

a. Reading: % children in grade V with the skill

no skill 2%
letters 7%
words 13%
grade II text 53%
grade I text 25%

b. Arithmetic: % children in grade V with the skill

no skill 2%
recognize numbers 1 to 9 7%
divide 38%
recognize numbers 10 to 99 20%
subtract 33%

Source: Pratham 2010.
Note: The panels are to be interpreted as follows: 7 percent of children in grade V can only recognize letters, 13 percent can recognize both letters and words, and so on.

the 51 countries in the sample (Das and Zajonc 2009). Although the median enrolled child failed to meet the lowest international benchmark, the top 5 percent tested scored much higher than the best in several other low-income countries, with scores comparable to those in some high-income countries.

This research is relatively recent, and little consensus exists on the nature and extent of sociodemographic variation in achievement levels. Some studies report better learning outcomes for boys and students from upper castes and richer and more educated families, while others find no gender or caste differences.

Improving human development outcomes for the poor, but not just the poor, remains a key challenge for India. That challenge is central to improving income-earning opportunities and directly improving welfare. Education is an essential tool for breaking the intergenerational transmission of poverty. It is becoming increasingly important if the poor are to share in the benefits of growth, as the economy transforms away from agriculture toward a greater role of urban and nonfarm growth. Poor health outcomes are not just a loss for the people concerned. Because they have high out-of-pocket expenditures and little health care coverage, ill health can be a catastrophe for poor families. Undernutrition can itself become a critical factor in perpetuating poverty. The evidence unambiguously suggests that childhood deprivation is associated with poorer childhood development, results in significant long-term impairment in later life, and may also adversely affect future generations.

Although gaps remain between the poor and others in outcomes, the burdens of undernutrition and poor learning outcomes, for example, are borne not just by the poor. Rates of malnutrition among India's children (as measured by the percentage underweight and stunted) are nearly one-and-a-half times the percentage of the population below the official poverty line. Given the recent record, it is simply not the case that continued rapid economic growth will automatically translate to commensurate improvements in human development outcomes. These challenges have led to vigorous debate and discussion on what actions are needed to improve delivery of services. Although that debate is beyond the scope of the report, it is clear from the findings reported that reducing nonconsumption poverty in India is a task that will require systemic improvements, not simply better targeting of existing systems to the consumption poor.

Rising Inequality: Cause for Concern?

Inequality may be greater in India than often thought. It affects poor and rich communities alike. Although comparisons based on consumption data have been used to argue that inequality in India is low by international standards, chapter 5 shows that when income, rather than NSS consumption data, is used, inequality in India appears to be in the same league as that in Brazil and South Africa, both high-inequality countries (figure 14).[8] Why the gap between India's consumption and income Gini measures of inequality is so large remains to be explained, but this finding at a minimum casts doubt on the often-rehearsed notion that inequality is low in India. (It also serves as a useful reminder of the difficulty of making international inequality comparisons, a difficulty too often overlooked when cross-country comparisons and regressions are undertaken.)

Inequality affects poor and rich communities alike. Chapter 5 challenges conventional wisdom at the local as well as the international level. The poverty mapping exercise mentioned earlier shows that consumption inequality seems to be at least as high among poorer rural communities as among better-off ones. Indeed, in Andhra Pradesh inequality seems to be even greater in poorer rural communities than in better-off ones. If local inequality of consumption is also an indication of concentration of power and influence, then resources allocated to poor communities—for example, under

24

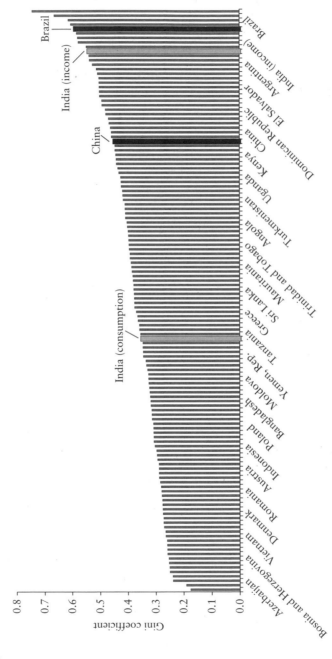

Figure 14 India in International Comparisons of Inequality

Sources: Consumption Gini from NSS 61st round; income Gini from 2004–05 NCAER–University of Maryland India Human Development Survey (Dubey 2008).

Note: Consumption Gini = 0.325; income Gini = 0.535.

"community-driven development" approaches—will not necessarily reach the poor and might instead be at risk of elite capture.

Consumption inequality has fallen over the longer term in India but is now on the increase. Turning from levels to trends, inequality is on the rise in India. This is a recent phenomenon. As figure 7 illustrated, the last five decades show a long-term trend in rural areas of declining inequality; a decline in inequality in urban areas until the 1980s, and since then a rise; and a long-term upward trend in the urban-rural gap. What this would mean for total inequality depends on how adjustments are made for urban-rural cost of living differences, but given that the great bulk of the population still lives in rural areas, a long-term downward trend would be expected.

Focusing in greater detail on the more recent past, however, tells a different story. Rural growth switched from being pro-poor (largely benefiting the poorer) between 1983 and 1993–94, to being largely distribution neutral between 1993–94 and 2004–05. In urban areas, over the same period, growth went from being distribution neutral to being pro-rich. And the gap between rural and urban areas continued to widen. Again, aggregate comparisons are difficult, but this set of findings would suggest an upward trend in national inequality. When one uses the official urban and rural poverty lines to correct for cost-of-living differences over time and between urban and rural areas, for most inequality indicators, no increase or a decrease in national inequality is apparent between 1983 and 1993–94, and a small increase is seen between 1993–94 and 2004–05. Figure 15 illustrates the Gini coefficients.

These results understate the increase in inequality, likely because the household consumption surveys are missing increases in top-end incomes. Increases in wealth holdings are also driving perceptions of increased inequality. Although the survey data we examine show an increase in inequality, it is not a dramatic increase. We have already noted, however, that the survey data likely underreport consumption at the top end. It is certainly popularly perceived that inequality has increased sharply, very likely driven by the observation that rich Indians did extraordinarily well during the boom of the 1990s. According to one study, in 1999–2000, the gap in per capita income between the 99th and 99.5th percentile was almost four times as large as the gap between the median person and the 95th percentile. Incomes of the super-rich at the 99.99th percentile grew by over 285 percent between 1987–88 and 1999–2000 (Banerjee and Piketty 2003). Wealth inequalities are also on the rise. Between 1996 and 2008, wealth holdings of Indian billionaires are estimated to have risen from 0.8 percent of GDP to 23 percent (Walton 2010).

Figure 15 Recent Trends Show Inequality on the Rise

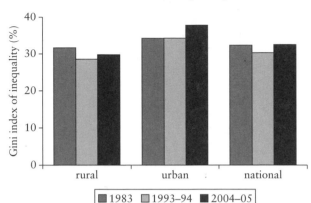

Source: Authors' estimates from respective NSS rounds.

Note: Gini index of uniform recall-period consumption corrected for cost-of-living differences across states using poverty line deflators.

Growing divergence across states in mean incomes does not explain the increase in inequality observed in the survey data. Divergence across states is often pointed to as the main source of rising inequality. Indeed, inequality in mean incomes across states is increasing, according to national accounts data (figure 16). Rich states used to have average incomes twice those of poor states in the 1970s; now the ratio is closer to four times. However, despite the clear evidence of divergence across states in incomes as measured by the national accounts, a decomposition analysis of inequality, using survey data between states, or between high-growth and low-growth regions, reveals that only a very small, albeit growing, share of overall consumption inequality can be attributed to differences in mean consumption levels between states. In other words, inequality of consumption within states, and within regions, dominates.

Increased returns to education appear to be an important factor. A similar inequality decomposition exercise (figure 17) shows that in urban areas, the share of inequality explained by a simple division of the population into those with and those without a primary education shows very little change. But the share of inequality explained when the population is divided into those with and those without a graduate education doubles to almost 20 percent in 2004–05, up from only 11 percent in 1983. The rural analysis tells a slightly different story. There, the share in inequality using both decompositions rises, more so for the graduates, but from a very low base.

Figure 16 Spatial Differences Have Grown

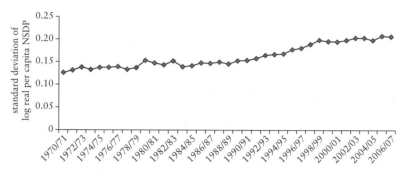

Source: Walton 2008.
Note: Based on data from 23 Indian states.

Figure 17 Increased Returns to Education Are Driving
Rising Inequality

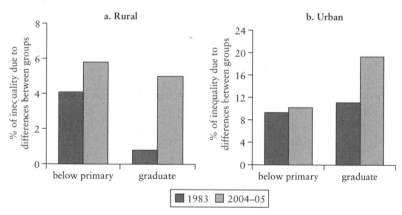

Source: Authors' estimates from respective NSS rounds.
Note: Percentage of inequality due to difference between given education category
compared with the rest of the population.

This evidence fits well with the story of the growing nonfarm sector told earlier, as we know that the less the countryside is dominated by agriculture, the more important education is. Even completing primary education increases the chances of escaping the farm. That education is a source of rising inequality appears paradoxical inasmuch as access to education is becoming much more equitable over time. However, inequalities in learning are high in India—among the highest in the world, and rewards to skills are becoming more unequal (Dutta 2006; Kijima 2006).

Some types of inequality, but not all, are harmful for growth and economic development. The link between inequality and poverty is far from straightforward. Everything else being equal, a rise in inequality will dampen the poverty-reducing impact of an increase in mean incomes. But everything else is not equal, and some growth accelerations might not be possible without an increase in inequality. The analysis suggests that the recent experience of India might fall into such a category, with increasing returns to education a necessary requirement for its recent rapid growth.

Even so, rising inequality can be of concern for other reasons. Some inequalities may be more structural and exclude groups from the development process.

Social Exclusion: Who Is Being Left Behind?

Although increases in inequality due to increasing returns to education might be growth enhancing and ultimately poverty reducing, other inequalities in India are structural and are more likely to act as a brake on, rather than enhance, poverty reduction. The final chapter of the report examines inequalities across social groups, with a particular focus on scheduled castes and tribes and on gender.

At the all-India level, differences between social groups explain only a small share of total consumption inequality in India; but in some states, group differences are important and growing. A decomposition inequality analysis shows that dividing households into those belonging to scheduled castes (SC), scheduled tribes (ST), Muslims, and others explains only about 4 percent of India's consumption inequality. At the state level the picture is less reassuring. In some states, notably rural Bihar, scheduled caste households appear, as a group, to be falling behind the rest of the population. More frequently the analysis shows that it is the more advantaged segments that are pulling ahead from the traditionally disadvantaged groups (scheduled castes, scheduled tribes, and Muslims taken together).

It is widely noted in the sociological and anthropological literature that social groups are highly heterogeneous. Our analysis of within-group inequality confirms that and shows that within-group inequalities are more important than those across groups. In other words, the gaps between elites and the poorest within the excluded groups are greater than the average gaps between groups.

That is not to deny that social group membership continues to be an important welfare determinant. Progress indicators are particularly worrying for scheduled tribes.

Welfare indicators for SCs and STs are improving, but the gap between them and the general population is large and persistent. Poverty rates for SCs and STs and for the general population have fallen by about 20 percentage points over the last two decades (figure 18). STs today (2004–05) experience levels of poverty seen in the general population 20 years earlier (1983), whereas SCs lag 10 years behind the general population.

Education indicators tell a similar story, with improvements but also large and persistent differences (figure 19). Scheduled tribe and scheduled caste women, in particular, are falling behind, with slower-paced improvements particularly in postprimary education.

Higher child mortality among STs is the starkest marker of deprivation. Mortality of rural ST children starts off on par with that of other groups but rapidly worsens by the time the children are five years old. A disproportionately high number of child deaths are concentrated among STs and in those states and districts with a high proportion of STs.

Figure 18 In Terms of Poverty, Scheduled Tribes Are 20 Years Behind the General Population, and Scheduled Castes Are 10 Years Behind

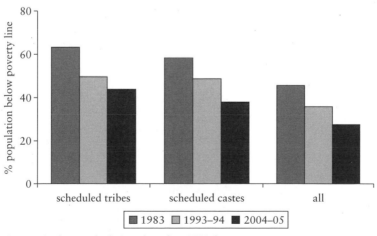

Source: Authors' calculations based on NSS data.

Figure 19 Changes in Postprimary Education by Social
Groups and Gender, 1983–2005

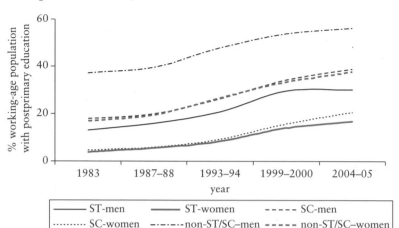

Source: Authors' calculations based on working-age population data from NSS
Schedule 10, various rounds.

*Occupational segregation and wage differentials between Dalits
and other groups are still evident.* Nearly 30 percent of Dalits are
engaged in low-skill casual jobs, compared to 8 percent in the general category (non-SC/ST/OBC [other backward caste]) individuals.
They are also less likely than other groups to have their own business
enterprises, particularly in urban areas. Concentration of Dalits in
casual work or in lower-paid occupations relative to other groups is
in part related to differences in education levels, but the differences
persist even after controlling for education and other characteristics.

Difference in access to occupations—or "glass walls"—is an
important determinant of the wage gap. Various studies show that
small-scale Dalit entrepreneurs, especially in rural areas, are prevented from moving out of caste-based occupations into self-
employed ventures. Even in the urban private formal sector, recent
research establishes, they are less likely to secure a job despite being
as qualified as applicants of other castes (Deshpande and Newman
2007).

*Some positive signs of dynamism are visible within the caste
hierarchy.* With the expansion of the nonfarm sector, discussed earlier, Dalits are moving out of agricultural labor to relatively higher
paying, nonfarm casual work and into trade and self-employment.
At the margin, an increasing number of new workers entering the
nonfarm sector are from a scheduled caste or tribe background.

With casual nonfarm employment paying significantly better than agriculture, the shift from agricultural labor to casual nonfarm labor is a sign of mobility, albeit limited. Other studies also present evidence of greater Dalit entrepreneurship and social change. Expanding economic opportunities, improvements in education, and greater political voice for scheduled castes have been drivers of change.

One of the most worrying trends is the increasing exclusion of scheduled tribes from the growth process. Scheduled tribes have historically lived in remote areas, and that has made the delivery of services to them particularly challenging. In addition, over the years they have been increasingly alienated from the traditional sources of their livelihood—land and forests (GoI Planning Commission 2008). Combined with their limited voice in decision making, that has caused them to lag behind other groups on a range of indicators. Scheduled tribes have also suffered more mass displacement as a result of infrastructure projects than any other group: they make up 8 percent of India's population but 40 percent of the 21 million people displaced between 1951 and 1990 (Burra 2008). Though consumption inequalities are not yet increasing, there are worrying indicators that India's educational expansion is leaving scheduled tribes behind. They show the least improvement in intergenerational mobility in education, as well as the worst indicators of child nutrition and mortality. Scheduled tribes are at risk of being locked out of India's growth and prosperity.

Although considerable progress has been achieved, female disadvantage in India continues, and women die unnecessarily both in infancy and in motherhood, with the poorest outcomes among women of scheduled castes and tribes. Female disadvantage is most starkly evident in the lower survival chances of baby girls compared to boys. India and, to a lesser extent, Nepal are the only two countries where the survival of infant girls is known to be lower than that of boys. At the same time, notable areas of progress can be seen. Fertility decline, for instance, frees up women from the cycle of childbearing and child rearing and allows them to enter into other arenas. In India, fertility rates in several states are now below replacement levels and resemble levels in developed countries; in other states the figures resemble those in much poorer countries (figure 20). Use of contraception is much higher than even a decade ago, and maternal mortality—although at stubbornly high levels across the South Asia region (except Sri Lanka)—is declining more sharply in India than in other countries. Progress has, however, been highly uneven, and Dalit and Adivasi women's outcomes are much worse than those of other women.

High levels of gender inequality persist in the labor market despite improvements in other areas. Female participation in the

Figure 20 Fertility Is Declining, and Many Indian States Resemble More Developed Countries

births per women

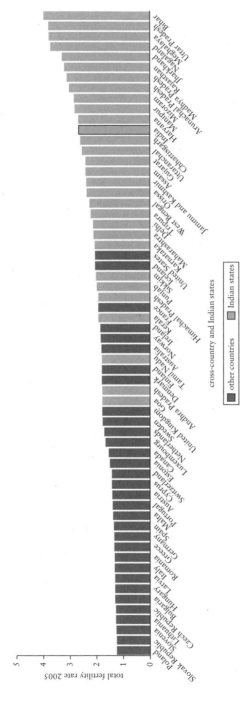

Sources: National Family Health Survey for India and Indian states; EUROSTAT 2008 for European countries; StatCan for Canada; AUSTATS for Australia; and Demographic Health Surveys for selected countries.

Note: Data from 2005, or closest year available.

labor force remains low in India, with only 40 percent of women employed in full-time work. That is so despite the fact that a very large share of women say that they aspire to work outside their homes. Economic and social outcomes for women are underpinned by low levels of security for them both within and outside their homes. Several policies and programs are under way to promote women's empowerment and better gender outcomes. Both vision and implementation count.

Concluding Remarks

Poverty has been falling in India for the last 30 years and continues to decline steadily, if not rapidly. In contrast, India's record on improving basic health and education indicators is mixed. Some outcomes have improved with rising income. In other dimensions, most notably nutrition, problems remain stubborn and are worse for the poor, but not only the poor.

India's structural transformation is affecting poverty. Underlying the long-term reduction of poverty is a gradual transformation of India's economic geography. This report has drawn on survey evidence to point to the emergence of new drivers of poverty reduction. India is slowly becoming urbanized, and urban growth has outpaced rural. Since the 1990s, a much stronger link from urban growth to a reduction of rural poverty is evident. In urban areas, it is small and medium-size towns, rather than large cities, that appear to demonstrate the strongest urban-rural growth linkages.

Rural areas are diversifying away from agriculture toward the nonfarm sector. Agriculture remains an important determinant of rural poverty, but the link between the two is weaker than it used to be. That is why poverty has continued to fall apace, even as agricultural growth has slowed. Expansion of the nonfarm sector has been poverty reducing both directly, because of the premium that even low-wage nonfarm jobs offer over agricultural wages, and indirectly, by driving up agricultural wages.

Inequality is on the increase. But at least some of the factors driving inequality up, such as increasing returns to education, seem to be associated with India's accelerating growth rather than with an intensification of structural inequality. Some signs are also apparent of dynamism within caste hierarchies. But structural inequalities also remain present and visible. Caste is still a potent indicator of social status. Female disadvantage continues despite high rates of growth, with deaths of females both in infancy and in motherhood and with poorer outcomes for women from scheduled castes and tribes. Worrying indicators are appearing that India's educational expansion is leaving scheduled tribes behind, and that group also displays the worst indicators of child nutrition and mortality.

This diagnosis of patterns and trends of poverty and inequality in India suggests some policy directions.

A multisectoral response to India's poverty seems indicated. Given the results that we report, continued debate about the appropriate sectoral focus for poverty reduction efforts is warranted. Agriculture is still the employer of too many of India's poor (especially the female and the elderly poor) to be ignored, but nonfarm rural employment and urban growth deserve greater attention. The rural nonfarm sector, as a sustainable source of poverty reduction, will need close scrutiny—the quality of nonfarm employment has been falling in a trend toward growing "casualization" of the sector. Within the urban sector, large cities may well continue to drive India's growth. But given that small and medium-size towns are currently home to 80 percent of India's urban poor, and given the strong links between such towns and rural areas, it will be necessary to ensure that no barriers exist to small-town growth and that no policy biases prevent small towns from realizing their potential. One place to look for such biases is in access to basic infrastructure services.

Improving India's human development indicators will require systemic change. The report shows very mixed progress with respect to human development indicators. Disaggregating outcomes between the poor and others shows that outcomes are worse for the poor. But the burden of undernutrition, for example, is not confined to the poor. These challenges have led to a vast debate about what actions are needed to improve delivery of services. Although that debate is beyond the scope of the report, it is clear that reducing nonconsumption poverty in India is a task that will require systemic improvements, rather than simply better targeting of existing systems to the consumption poor.

A redoubling of efforts to get scheduled tribe children into school is needed. Social status and gender continue to be important indicators of disadvantage. The report's analysis draws attention to the risk that scheduled tribes, in particular, might be locked out of the modern economy by their lagging participation in India's schooling expansion above the primary school level.

Data inconsistencies need to be addressed. As stated at the outset, India enjoys a rich pool of primary data from which analysts can draw. It is no surprise that data inconsistencies and contradictory trends appear. From our vantage point, a high premium should be placed on resolving inconsistencies around India's poverty line, understanding the growing divergence between the national accounts and household consumption survey data, and reconciling the divergent trends in India's two household health monitoring surveys.

Notes

1. India's official poverty estimates are based on the "thick" rounds of the consumption expenditure surveys carried out (roughly) every five years by the National Sample Survey (NSS) Organization. The most recent thick round for which data are available is 2004–05. Trends in education attendance are also based on the NSS. Trends and patterns of health and nutrition outcomes are primarily based on the National Family Health Surveys. The most recent data available from that source are from 2005–06.

2. Rupees converted to international purchasing power parity (PPP) $ using 2005 PPP rates of Rs 11.4 to the dollar in rural areas and Rs 17.24 to the dollar in urban areas.

3. See Bhalla 2002 and the arguments summarized in Deaton and Kozel 2005 for differing views on whether the national accounts estimates of consumption are more or less reliable than NSS estimates.

4. See Deaton and Drèze 2009 for a comprehensive review.

5. However, problems related to public amenities were seen as worse, possibly as a result of increasing population pressure (Praxis 1999). Small city-specific studies also reveal that despite some evidence of limited income mobility, little or no improvement has occurred in living conditions such as shelter, basic amenities like water and sanitation, and the living environment (see, for example, Swaminathan 1995; Praxis 1999).

6. Some surprises appear as well. For example, states such as Madhya Pradesh, Chhattisgarh, and Bihar outperform the southern states with respect to learning achievement (Pratham 2009).

7. See Das, Pandey, and Zojanc 2006 for a summary.

8. Income estimates are from a fairly comprehensive measure of income obtained from the 2004–05 India Human Development Survey collected by the National Council of Applied Economic Research (NCAER) and University of Maryland.

References

Banerjee, A., and T. Piketty. 2003. "Top Indian Incomes: 1956–2000." *World Bank Economic Review* 19 (1): 1–20.

Bhalla, S. 2002. "Imagine There's No Country: Poverty, Inequality and Growth in the Era of Globalization." Institute for International Economics, Washington, DC.

Burra, N. 2008. "The Political Economy of Tribals in India in the Context of Poverty and Social Exclusion." Paper prepared for the India Poverty and Social Exclusion Report, New Delhi.

Das, J., P. Pandey, and T. Zojanc. 2006. "Learning Levels and Gaps in Pakistan." Policy Research Working Paper 4067, World Bank, Washington, DC.

Das, J., and T. Zajonc. 2009. "India Shining and Bharat Drowning: Comparing Two Indian States to the Worldwide Distribution in Mathematics Achievement." *Journal of Development Economics* 92 (2): 175–87.

Datt, G., and M. Ravallion. 2009. "Has Poverty in India Become Less Responsive to Economic Growth?" Background paper prepared for India Poverty Assessment Report, World Bank, Washington, DC.

Deaton, A. 2006. "Global Patterns of Income and Health: Facts, Interpretations and Policies." National Bureau of Economic Research Working Paper 12735, Cambridge, MA.

Deaton, A., and J. Drèze. 2009. "Food and Nutrition in India: Facts and Interpretations." *Economic and Political Weekly* 44 (7): 42–65.

Deaton, A., and V. Kozel. 2005. *The Great Indian Poverty Debate.* New Delhi: Macmillan.

Deshpande, A., and K. Newman. 2007. "Where the Path Leads: The Role of Caste in Post-University Employment Expectations." *Economic and Political Weekly* 42 (41): 4133–40.

———. 2008. *Development Challenges in Extremist Affected Areas: Report of an Expert Group to Planning Commission.* New Delhi: Planning Commission. http://planningcommission.nic.in/reports/publications/rep_dce.pdf. Accessed April 2009.

Dubey, A. 2008. "Consumption, Income and Inequality in India." Background paper prepared for India Poverty Assessment Report, World Bank, Washington, DC.

Dutta, P. V. 2006. "Returns to Education: New Evidence for India, 1983–1999." *Education Economics* 14 (4): 431–51.

GoI (Government of India, Planning Commission). 2008. *Eleventh Five Year Plan 2007–12.* New Delhi: Oxford University Press.

———. 2009. *Report of the Expert Group to Review the Methodology for Estimation of Poverty.* http://planningcommission.nic.in/reports/genrep/rep_pov.pdf.

Haddad, L., H. Alderman, S. Appleton, L. Song, and Y. Yohannes. 2003. "Reducing Child Malnutrition: How Far Does Income Growth Take Us?" *World Bank Economic Review* 17 (1): 107–31.

IIPS (International Institute for Population Sciences) and ICF Macro. 2007. National Family Health Survey (NFHS-III), 2005–06. IIPS, Mumbai.

Jalan, J., and R. Murgai. 2008. "Intergenerational Mobility in Education in India." Manuscript, World Bank, New Delhi.

Kijima, Y. 2006. "Why Did Wage Inequality Increase? Evidence from Urban India 1983–99." *Journal of Development Economics* 81 (1): 97–117.

NCERT (National Council of Educational Research and Training, India). 2009. *Learning Achievement of Children in Elementary Education: A Journey from Baseline to Midterm.* New Delhi: NCERT.

Pandey, P., S. Goyal, and V. Sundararaman. 2008. "Public Participation, Teacher Accountability, and School Outcomes." Policy Research Working Paper 4777, World Bank, Washington, DC.

Pratham. 2009. "ASER 2008—Annual Status of Education Report (Rural) 2008 (Provisional)." New Delhi: Pratham Resource Center.

———. 2010. "ASER 2009—Annual Status of Education Report (Rural) 2009. Pratham Resource Center, New Delhi.

Praxis. 1999. "Consultations with the Poor: India 1999." Prepared as a background paper for the *World Development Report 2000–01,* World Bank, Washington, DC.

Riboud, M., Y. Savchenko, and H. Tan. 2007. "The Knowledge Economy and Education and Training in South Asia: A Mapping Exercise of Available Survey Data." Human Development Unit, South Asia Region, World Bank, Washington, DC.

Srinivasan, R. 2007. "A Decade of Economic Growth in India and China: Its Impact on Well-Being." Presentation, World Bank, New Delhi, November.

Sundaram, K. 2007. "Employment and Poverty in India, 2000–2005." *Economic and Political Weekly,* July 28.

Swaminathan, M. 1995. "Aspects of Urban Poverty in Bombay." *Environment and Urbanization* 7 (1): 133–44.

Walton, M. 2008. Presentation to the Indian Planning Commission.

———. 2010. "Inequality, Rents and the Long-Run Transformation of India." Unpublished manuscript, Kennedy School of Government, Harvard University, Cambridge, MA.

1

Consumption Poverty
and Growth

Twenty years ago the common image of India was one of a vast, populous country blessed with a vibrant democracy but afflicted by a highly rigid social structure, low levels of human development, and widespread and deep consumption poverty and doomed to eternal economic underperformance. Recent decades have seen significant change. Following the economic reforms that took hold in the 1990s, India has raced to the top of world charts in aggregate economic performance. Little doubt remains that the newly unleashed Indian economy has settled into a new, more rapid growth trajectory. Indeed, on the economic front the country now faces challenges that are linked to success—moving to the next generation of reforms to sustain growth and extending the benefits of rapid growth across sectors, regions, and people.

Economic growth is only a means, not an end. It is critical that rising incomes and the new opportunities ushered in by a reinvigorated economy translate into welfare improvements. Since the 1970s India has recorded steady progress in reducing poverty. Proportionally, poverty declined slowly during the prereform decades, but in the face of population growth it proved very difficult to reduce the total number of people suffering from staggering levels of material deprivation. Whether the newly galvanized, postreform Indian economy has brought a faster reduction of poverty is a key question of interest.

Fortunately for efforts to understand poverty, India benefits from a much higher quality and more substantial evidence base than most other countries. Questions around poverty in India have engaged a large community of researchers over the years. But in recent decades, because difficult measurement issues have arisen, a disproportionate amount of attention has been devoted to assessing the extent of poverty and the rate of its decline. Much less is known about how the rapidly changing economic landscape has altered the underlying profile of poverty and how that affects the search for its causes and cure. This book seeks to fill that gap.

The Book Is Structured around Three Themes: Consumption Poverty and Growth; Human Development; and Inequality and Social Exclusion

Chapters 1 to 3 analyze trends in consumption poverty and in the pattern of economic growth and the links between them. Focusing on trends and patterns of poverty,[1] chapter 1 shows that the pace of poverty reduction has increased in the postreform period, compared to the previous 30 years, although it is still too early to say whether this marks a new trend. Because of considerable data uncertainties, we cannot be certain that the responsiveness of poverty reduction to growth has increased, or decreased, postreform. The main data uncertainty is the large and growing discrepancy between household survey and national accounts estimates of consumption. The analysis in this chapter points to two emerging drivers of poverty reduction in India: urban growth and rural nonfarm employment. They are the focus of the following two chapters.

Chapter 2, on urban poverty and the links between urban growth and rural poverty reduction, proposes a normative and instrumental case for a greater focus on the development of small and medium-size towns. The vast majority (80 percent) of India's urban poor reside in these towns, rather than megacities. Within the urban sector, it is also small and medium-size towns, rather than large cities, that appear to demonstrate the strongest urban-rural growth links. Chapter 3 considers the rural nonfarm sector, in which employment has grown about four times as fast as farm employment; more rural jobs have been created off farms than on since the mid-1990s. The chapter argues that that transformation, albeit slow by international standards, has reduced poverty. Nonfarm growth has reduced poverty, both directly—by providing jobs that pay better than agricultural jobs—and indirectly—by placing pressure on agricultural wages. That said, an increasing "casualization" of nonfarm work has occurred, and nonfarm employment growth is neither rapid nor inclusive enough to displace agriculture as an important determinant of rural livelihoods in India.

Chapter 4 turns to the nonincome dimensions of poverty. It analyzes trends in relation to education and health, including nutrition.

In contrast to the steady reduction in consumption poverty, India's record in improving human development indicators is mixed. In several dimensions, problems remain stubborn. Outcomes are worse for the poor, but not only the poor, suggesting the existence of systemic issues in the delivery of those services that need to be tackled.

Chapters 5 and 6 examine and attempt to understand inequality in India, which is on the rise since the 1990s, and participation of disadvantaged groups in the development process. That one of the factors driving more inequality has been increasing returns to education—as argued in chapter 5—suggests that the increase in inequality was a price for increased growth and the accompanying poverty reduction. Even so, rising inequality is of concern for other reasons. Some inequalities may be more structural in nature, reflecting inequalities of opportunity that hold back particular groups. Chapter 6 further probes the question of structural inequalities and asks how scheduled castes, scheduled tribes, and women have fared. It shows that improvements are evident but not similar for all. In the aggregate, scheduled tribes have the slowest pace of improvements in a range of areas. Caste seems to be "reinventing" itself in response to economic opportunities, and far from its static stereotype, it is an evolving, dynamic institution. Results from this reinvention are mixed, however. Female disadvantage in India continues, despite high rates of growth, and women die unnecessarily both in infancy and in motherhood, with poorer outcomes for women from scheduled castes and tribes.

Consumption Poverty: Trends and Patterns

Stepping back even from the difficult question of attributing progress in poverty reduction to reform, it has proved difficult even to establish *whether* the pace of poverty reduction in India has accelerated since the late 1980s. Official estimates of poverty are based on the "quinquennial" or "thick" rounds of the nationally representative National Sample Surveys (NSS).[2] Changes in the questionnaire design of the 1999–2000 NSS rendered consumption measures from that round not comparable to earlier survey rounds, leading to a massive intellectual effort devoted to basic questions surrounding the pace of poverty decline. The current, best statement on the outcome of that debate is that progress in poverty reduction since the 1990s seems not to have matched the performance of the Indian economy at the aggregate level and seems closer to India's historical record. Release of the 2004–05 NSS round, which uses the same methodology as the pre-1999 rounds, provides an opportunity to reexamine the pace of poverty decline, setting aside at least measurement concerns related to questionnaire design, though, as discussed below, other critical measurement issues remain.

India Has Continued to Record Steady Progress in Reducing Consumption Poverty

In the two decades between 1983 and 2004–05 the poverty rate—the percentage of people whose overall consumption is too low to purchase a basket of goods as measured by the poverty line—in both rural and urban India has come down. In 2004–05, 28 percent of people in rural areas and 26 percent of people in urban areas lived below the poverty line, down from 47 percent and 42 percent in 1983.[3] The depth and severity of poverty fell even faster than the poverty head-count rate (figure 1.1). Thus, the decline of poverty was not simply a process of income gains by people in the vicinity of the poverty line, with others left unaffected. Rather, the process through which poverty was being reduced also improved the consumption of those well below the poverty line (see box 1.1 on poverty lines and poverty measures). These are significant improvements.

Because of population growth, however, it has proved difficult to reduce the numbers of poor at a comparably rapid pace. Although the poverty rate has declined by 2.3 percent per annum in the last two decades, the absolute number of poor people has fallen by only 0.3 percent per year. So despite India's success in bringing down its poverty rate, more than 300 million people remained in poverty in 2004–05.

Improvements in the last two decades represent a continuation of a long-term secular decline of both urban and rural poverty under way in India since the mid-1970s (figure 1. 2).

Some Signs Indicate a Steeper Decline in Consumption Poverty after 1991, Although It Is Too Early to Say That It Is a (Statistically) Robust New Trend

Views are divided on whether the pace of poverty reduction picked up commensurately with growth in the 1990s. One source of difference in views arises from whether the yardstick for measuring the pace of progress is absolute change in poverty rates (that is, percentage points per year) or proportionate change (percentage change from the baseline poverty rate). A reading of the evidence based on absolute changes would conclude that poverty reduction suffered a setback in the 1990s compared to the 1980s, but proportionate changes, which take account of the lower base poverty rate against

Figure 1.1 Evolution of Poverty since the Early 1980s

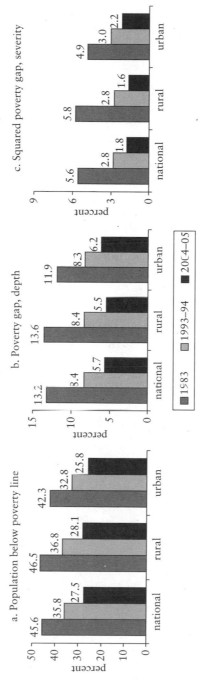

Source: Authors' estimates using unit-record NSS Schedule 1.0 data.
Note: Data based on uniform recall period consumption aggregates and official Planning Commission poverty lines.

Box 1.1 Poverty Lines and Poverty Measures

India's official poverty line in monthly per capita expenditure, in 1973–74 all-India prices, is Rs 49 in rural areas and Rs 57 in urban areas, with people below those expenditure levels considered poor. These figures correspond to a total household expenditure estimated as sufficient to provide 2,400 calories daily in rural areas and 2,100 calories daily in urban areas, plus some basic nonfood items. From the late 1970s into the mid-1990s, only these two lines were used. On the recommendation of the 1993 Planning Commission Expert Group on Estimation of the Proportion of the Poor, the lines were modified to incorporate interstate differences in price levels, as well as variations in intrastate rural-to-urban differentials. Poverty lines are thus defined at the state level, separately for rural and urban areas. Each line is updated by a set of state-specific price indexes based on the food and nonfood components of the state consumer price index of agricultural laborers for rural lines and the state consumer price index for industrial workers for urban lines, weighted by the 1973–74 food shares of households near the poverty line. This book primarily uses the lines proposed by the 1993 expert group.

In addition, for the purpose of examining changes in poverty over the past few decades and its relationship to growth, we use a new and consistent time series of poverty measures for rural and urban India over the period 1951 to 2006. This series is also based on NSS consumption data and the original Planning Commission poverty lines but uses slightly different price indices for updating the lines over time. The new series adds 14 survey rounds to the Ravallion and Datt (1996) series. In addition, the new series improves on the original one by using chain price indexes that incorporate evolving food and nonfood budget shares of the poor (for a full discussion of the new series, see Datt and Ravallion 2009).

Three measures of expenditure poverty are used: (a) *head-count index* (H), given by the percentage of the population who live in households with consumption per capita less than the poverty line; (b) the *poverty gap index* (PG), defined by the mean distance below the poverty line expressed as a proportion of that line, where the mean is formed over the entire population, counting the nonpoor as having zero poverty gap; and (c) the *squared poverty gap index* (SPG), defined as the mean of the squared proportionate poverty gaps. Unlike PG, SPG is sensitive to distribution among the poor, in that it satisfies the transfer axiom for poverty measurement. All three measures are members of the Foster-Greer-Thorbecke (FGT) class,

$$P_{\alpha t} = \frac{1}{n_t} \sum_{i=1}^{n_t} \max[(1 - y_{it}/z)^{\alpha}, 0],$$

(continued next page)

in which y_i is consumption expenditure of the ith person in a population of size n, z is the poverty line, and α is a nonnegative parameter. The head-count index is obtained when $\alpha = 0$, the poverty gap index is obtained when $\alpha = 1$, and the squared poverty gap index has $\alpha = 2$.

Figure 1.2 Evolution of Poverty, 1951–2006

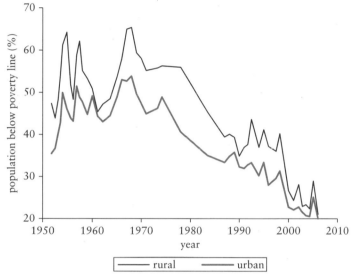

Source: Datt and Ravallion 2009.
Note: Data based on Datt-Ravallion poverty lines and annual rounds of NSS consumption data, except between 1978 and 1988, for which only four rounds of NSS data are available.

which progress is evaluated, suggest that the pace has been marginally faster.

Taking the long view shown in figure 1.2 suggests the emergence of a new trend. Progress in poverty reduction evident since the mid-1970s slowed somewhat in the early 1990s, but since then it appears to have regained momentum. The annual percentage point reduction in the head-count index, which had been about 0.5 percentage point per year during 1958–91, increased to nearly 0.8 percentage point during 1991–2006. Thus, the *proportionate* rate of progress against poverty was considerably higher in the post-1991 period. Moreover, unlike the pre-1991 period, the higher trend rate after 1991 was sufficient to bring down the number of poor.

Thus, the pace of poverty reduction has picked up, but with two important caveats. First, the pre-1991 trend is sensitive to the starting year.[4] Second, the difference between the trend rates of poverty reduction for the two periods is not statistically significant; it is too early to say if a statistically robust trend has emerged.

Definitive views on the pace of poverty decline are also hostage to a number of additional measurement issues. First, as mentioned earlier, changes in questionnaire design of the 1999–2000 NSS and attempts at restoring comparability have yielded quite contrasting conclusions about whether poverty reduction between 1993–94 and 2004–05 took place in the first or second half of the decade (before or after 1999–2000).[5] Second, concerns have been raised that the price indexes used to update India's poverty lines are "at best outdated and at worst simply incorrect" (Deaton 2008). Deaton (2008) estimates that for the 1999–2004 period, correcting for outdated weights in the price indexes eliminates more than three years of progress. Some of the key concerns are summarized in box 1.2. In response to such concerns, the government has constituted an expert group to propose a revised set of official poverty lines for India. Finally, India's poverty measures are threatened by the long unresolved and increasing discrepancy between consumption as measured in the surveys and the national accounts, an issue addressed in the next section.

Consistent with the Decline in Consumption Poverty, Communities Also Self-Report Improvements in Well-Being or Declining Perceived Poverty

Improvements are seen in terms not only of increases in incomes and purchasing power, but also in some education and health outcomes and an increase in personal freedom and choices (related to reduced dependence on patrons in rural areas and greater enterprise in urban areas).[6] In self-reported evaluations of well-being in the 2006 World Gallup Poll survey for India, half the respondents said that their life is "getting better." Only 12 percent of respondents felt that their lives had been getting worse over time.[7]

Calorie Poverty Has Not Declined

Although consumption poverty has declined steadily in India, caloric intake has been falling. Do such trends indicate rising poverty, or do they reflect response to changes in patterns of caloric requirements, substitutions away from some foods, and other processes consistent with rising living standards?[8]

Box 1.2 India's Poverty Lines Need to Be Overhauled

In recent years India's poverty lines have come under the scanner for several reasons. One serious problem is that the urban-to-rural price differentials that the measures imply are very large, perhaps too large to be credible for some states. In 2004–05, the average ratio of urban to rural poverty lines is 1.5, and the ratio varies widely across states. It is over 1.8 in Andhra Pradesh, and nearly as great in Maharashtra, Karnataka, and Madhya Pradesh, but actually slightly less than unity in Assam. As a result, in some states urban poverty rates are much higher than rural, a finding that does not always square with other evidence on living standards. Alternative price indexes (for example, Deaton and Tarozzi 2005) based on NSS data are very different from the official indexes and suggest a closer price differential between rural and urban areas and higher rural poverty rates.

Another issue is the state-level price indexes used for updating lines within sectors. As mentioned in box 1.1, poverty lines fixed in the mid-1970s are held constant in real terms and are updated using the food and nonfood components of the state-level Consumer Price Index for Agricultural Laborers (CPIAL) and Consumer Price Index for Industrial Workers (CPIIW), weighted by the food shares of households near the poverty line. Weights in the CPIs have not been updated since 1983; compared to current consumption patterns they place too high a weight on food, and within food on coarse cereals. For these reasons, between 1999–2000 and 2004–05, when prices of food fell relative to nonfoods, and within foods coarse cereals became comparatively cheaper, the CPIAL is estimated to have understated the rate of inflation by nearly four percentage points. To compound the problems, the indexes used to update poverty lines also put too high a weight (from a 1973–74 survey) on the food component of the CPIs. Ignoring other problems in poverty lines, it is estimated that this issue alone implies that the official poverty rates for rural India in 2004–05 are too low; at current rates of rural poverty reduction, correcting for understated inflation eliminates three years of progress. It is clear that the weights used for price indexes should be updated more frequently than they are presently.

A third issue is that the poverty line is considered by some to be so low that it "systematically underestimates poverty and related deprivation" (Sengupta, Kanan, and Raveendran 2008). Social acceptability and comparability over time and in different locations are the key criteria for a poverty line. The Indian poverty lines have come under criticism on both counts.

In response to such concerns, the Planning Commission set up an expert group to review methods for poverty estimation in India. The expert group report, submitted in November 2009, makes four

(continued next page)

major departures from the present method (GoI 2009). First, it moves away from anchoring poverty lines to caloric norms, in view of the fact that calorie consumption is found to be poorly correlated with nutritional outcomes either over time or across space. The new norm is taken as the current (official) poverty line in urban India, taking into account consumption of all goods and services. Second, all state urban and rural poverty lines are calculated by a purchasing power parity (PPP) cost-of-living adjustment of the current all-India urban poverty line (with a minor modification for a switch from a uniform to a mixed reference period measure of consumption). Third, for both spatial and intertemporal price adjustments, it advocates use of unit values obtained from the NSS consumption-expenditure survey itself, instead of the relevant CPIs. Finally, the price indexes now include private expenditures on health and education, which have been increasing over time.

One significant outcome of the expert group approach is that the new price indexes imply smaller cost-of-living differences between urban and rural areas. Since the present official urban poverty line is set as the anchor, in the new estimates the rural poverty line and poverty rate are revised upward. Thus, the expert group method yields poverty head-count rates in 2004–05 of 25.7 percent in urban and 41.8 percent in rural areas. There are significant state-level changes as well, because of changes in the urban and rural indexes of individual states relative to all of India, and changes in rural-relative-to-urban comparisons within states. A number of states show less urban poverty than the present official poverty estimates; rural poverty estimates are higher than the official ones in almost every major state. The interstate coefficient of variation in both urban and rural poverty rates is smaller. And no state shows a higher incidence of urban than of rural poverty. However, the broad clustering of high-poverty states (Bihar, Jharkhand, Madhya Pradesh, Chhattisgarh, and Orissa), low-poverty states, and the rest remains unchanged.

The proposal of the expert group has attracted public scrutiny and debate. Official communication from the government on revision of India's poverty lines based on the expert group's recommendations is still pending. Further work is also needed to develop a sound methodology for updating and back-casting new poverty lines over time.

Sources: Drawn primarily from Deaton 2008; Deaton and Kozel 2005; and GoI 2009.

A few observations characterize the broad nature of the decline in food intake.[9] First, not only did overall caloric intake decline, but so did the intake of proteins and other nutrients. Between 1983 and 2004, per capita calorie consumption fell 9 percent in rural areas and 2 percent in urban areas (figure 1.3). Per capita protein

Figure 1.3 The Calorie-Income Puzzle: Declining
Calorie Consumption during a Period of Rising
Per Capita Expenditure

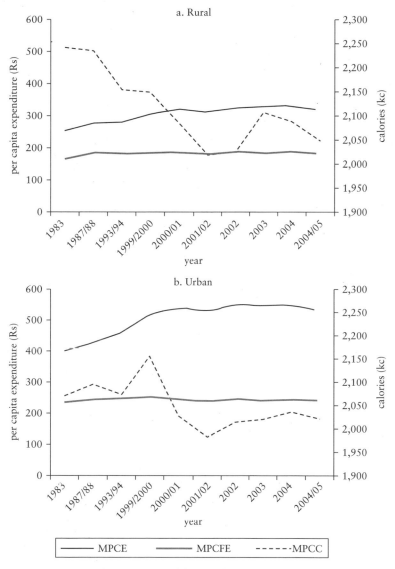

Source: Deaton and Drèze 2009, tables 1 and 2.
   Note: MPCE = monthly per capita (total) expenditure; MPCFE = monthly per capita
food expenditure; MPCC = monthly per capita calorie consumption.

consumption fell by 12 percent in rural and 5 percent in urban areas. The only exception is fat consumption, which increased during the period by 31 percent in rural and 28 percent in urban areas.[10]

Second, although urban areas historically reported *lower* caloric intake (typically attributed to lower activity levels), a gradual convergence has taken place between urban and rural regions during this time. In addition, rural areas with higher levels of farm mechanization (such as Punjab) witnessed a larger decline in calorie consumption. Third, "calorie Engel curves"[11] show that the decline was similar across different parts of the income distribution. There is some evidence that the decline was greater among better-off households, with a marginal increase among the bottom decile (Deaton and Drèze 2009; Rao 2005).

These trends naturally imply a very different picture of poverty depending on whether one uses consumption expenditure or calorie consumption as the yardstick (table 1.1). The decline in calorie consumption over time translates to an increasing proportion of households with calorie consumption lower than the specified minimums of 2,400 and 2,100 kilocalories in rural and urban areas, respectively. As a result, calorie-based estimates of poverty suggest that in 2004–05, 80 percent of the rural population and 64 percent of the urban population were calorie poor.

A Possible Explanation for the Paradox of Declining Consumption Poverty and Rising "Calorie Poverty" Is a Shift in Food Preferences and Reduced Calorie Requirements

One view is that the rise in calorie poverty is a direct consequence of a significant reduction in purchasing power, especially in rural

Table 1.1 Calorie Poverty Rises Even as Consumption Poverty Falls

	Consumption poverty (%)		Calorie poverty (%)	
Year	Rural	Urban	Rural	Urban
1983	46.5	42.3	66.1	60.5
1987–88	39.3	39.2	65.9	57.1
1993–94	36.8	32.8	71.1	58.1
1999–2000	..	..	74.2	58.2
2004–05	28.1	25.8	79.8	63.9

Sources: Deaton and Drèze 2009, table 5, for calorie poverty data and World Bank staff estimates for consumption poverty data.

Note: Consumption poverty estimates for 1999–2000 are not reported because of changes in questionnaire design, which rendered consumption measures from that round incomparable to previous survey rounds.

areas, as a result of which the poor are simply unable to afford sufficient food and move into hunger and starvation (Patnaik 2007).

However, the prevalence of self-reported hunger has declined over the last three decades: the percentage of individuals reporting inadequate food fell from 17 percent to 3 percent between 1983 and 2004–05 in rural areas. Also, it does not appear that households, even poor households, cannot buy enough food to meet caloric requirements (Banerjee and Duflo 2006; Sen 2005). Sen (2005) shows empirically that households around the poverty line could meet the recommended caloric intake within their *current* food budget by spending it according to the food consumption patterns of people below the poverty line. That would entail reallocating their food budget toward cheaper food items that yield calories equivalent to those that poor people purchase.

What, then, explains declining caloric intake? Tentative support exists for two factors.[12] First, some evidence appears of a shift in food preferences from cheaper sources of calories toward more expensive foods. Although cereals remain the chief source of calories, the share of cereals in total calorie intake fell from 75 percent to 68 percent in rural areas and from 63 percent to 57 percent in urban areas between 1983 and 2004–05. Similarly, within the cereals category a shift has occurred from "inferior grains" to higher-priced rice and wheat (Chandrashekhar and Ghosh 2003). That change may be due to changes in incomes and relative food prices, as well as nonincome factors such as exposure to new foods, imitation of consumption patterns of the wealthy, the influence of advertising, and changes induced by public policy.[13] Second is the suggestion of reduced caloric requirements as a result of improvements in the public health environment. Moreover, a number of developments over the last two decades imply a fall in activity levels, particularly in rural areas, including greater mechanization of agricultural activities and domestic work, greater ownership of consumer durables, greater access to safe drinking water, and expansion of transportation networks. In other words, the decline in food intake appears to reflect a voluntary shift toward a more diversified basket of consumption. This hypothesis, however, remains somewhat tentative because direct evidence on how activity levels have changed is unavailable.

Whether It Makes Sense to Measure Poverty through Calorie Consumption Remains Controversial

It is interesting to note that the recent Planning Commission report on the revision of India's poverty lines has explicitly moved away from anchoring the poverty line in calorie norms (GoI 2009; see box 1.2). Such a shift is warranted for several reasons. First, it is likely that the original calorie norms were too high. For example, UN Food and Agriculture Organization's minimum calorie norm for India is currently around 1,800 calories per capita per day, well below the original norms and closer to the average calorie intake of people near the new poverty lines that the Planning Commission Expert Group has proposed. But second, and more important, it is unclear what implications, if any, these trends hold for nutritional outcomes more generally. For example, child nutrition status in India is negatively correlated with average calorie consumption across districts. Third, to the extent that declining caloric intake reflects food preferences for a more varied diet (as discussed above), calorie shortfalls are a matter of choice rather than markers of impoverishment.

Large Differences in Poverty Levels Persist across India's States and Are Growing in Urban Areas

Urban and rural poverty rates have been converging, and although rural poverty rates still exceed urban (the latest figures are 28 percent and 26 percent), by other measures (depth and severity) urban poverty has surpassed rural poverty (figure 1.1). The pattern of rising urban relative to rural poverty has been found in the developing world as a whole, as shown in Ravallion, Chen, and Sangraula (2007).

Although poverty is clearly becoming more urban, because India remains a predominantly rural country it will be many decades before a majority of India's poor live in urban areas. India and poverty in India both remain predominantly rural: nearly three out of every four persons, and roughly the same share of poor persons, live in rural areas.

Wide disparity in poverty across the states is a key feature of poverty in India (figure 1.4). In rural areas, the seven poorest states—Bihar, Chhattisgarh, Jharkhand, Madhya Pradesh, Orissa, Uttarakhand, and Uttar Pradesh—have poverty rates between 33 percent and 47 percent. The least-poor rural states, such as Punjab, Haryana, Kerala, Himachal Pradesh, and Andhra Pradesh, have poverty rates that are a third or a quarter of those in the poorest states. Differences in urban poverty rates across states are equally dramatic, ranging from a low of 3 percent to 4 percent in Assam and Himachal Pradesh, to over 40 percent in Chhattisgarh, Madhya Pradesh, and Orissa.

These disparities are even more pronounced if one looks below the state level. Information on poverty rates below the state level is typically not available because household surveys lack sufficient sample size to produce statistically reliable estimates. A poverty

Figure 1.4 Evolution of Poverty across Indian States

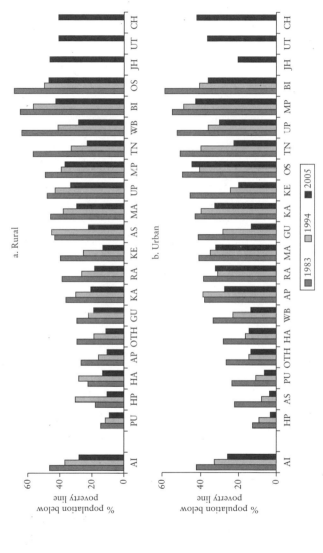

Source: Authors' estimates using unit-record NSS Schedule 1.0 data.

Note: Poverty rates for the newly created states of Chhattisgarh, Jharkhand, and Uttarakhand are only reported after the states were formed. For comparability over time, poverty trends reported for Madhya Pradesh, Bihar, and Uttar Pradesh in all three years are for the divided states. States are sorted in ascending order of 1983 poverty rates. AI = All India, PU = Punjab, HP = Himachal Pradesh, HA = Haryana, AP = Andhra Pradesh, OTH = Other States, GU = Gujarat, KA = Karnataka, RA = Rajasthan, KE = Kerala, AS = Assam, MA = Maharashtra, UP = Uttar Pradesh, MP = Madhya Pradesh, TN = Tamil Nadu, WB = West Bengal, BI = Bihar, OS = Orissa, JH = Jharkhand, UT = Uttarakhand, CH = Chhattisgarh.

mapping exercise, which uses small-area estimation techniques to combine National Sample Survey (NSS) household survey data with Population Census data, was carried out for three states—West Bengal, Orissa, and Andhra Pradesh—and provides an opportunity to examine a more disaggregated spatial poverty profile (see box 1.3 for a description of poverty mapping methods). Results from that exercise

---

Box 1.3 Developing Poverty Maps Using the Small-Area Estimation Method

Since the late 1990s researchers in the World Bank research department and in academia have been developing detailed "poverty maps" in a growing number of developing countries. These maps provide estimates of poverty and inequality at the local level, such as the district, subdistrict, and even the village level. Such information is not commonly available because household surveys are typically too small in sample size to permit sufficiently fine disaggregation. Yet with ongoing efforts to apply detailed spatial targeting of public interventions, or to realize gains from decentralization and community-centered development, the need has become pressing for information on distributional outcomes at the local level.

The poverty mapping method was originally introduced in Hentschel et al. (2000) and refined further in Elbers, Lanjouw, and Lanjouw (2003) (hereinafter the "ELL" approach). It combines household survey data with unit record data from the Population Census to expand the availability of pertinent information. Poverty maps provide estimates of poverty and inequality at the local level. It is important to bear in mind that poverty mapping uses statistical techniques to circumvent the absence of statistically representative household data at a disaggregated level, and that can introduce imputation errors. Procedures suggested in ELL can be applied to obtain a sense of the precision of the estimates.

A pilot effort has been undertaken in India to produce poverty maps for three states: West Bengal, Orissa, and Andhra Pradesh. This exercise combined National Sample Survey (NSS) and census data by applying ELL small-area estimation techniques. The project has been a collaborative effort involving the Indian Planning Commission, the Registrar General of the Indian Census, the India Development Foundation, and the World Bank.

Assessment of the statistical properties of the poverty estimates suggests that for rural areas, the poverty estimates are statistically reliable at the tehsil (or block) level, whereas for urban areas, the estimates are statistically reliable at the district level. Further details on the poverty mapping procedure and on the validity of the resultant estimates can be found in Gangopadhyay et al. (2010).

Source: Authors, based on the references cited.

show substantial variation in poverty within states (map 1.1). For instance, in Anantpur district of Andhra Pradesh, the rural poverty head-count rate (23.8 percent) is more than double the state's rate of 10.5 percent. In West Bengal, two areas are strikingly more affluent than other parts of the state—those surrounding Kolkata and areas in the northern part of the state. Drilling down further to poverty rates at the block level shows that districts can be very heterogeneous as well (Gangopadhyay et al. 2010).

Given such disparities, an obvious but important fact is that where people live is important: location-specific features are important parts of the overall experience of poverty. States matter. India's states are so different in their poverty levels that they range from the best in the developing world to the worst. As depicted in figure 1.5, rural areas of the poorest states have poverty rates that are comparable to the highest in the developing world. In contrast, urban areas of Punjab and Himachal Pradesh have poverty rates that are similar to those of Turkey and the richer Latin American countries. Even in poor states, some regions are thriving, and in richer states some regions resemble the poorest areas in the country.

The pace of poverty reduction has been uneven across states (figure 1.6). In general, in urban areas better-off states have remained relatively affluent and reduced poverty, while poorer states remained

Map 1.1 Location Matters: Rural and Urban Poverty Rates Vary Significantly within States

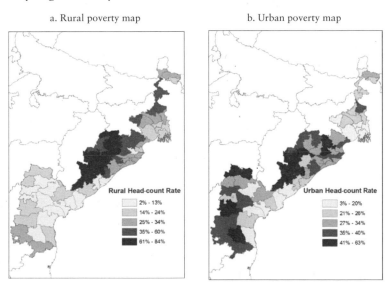

Source: Estimates based on poverty mapping results in Gangopadhyay et al. (2010).

Figure 1.5 Poverty Rates in Indian States Span the Best in
the Developing World to the Worst

Percent

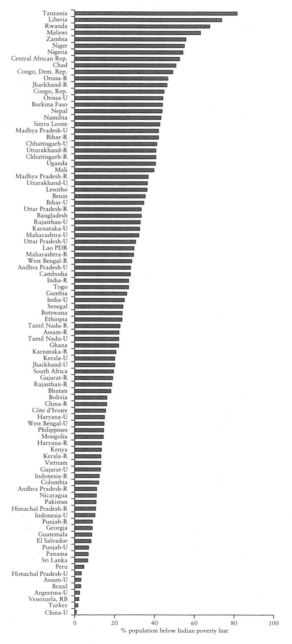

Source: Authors' estimates based on data from http://iresearch.worldbank.org/
PovcalNet/.

Note: R = rural; U = urban.

Figure 1.6 Uneven Progress in Reducing Poverty across States

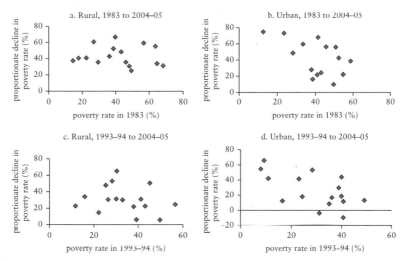

Source: Authors' estimates using unit-record NSS Schedule 1.0 data.

Note: Data based on uniform recall period consumption aggregates and official Planning Commission poverty lines. Only 16 major states are shown.

poor and made less progress in poverty reduction. The picture is more mixed in rural areas, where also in some cases poorer states made major progress in poverty reduction. In Kerala, for example, rural poverty declined by 4.5 percent per annum in the two decades between 1983 and 2004–05. Other major states where rural poverty declined substantially (as a percentage of the original level in 1983) include Andhra Pradesh, Tamil Nadu, West Bengal, Rajasthan, and Assam. Notably poor performers include Bihar, Orissa, Uttar Pradesh, and Madhya Pradesh. The stronger-performing states managed to reduce rural poverty at a rate of 3 percent to 5 percent (or more) per annum. Poor-performing states averaged less than 2 percent per year. It is important to note, however, that large differences in progress *within* states exist as well. In rural areas, while poverty declined in most NSS regions, it is estimated to have risen in roughly one in six regions between 1993 and 2004 (Lanjouw and Murgai 2009). In the next two chapters we use the regional and temporal variations in poverty reduction in India to understand the drivers of poverty reduction.

    With these patterns of progress, it is still the case that because poorer states in general are also the most populous, a large proportion of the poor are concentrated in the poorest states. Thus, the seven states with highest rural poverty incidence account for 44 percent of the rural population but an even greater share,

60 percent, of the rural poor. Urban poverty is less concentrated than rural, with the poorest seven urban states home to a third of the urban poor and a quarter of the urban population. Accelerating progress in the poorest states is important, as these are also the states where fertility rates are particularly high (see chapter 6).

Has Poverty Become Less Responsive to Economic Growth?

Much debate has taken place about whether the faster pace of economic growth since the early 1990s has helped put India's poor on a new trajectory of more rapidly rising living standards. This section revisits that question using a new series of consumption-based poverty measures spanning 50 years and including a 15-year period after economic reforms began in earnest.

In an old but formative debate in the literature, some scholars argued that the agricultural growth process stimulated by the green revolution brought little or no gain to the rural poor, while others pointed to farm output growth as the key to rural poverty reduction (Ahluwalia 1978, 1985; Saith 1981; van de Walle 1985; Gaiha 1989; Bhattacharya et al. 1991; Bell and Rich 1994; and Datt and Ravallion 1998). Also debated has been how much urban growth has benefited the poor. The optimism of many of India's postindependence planners that the country's (largely urban-based) industrialization would bring lasting, long-term gains to both the urban and rural poor was not always shared by other observers, then and more recently (see, for example, Eswaran and Kotwal 1994). These intellectual debates about growth and the poor lie at the very heart of broader policy debates on development strategy in all developing countries.

The evidence suggests that prior to the 1990s economic growth in India had tended to reduce poverty. Using data from 1958 to 1991, Ravallion and Datt (1996) found that the elasticity of the incidence of poverty with respect to mean household consumption was −1.3, though somewhat lower (in absolute value) with respect to either consumption or Net Domestic Product (NDP) per capita, as measured from the National Accounts Statistics. Absolute elasticities for measures of the depth and severity of poverty were higher, indicating that those well below the poverty line, as well as those near the poverty line, have benefited from growth. Nor was any convincing evidence found that economic growth in India before the 1990s tended to be associated with rising overall inequality (Bruno, Ravaillion, and Squire 1998). On the basis of the evidence it cannot be argued that the pre-1990s growth in India tended to leave the poor behind. Arguably the bigger concern for India's poor was that too little growth was occurring.

Thus, it was hoped that the higher growth rates attained in the wake of India's economic reforms would bring more rapid poverty reduction. But echoing the earlier debates have been conflicting opinions on the extent to which India's poor have shared in postreform growth. Concerns were expressed about geographic and sectoral divergence, which appeared to have attenuated the impact on poverty of aggregate growth in the immediate postreform period (Datt and Ravallion 2002; Bhattacharya and Sakthivel 2004; Jha 2000a, 2000b; Purfield 2006). More recently, evidence of rising inequality has appeared, particularly in urban areas, which may have blunted the effectiveness of growth as a poverty reducer.[14] Topalova (2008), for example, shows that in the 1990s, had growth not been accompanied by rising inequality, it would have generated a decline in rural poverty that was 22 percent greater; in urban areas the decline in poverty would have been 76 percent greater.

Statements about the evolution of inequality and its impact on growth must remain qualified, however, because a number of measurement issues remain unresolved (see box 1.4, below, and chapter 5 for a discussion in greater detail of trends and patterns

Box 1.4 National Sample Surveys versus National Accounts Statistics: Implications for Poverty and Inequality Measurement

The implications for poverty and inequality measurement of the large and growing gap between consumption as measured in the NSS and the NAS depend on the sources of the discrepancy. Several studies have been carried out to investigate possible sources, including a recent one by an Expert Group of the Central Statistical Organisation (CSO 2008) based on comparisons of the 1999–2000 and 2004–05 consumption expenditure surveys.

Some of the gap is due to errors in NAS consumption figures, which are determined residually in India, after subtracting other components of domestic absorption from output at the commodity level. There are also differences in the definition of "consumption," and some things are included in NAS consumption that one would not use in measuring household living standards (for further discussion of the differences between the two data sources, see Sundaram and Tendulkar 2001; Ravallion 2000, 2003; Sen 2005; and Deaton 2005). But not all of the gap can be explained this way. The Central

(continued next page)

Statistical Organisation (2008) estimates that the NSS consumption aggregate represents 60 percent to 65 percent of private consumption from the NAS, after accounting for differences in certain notional components (imputed services and financial intermediation services).

Some of the gap is likely due to errors in the NSS. By international standards, the National Sample Survey Organisation's methods appear to have changed little over many decades. Although that is probably helpful for comparability purposes, it raises questions about whether NSS methods are properly picking up consumption of some goods and services whose consumption was previously unimportant. NSS design may also account for at least some of the discrepancy because switching to a mixed recall period for consumption helps close the gap between the NSS and NAS consumption aggregates.

Although we cannot rule out the possibility that such problems lead to overestimates of poverty in India, it is likely that the surveys do a better job of measuring poverty than inequality. Some degree of underreporting of consumption by respondents, or selective compliance with the NSS's randomized assignments, is also likely (as in any survey), although it is expected that this is more of a problem for estimating the levels of living of the rich than of the poor. Evidence from other sources is consistent with that expectation (Banerjee and Piketty 2003).

Preliminary analysis by Himanshu (2009) also suggests that NSS estimates of poverty may be less prone to error than inequality estimates. Comparing estimates of wage and salary incomes in the NSS to estimates of compensation to employees in the NAS, he finds that the difference increased from 34 percent in 1993–94 to 47 percent in 2004–05. These differences are remarkably similar to estimated differences in aggregate private consumption between the two sources. A breakdown by industry shows that estimates of wage income in the primary sector match almost exactly (2 percent difference in 1993–94), though the gap grew to 9 percent in 2004–05. The gap in industries such as manufacturing, utilities, trade, and transportation is much larger but has not grown over time. It is sectors such as construction, finance, and social services where the NSS is increasingly falling behind in aggregate estimates of wage earnings. However, the industry groups for which the difference has remained stable over the years together represent 80 percent of poor households (based on principal industry affiliation in 2004–05). Disaggregating estimates into organized and unorganized sector compensation shows that underestimation in the NSS is much smaller for the unorganized sector, which is the sector of employment for nearly all the poor. These are preliminary findings and need to be probed further. However, the evidence suggests that NSS estimates may do a better job of picking up the poor than the rich.

Sources: Datt and Ravallion 2009 and citations therein; Himanshu 2009.

of inequality). It is also possible that growth may not have been as high had inequality not risen.

Table 1.2 reports estimates of the elasticities of all three poverty measures with respect to three measures of economic growth: (a) the mean consumption per person, as estimated from the NSS; (b) the mean consumption per person, as estimated by the National Accounts Statistics (NAS) and the Population Census; and (c) the mean NDP per person, also from the NAS and census. In all cases, the elasticities are estimated by regressing the log poverty measure on the log consumption or income.

Growth Has Tended to Reduce Poverty, Including Growth in the Postreform Period

The national poverty measures responded significantly to growth in all three measures of consumption growth. The growth elasticities tend to be higher (in absolute value) for the poverty gap and squared poverty gap than the head-count index. That implies that the depth of poverty and inequality among the poor are reduced by growth. Thus, the impacts of growth are not confined to households around the poverty line.

However, No Robust Evidence Appears That the Responsiveness of Poverty to Growth Has Increased (or Decreased) Since Reform

As table 1.2 shows, the evidence on whether poverty was more responsive to growth, or less so, in the postreform period is

Table 1.2 Growth Matters; Whether It Has Become More or Less Potent at Reducing Poverty Postreform Is Unclear

	Elasticity of head-count index		
Period	*NSS consumption*	*NAS private consumption*	*NDP*
1958–2006	–1.6	–0.9	–0.7
Pre-1991	–1.6	–1.0	–0.7
Post-1991	–2.1	–0.7	–0.5
HO: pre-1991 elasticity = post-1991 elasticity (probability)	(0.00)	(0.23)	(0.24)

Source: Datt and Ravallion 2009.

Note: Data based on regressions of first differences of the log poverty measures against first differences of the log consumption, or NDP, using 37 surveys spanning 1958–2006. All regressions include a control for surveys that use a mixed-recall period. All elasticity estimates are significantly different from zero at the 1 percent level.

inconclusive. In both periods, the elasticity of poverty reduction is greater using growth rates calculated from household surveys than using national accounts. But comparing the two periods, the elasticity with respect to the survey mean is greater in the postreform period, whereas the opposite is true using consumption from the national accounts.[15] It is also notable how much difference appears in the elasticity, based on the NSS consumption growth rates versus the NAS rates, for the post-1991 period.

Data Issues Cloud Our Assessment of Whether the Growth Process Has Become More or Less Pro-Poor in the Postreform Period

The most significant reason for lower (absolute) elasticities with respect to NAS consumption or income has to do with the increasing divergence between NSS and NAS growth rates of mean consumption of income; the NSS series does not fully reflect the gains in mean consumption indicated by the NAS. Figure 1.7 shows that the proportion of NSS consumption to NAS private consumption has been declining over time. The estimate of aggregate household consumption implied by the NSS is now only about half of the household component of the NAS. The gap is unusually large for India. It is also notable that the NSS series does not reflect the large gains in mean consumption that the NAS indicates from the early 1990s onward.

The growing divergence between the consumption growth rates implied by the surveys and the national accounts confounds our

Figure 1.7 NSS and NAS Consumptions Are Diverging

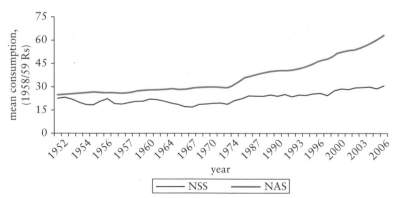

Source: Datt and Ravallion 2009.

ability to assess whether growth has become more pro-poor in the postreform period.

On the basis of our results, it certainly cannot be argued that postreform growth has left the poor behind. However, the answer to the question of whether poverty in India has become more responsive to economic growth or less so depends crucially on whether one is talking about growth in mean household consumption, as measured in the surveys, or growth based on the national accounts. As it is, we do not see in these data a robust case for saying that poverty elasticity has either fallen or risen.

A High Premium Should Be Placed on Understanding the Sources of Discrepancies between the National Sample Surveys and National Accounts Statistics Estimates of Consumption

Discrepancies such as we have been discussing will also have implications for measurements of poverty and inequality. The use of NSS household surveys in measuring poverty has been questioned by some observers. Bhalla (2002), in particular, has argued that the national accounts estimates of consumption are more reliable than NSS estimates, leading to an overestimation of the level of poverty in India and underestimation of the pace of poverty reduction. Others have argued that the national accounts are inferior as a measure of living standards (see the arguments summarized in Deaton and Kozel 2005).

The extent of bias in poverty estimates depends on how much of the discrepancy is attributed to the NSS or the NAS. Choosing between the NSS and NAS is not easy and is well beyond the scope of this book. With the evidence available, as summarized in box 1.4, it is likely that surveys do a better job of measuring poverty than of measuring inequality. Getting to the bottom of the sources of differences and resolving them should be a priority for India's statistical system.

Changing Drivers of Poverty Reduction

This section examines the effects on poverty of the sectoral—rural and urban—pattern of economic growth. We measure the importance to India's poor of growth in the rural and urban sectors, rural-to-urban migration, and spillover effects between sectors. We also focus on the changing composition of gross domestic product (GDP) in India, among agriculture, industry, and services, to associate growth in different sectors to observed patterns of poverty reduction.

The Analysis Suggests a Striking Change in the Relative Importance of Urban and Rural Economic Growth: Urban Economic Growth Is Now Much More Strongly Linked to Reduction of Rural Poverty Than It Was before Reform

Consumption levels have grown more rapidly in urban areas than in rural ones in the past few decades. As a result, India has seen divergence over time between urban mean consumption and the rural mean, as measured from the NSS (figure 1.8). Urbanization of the population has also been more rapid since 1990 (though these data rely heavily on extrapolations between census years). In the 40 years after 1950, the urban sector's share of India's population rose only from 17 percent to 26 percent, but in just 15 years after 1990 it is projected to have risen to 29 percent.

Confirming earlier analysis, Datt and Ravallion (2009) found that before 1991, urban economic growth helped reduce urban poverty but brought little or no overall benefit to the rural poor; in fact, the

Figure 1.8 Urban and Rural Consumption Levels Are Diverging

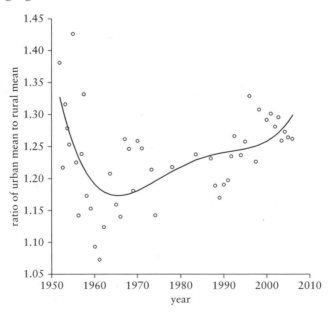

Source: Datt and Ravallion 2009.

main force driving overall poverty reduction was rural economic growth (table 1.3).

The picture looks very different after 1991, as urban economic growth has become the more important driver of poverty reduction. As before, urban growth reduced urban poverty, and rural growth reduced rural poverty. But after 1991 a much stronger link from urban economic growth to rural poverty reduction is evident. Rural economic growth remains important to rural poverty reduction, but its spillover effect to the urban poor has largely vanished in the period after 1991.[16] Figure 1.9 shows the estimated impact of urban economic growth in the periods before and after 1991. For each period, the figure plots the change in log national head-count index that remains unexplained by rural growth, against the change in log urban mean consumption. We see no significant poverty-reducing effect of growth in mean urban consumption in the earlier period, but a significant impact emerges after 1991.

The increasing impact of urban growth on poverty nationally and its beneficial effect on rural poverty accord with evidence over time and across countries that suggests that a faster pace of urbanization, consistent with higher growth, can bring greater overall progress against poverty, though urban poverty incidence may well increase in the process (Ravallion, Chen, and Sangraula 2007).

In what ways may the fortunes of urban and rural areas be linked? Migration from rural to urban areas is clearly one of them, but in India, views conflict sharply on how much migration occurs.[17] Munshi and Rosenzweig (2007) argue, "Among developing countries, India stands out for its remarkably low levels of

Table 1.3 Urban Growth Has Become the More Important Driver of Poverty Reduction Compared with Rural Growth

Growth	Elasticity of poverty measures		
	National poverty	Urban poverty	Rural poverty
Urban growth			
Up to 1991	−0.1	−0.9	0.1
After 1991	−1.2	−1.3	−1.3
Rural growth			
Up to 1991	−1.1	−0.4	−1.3
After 1991	−0.7	−0.1	−0.9

Source: Datt and Ravallion 2009.

Note: Elasticities are evaluated at means for the periods up to and following 1991 using parameter estimates from regressions of changes in poverty rates for urban and rural growth, as well as the population shift from rural to urban areas using surveys spanning 1951–2006.

Figure 1.9 The Postreform Process of Urban Economic
Growth Has Brought Significant Gains to the Poor

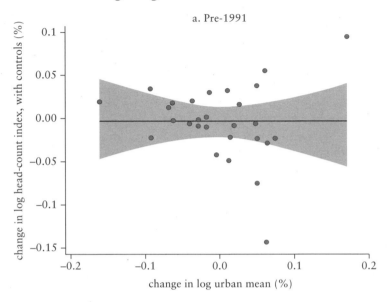

a. Pre-1991

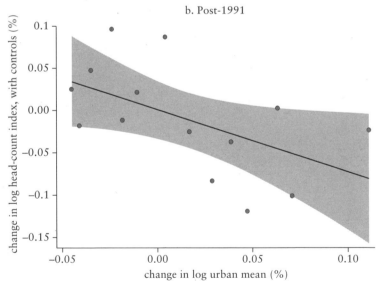

b. Post-1991

Source: Datt and Ravallion 2009.
Note: The shaded area shows the 95 percent confidence intervals.

occupational and geographic mobility"; they cite low levels of urbanization in India compared to other countries as one piece of evidence. In contrast, Gardner and Osella (2003) claim that there is "irrefutable evidence that movement, both within rural areas and between villages, towns and cities, has always been, and continues to be, a central feature of life within the subcontinent." A significant discrepancy also appears between analyses of spatial mobility in India based on large surveys and village-level studies. The former find less migration (whether based on census, NSS, or other nationally representative surveys) than the latter. It is very likely that spatial mobility from rural India is not as small as large-scale survey data suggest; the reality of seasonal migration and short-duration migration is not captured in the sample surveys (Kapur and Witsoe 2008).

Even without labor mobility, integration of urban and rural sectors can arise through trade in goods; the living standards of households that are in different sectors but share similar factor endowments will tend to move together, to the extent that trade in goods eliminates differences in factor costs at the margin. But even without factor-price equalization, the fact that the rural sector produces food partly consumed in the urban sector can mean that agricultural growth raises urban welfare by lowering food prices, which are not well integrated with global markets.

A more detailed analysis of the evidence that economic growth in urban India may be contributing to lower rural poverty, and the channels through which that is taking place, is undertaken in chapters 2 and 3.

Prima Facie, Aggregate Trends Suggest Growing Importance of the Nonagricultural Sectors as Drivers of Rural Poverty Reduction

Historical evidence in India from the 1970s to the early 1990s has shown agricultural growth to be a major factor in reducing poverty. States with higher rates of agricultural growth and associated real wage increases experienced faster poverty decline; growth in India's tertiary sector (primarily services) was also important, but growth in the secondary (manufacturing) sector had little impact on poverty (Ravallion and Datt 1996).

Since the 1990s, however, agricultural performance has lagged other sectors. The tertiary sector (primarily services and trade) has grown fastest, doubling in the postreform period from 3 percent per annum up to 1991, to almost 6 percent after 1991. The share of services in output rose from 43 percent in 1991 to 56 percent in

2006. Agriculture has been a shrinking sector, with its contribution down to only a fifth of overall GDP by the mid-2000s. National trends are mirrored in rural GDP: agriculture used to account for three-quarters of rural GDP in the 1970s, but by the latest available estimates, it is now down to less than 50 percent of the rural economy. Industry and services are about equally important, each contributing about a quarter of rural GDP.

The growth of real daily wages in rural areas—a key link between agricultural growth and poverty reduction—also slowed in the 1990s. According to NSS data, in the two decades between 1983 and 2004–05, real agricultural wages grew at the rate of 3.2 percent per year. The rate of growth was higher in the first decade—1983 to 1993–94—but slowed to 2.3 percent per year in the decade that followed, and much more drastically, to 1.7 percent per year, between 1999–2000 and 2004–05.

These aggregate trends in agricultural growth and wages would support a slowdown in poverty reduction since the early 1990s, but poverty trends suggest otherwise. As noted earlier, no strong evidence is present of either acceleration or deceleration in poverty reduction. That is true both nationally and in rural areas.

That hypothesis, however, requires closer investigation. Views are divided, and the evidence is not clear-cut. The rural nonfarm sector was the primary source of new jobs in the 1990s (although the pace of transformation remains slow compared to other countries). Some observers (Himanshu 2007; Dev and Ravi 2007) speculate that the rural nonfarm sector may be a key factor underlying the decline in rural poverty despite a collapse in agricultural wage growth. Others express concern that accelerating nonfarm employment reflects agrarian distress rather than the pull of better nonfarm jobs.

A separate concern exists that service sector–led growth disproportionately benefits the rich and thus cannot be as effective as agricultural or industrial growth in reducing poverty. Topalova (2008) uses variation across India's states and over time to show that faster growth in agriculture and industry in the 1980s and 1990s was associated with a diminishing gap between the consumption growth of the poor and the rich. Faster service sector growth has been associated with the opposite. It is important to note that although these observations imply that service sector growth may prove to be less potent at reducing poverty, they say nothing about whether or not service sector growth is associated with absolute gains for the poor. A more detailed analysis of the nature of rural transformation and changes in the rural nonfarm sector, attempted in chapter 3, is needed to understand the drivers of poverty reduction.

Thinking beyond the "Official" Poor

Although a large portion of this book is devoted to analysis of households falling below India's official poverty line, it also examines broader issues of inequality, human development (nonincome poverty), and social exclusion. Focusing only on the "official" poor can be limiting.

At any point in time, a cross-sectional survey cannot tell whether an individual who is counted as poor is experiencing chronic poverty or a shorter episode of poverty. Microstudies and research based on panel data that track individuals over an extended period show that the poor are a fluid group. One long-term, village-level survey of households in South India found that whereas only 12 percent of households were persistently poor over the nine years of data collection, two-thirds of those surveyed moved in and out of poverty (Dercon and Krutikova 2008). The World Bank's study *Moving Out of Poverty* (2009) shows that in West Bengal about 30 percent of those who began in poverty moved out over a 10-year period, but 21 percent of the nonpoor moved into poverty. The fact that "poverty is a condition, not a characteristic" (World Bank 2009) suggests that focusing only on the poor at a given time can underemphasize those among the nonpoor who face substantial risk of poverty.

Poverty dynamics aside, a second reason why a sharp distinction between the poor and nonpoor is unhelpful is that India's poverty line is very low by international standards. The official, all-India rural and urban poverty lines in 2004–05 were Rs 12 and Rs 18 per person per day, respectively. At 2005 purchasing power parity, these together represent a national poverty line of almost exactly $1 per day. That is well below the median poverty line among developing countries ($2 per day) and is also lower than the World Bank's international poverty line of $1.25 per day, defined as the average poverty line in the 15 poorest countries. India's line is also lower than what one would predict given the current level of India's mean consumption (Ravallion 2008).[18]

India's poverty lines are also low when compared to people's perceptions of what it means to be poor (box 1.5).

The point is not to discard the official poverty lines, as they serve the important and useful purpose of providing a common yardstick to track progress over time and across space (although even official poverty lines needed to be revisited from time to time, and India's are in urgent need of overhaul; see box 1.2). The point is simply to note that the combination of transitions in and out of poverty and a low poverty line suggests that policy design, and poverty analysis in general, must look beyond the "official poor."

Box 1.5 People's Perceptions of What It Means to Be Poor

Participatory methods, including techniques such as the ladder of life and community wealth rankings, have been used in a number of studies to elicit people's views about what it means to be poor and to specify a community poverty line—the threshold above which the community would consider its households to be no longer poor.

When people are asked to define who "the poor" are, the variety of responses is striking. Broadly classified, responses range among (a) economic indicators associated with livelihoods, assets, and income; (b) ability to meet basic needs for food, shelter, and clothing; (c) health and education; and (d) indicators of insecurity, exclusion, and lack of participation (Praxis 1999; Jayaram and Lanjouw 1999; Krishna 2004, 2006; Swaminathan 1995; Kozel and Parker 2005). These indicators may or may not correlate closely with consumption poverty (in India some, such as child nutrition status, do not).

Several studies also show that communities perceive the official poverty threshold to be too low. The World Bank's study *Moving Out of Poverty* (2009) found that two-thirds or more of the communities sampled in the four states covered—West Bengal, Assam, Andhra Pradesh, and Uttar Pradesh—felt that the official poverty-level figures were inadequate to meet basic needs. In those states, the community-defined poverty lines are much (10 to 20 percentage points) higher than the official ones.

Community-defined poverty lines have their own problems. For instance, such studies typically measure poverty in terms of the ranking of households relative to others in the locality, and not absolute poverty, and as a result, spatial comparisons of poverty are more difficult and ambiguous. Nonetheless, these findings suggest that the official poverty lines are better thought of as measuring absolute destitution than as capturing people's notions of what it means to be poor.

Source: Authors, drawing on the references cited.

This is particularly relevant to India where a large fraction of the officially nonpoor population, especially in rural areas, have consumption levels that are precariously close to the poverty line and thus have a tenuous hold on their nonpoor status (figure 1.10). That is particularly true of rural areas, where the median rural person (at the 50th percentile of the per capita consumption distribution) lives on Rs 15 per day, spending only Rs 3 more than a person at the poverty threshold. About 170 million rural households are in this lower middle class, consuming between Rs 12 and

Figure 1.10 India's Middle-Class Lives Barely or Not Far Above India's Poverty Line, and Below International Poverty Lines, Especially in Rural Areas

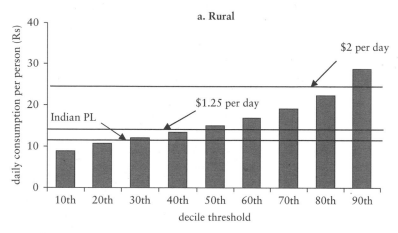

a. Rural

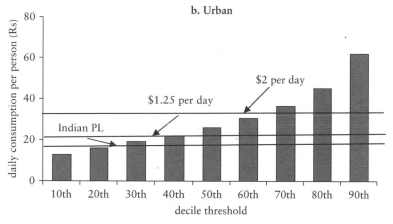

b. Urban

Source: Authors' estimates from NSS 2004–05 Schedule 1.0.

Note: Consumption estimates are in all-India rural or urban rupees and are corrected for cost-of-living differences between states using the official poverty lines. International poverty lines were converted to rupees using 2005 purchasing power parity rates of 11.4 Rs/$ in rural areas and 17.24 Rs/$ in urban areas. PL = poverty line.

Rs 15 a day. When that number is combined with the number of poor, it totals 390 million people in rural India who live on less than Rs 15 a day. With such a large number of people with consumption levels barely above the poverty line, it should come as no surprise that microstudies find the high frequency of transitions in and out of poverty described above.[19]

Compared to rural areas, in urban areas the middle class is more visibly different from the poor in consumption levels, with a near-doubling of expenditures between the 30th and 70th percentiles. The median urban person in 2004–05 lived on Rs 26 per day, spending about 40 percent more than a person at the urban poverty threshold.

In income terms, differences between the poor and middle-income groups are likely to be greater because of differences in savings rates. The National Sample Surveys do not collect data on household incomes. But information on ownership of selected durables is available, and it shows that middle-class households, in both rural and urban areas, are significantly more likely to own items such as radios, televisions, and electric fans. Asset ownership patterns are a reminder that small changes in consumption levels reflect real improvements in the quality of life. At the same time, however, vulnerability to shocks remains high when overall consumption levels are so low.

Tables 1.4 and 1.5 compare selected household characteristics for different groups of the expenditure distribution. Characteristics such as education level, social group status, and means of livelihood are clearly associated with poverty, in the expected directions. At the same time, the tables also reinforce the impression of tremendous heterogeneity within the middle class. In most dimensions, the lower tail of the rural middle class more closely resembles the attributes of the poor than of the rich. The urban middle class is more visibly different from the poor.

Table 1.4 Selected Characteristics of the Rural Poor, Middle Class, and Rich

Characteristic	Poor (lowest 30%)	Middle class (next 30%)	Middle class (next 20%)	Rich (top 20%)	Total
Social group					
Scheduled tribes	16.8	9.9	7.8	4.9	10.6
Scheduled castes	27.6	22.3	17.5	12.3	20.9
Other backward castes	39.2	45.3	44.1	43.0	42.8
General	16.4	22.5	30.6	39.7	25.7
All	100.0	100.0	100.0	100.0	100.0
Education: head of the household					
Illiterate	59.4	46.9	37.6	27.3	44.9
Literate and primary school	24.9	27.9	28.2	24.4	26.4
Middle school	9.9	14.4	17.7	18.9	14.6
Secondary and high school	5.1	9.4	13.6	21.4	11.4
Graduate school and higher	0.6	1.4	2.9	8.0	2.8
All	100.0	100.0	100.0	100.0	100.0
Main source of household income					
Self-employed: agriculture	14.1	16.9	16.9	19.3	16.5
Agricultural wage labor	38.8	25.9	17.5	9.9	24.9
Other labor	12.2	10.8	9.5	8.3	10.4
Self-employed: nonagriculture	30.4	40.5	46.9	44.1	39.5
Others	4.5	6.0	9.3	18.5	8.7
All	100.0	100.0	100.0	100.0	100.0

Source: Authors' estimates from NSS 2004-05 Schedule 1.0.
Note: Expenditure group classification based on uniform recall period measure of consumption. Expenditure corrected for cost-of-living differences across states using Government of India official poverty lines.

Table 1.5 Selected Characteristics of the Urban Poor, Middle Class, and Rich

Characteristic	Poor (lowest 30%)	Expenditure group Middle class (next 40%)	Rich (top 30%)	Total
Social group				
Scheduled tribes	3.7	2.7	2.4	2.9
Scheduled castes	23.8	15.6	7.6	15.7
Other backward castes	43.0	38.3	24.5	35.6
General	29.4	43.4	65.5	45.8
All	100.0	100.0	100.0	100.0
Education: head of the household				
Illiterate	39.1	16.9	5.3	20.1
Literate and primary school	29.3	23.8	10.0	21.3
Middle school	17.2	21.6	13.5	17.8
Secondary and high school	12.1	27.2	35.3	25.1
Graduate school and higher	2.3	10.5	35.9	15.6
All	100.0	100.0	100.0	100.0
Main source of household income				
Self-employed	45.7	44.1	38.8	43.0
Regular wage or salary earning	25.7	42.1	49.8	39.5
Casual labor	25.2	8.8	2.2	11.7
Others	3.4	5.1	9.2	5.8
All	100.0	100.0	100.0	100.0

Source: Authors' estimates from NSS 2004-05 Schedule 1.0.
Note: Expenditure group classification based on uniform recall period measure of consumption. Expenditure corrected for cost-of-living differences across states using Government of India official poverty lines.

Notes

1. This chapter draws from three background papers prepared for this report: Datt and Ravallion 2009; Deaton 2008; and Kapur and Witsoe 2008.

2. See, for example, Deaton and Kozel 2005, which includes a number of papers relevant to the debate.

3. The NSS 61st round from 2004–05 is the latest available thick round.

4. For example, using 1970 (instead of 1958) as the first year for the trend calculations would suggest a higher trend rate of poverty reduction in the pre-1991 period.

5. Some claim that the 1990s were "a lost decade for rural poverty reduction," suggesting that the poverty reduction between 1993–94 and 2004–05 was concentrated in the latter half of that period (Himanshu 2007). Others conclude exactly the opposite, arguing that most of the progress took place in the first half (Sundaram 2007).

6. However, problems related to public amenities were seen as worse, possibly because of increasing population pressure (Praxis 1999). Small, city-specific studies, despite some evidence of limited income mobility, also reveal little or no improvement in living conditions—shelter, basic amenities such as water and sanitation, and the living environment (see, for example, Swaminathan 1995; Praxis 1999).

7. Srinivasan 2007.

8. Progress in child malnutrition has also stalled. Trends in nutrition, health, and education outcomes are examined in chapter 4.

9. Real food consumption expenditure per capita has remained unchanged since the 1980s. The case of India is not unique. Several countries have experienced this phenomenon in the past, including China in the 1980s and 1990s (see Deaton and Drèze 2009; Patnaik 2007; Radhakrishnan et al. 2004; Rao 2005; and Sen 2005).

10. These estimates are derived from the NSS but are corroborated by other sources, including National Nutrition Monitoring Bureau (NNMB) data on declining calorie and protein consumption in nine states and declining aggregate food availability (Deaton and Drèze 2009; Patnaik 2007).

11. These are analogous to standard Engel curves and plot per capita calorie consumption against per capita household expenditure.

12. See Deaton and Drèze 2009 for a comprehensive review.

13. See Rao 2005; see also Jensen and Miller 2008 for a shift toward higher-quality but nutritionally inferior food in response to a simulated rice subsidy.

14. On rising inequality in India since the early 1990s, see Ravallion 2000; Deaton and Drèze 2002; and Sen and Himanshu 2004. On the

comparison with China, see Chaudhuri and Ravallion 2006. Taking the long view, between the 1950s and now, inequality in rural areas has tended to decline slightly (Datt and Ravallion 2009). Inequality within urban areas shows no clear trend in either direction over the period as a whole but since the 1980s shows a tendency to increase (see chapter 5).

15. The difference in survey-based post- and pre-1991 elasticities for the poverty gap and squared poverty gap measures is small and not statistically significant, consistent with the increase in inequality during the latter period.

16. This analysis is based on the urban-rural classification of the NSSO's tabulations. Over such a long period some rural areas would naturally have become urban areas. To the extent that rural (nonfarm) economic growth may help create such reclassifications, as successful villages evolve into towns, this may produce a downward bias in estimates of the (absolute) elasticities of rural poverty to rural economic growth.

17. Migration from rural (agriculture) to urban (industrial) settings has been a key driver in macromodels of economic development going back to the seminal work of Arthur Lewis (1954). It is known in theory that, under certain conditions, migration to urban areas can be very important to both growth and poverty reduction (Fields 1980; Anand and Kanbur 1985).

18. For India, the national poverty line of $1.03 per day is one-third below the value of $1.63 per day that is predicted based on India's NAS consumption per capita, based on the cross-country relationship in Ravallion, Chen, and Sangraula (2008).

19. The fact that a large share of India's nonpoor are clustered close to the poverty line has been noted previously by many. For a recent detailed discussion of characteristics of "India's common people," see Sengupta, Kanan, and Raveendran 2008.

References

Ahluwalia, M. S. 1978. "Rural Poverty and Agricultural Performance in India." *Journal of Development Studies* 14: 298–323.

———. 1985. "Rural Poverty, Agricultural Production, and Prices: A Reexamination." In *Agricultural Change and Rural Poverty*, ed. J. W. Mellor and G. M. Desai. Baltimore: Johns Hopkins University Press.

Anand, S., and R. Kanbur. 1985. "Poverty under the Kuznets Process." *Economic Journal* 95: 42–50.

Banerjee, A., and E. Duflo. 2006. "The Economic Lives of the Poor." MIT Department of Economics Working Paper 06-29. http://ssrn.com/abstract=942062.

Banerjee, A., and T. Piketty. 2003. "Top Indian Incomes: 1956–2000." *World Bank Economic Review* 19 (1): 1–20.

Bell, C., and R. Rich. 1994. "Rural Poverty and Agricultural Performance in Post-Independence India." *Oxford Bulletin of Economics and Statistics* 56 (2): 111–33.

Bhalla, S. 2002. "Imagine There's No Country: Poverty, Inequality and Growth in the Era of Globalization." Institute for International Economics, Washington, DC.

Bhattacharya, B., and S. Sakthivel. 2004. "Regional Growth and Disparity in India: Comparison of Pre- and Post Reform Decades." *Economic and Political Weekly* 39 (10): 1071–77.

Bhattacharya, N., D. Coondoo, P. Maiti, and R. Mukherjee. 1991. *Poverty, Inequality and Prices in Rural India*. New Delhi: Sage Publications.

Bruno, M., M. Ravallion, and L. Squire. 1998. "Equity and Growth in Developing Countries: Old and New Perspectives on the Policy Issues." In *Income Distribution and High-Quality Growth*, ed. Vito Tanzi and Ke-young Chu. Cambridge, MA: MIT Press.

CSO (Central Statistical Organisation). 2008. *Report of the Group for Examining Discrepancy in PFCE Estimates from NSSO Consumer Expenditure Data and Estimates Compiled by National Accounts Dvision*. Ministry of Statistics and Program Implementation, Government of India.

Chandrashekhar, C. P., and J. Ghosh. 2003. "The Calorie Consumption Puzzle." *Business Line*, February 11. http://www.blonnet.com/2003/02/11/stories/2003021100210900.htm.

Chaudhuri, S., and M. Ravallion. 2006. "Partially Awakened Giants: Uneven Growth in China and India." In *Dancing with Giants: China, India, and the Global Economy*, ed. L. Alan Winters and Shahid Yusuf. Washington, DC: World Bank.

Datt, G., and M. Ravallion. 1998. "Farm Productivity and Rural Poverty in India." *Journal of Development Studies* 34: 62–85.

———. 2002. "Has India's Post-Reform Economic Growth Left the Poor Behind?" *Journal of Economic Perspectives* 16 (3): 89–108.

———. 2009. "Has Poverty in India Become Less Responsive to Economic Growth?" Background paper prepared for India Poverty Assessment Report, World Bank, Washington, DC.

Deaton, A. 2008. "Price Trends in India and Their Implications for Measuring Poverty." *Economic and Political Weekly* 43 (6): 43–49.

Deaton, A., and J. Drèze. 2002. "Poverty and Inequality in India: A Re-Examination." *Economic and Political Weekly* 37 (36): 3729–48.

———. 2009. "Food and Nutrition in India: Facts and Interpretations." *Economic and Political Weekly* 44 (7): 42–65.

Deaton, A., and V. Kozel. 2005. *The Great Indian Poverty Debate*. New Delhi: Macmillan.

Deaton, A., and A. Tarozzi. 2005. "Prices and Poverty in India." In *The Great Indian Poverty Debate*, ed. A. Deaton and V. Kozel, chap. 16. New Delhi: Macmillan.

Deaton, Angus. 2005. "Measuring Poverty in a Growing World (or Measur ing Growth in a Poor World)." *Review of Economics and Statistics* 87: 353–78.

Dercon, S., and S. Krutikova. 2008. "Thirty Years Later: Welfare Dynamics of Some Well-Known Villages in Maharashtra and Andhra Pradesh." Background paper prepared for India Poverty Assessment Report, University of Oxford, U.K.

Dev, M., and C. Ravi. 2007. "Poverty and Inequality: All-India and States, 1983–2005." *Economic and Political Weekly* 42 (6): 509–21.

Elbers, C., J. O. Lanjouw, and P. Lanjouw. 2003. "Micro-Level Estimation of Poverty and Inequality." *Econometrica* 71 (1): 355–64.

Eswaran, M., and A. Kotwal. 1994. *Why Poverty Persists in India*. Delhi: Oxford University Press.

Fields, G. 1980. *Poverty, Inequality and Development*. Cambridge: Cambridge University Press.

Gaiha, R. 1989. "Poverty, Agricultural Production and Price Fluctuations in Rural India: A Reformulation." *Cambridge Journal of Economics* 13 (2): 333–52.

Gangopadhyay, S., P. Lanjouw, T. Vishwanath, and N. Yoshida. 2010. "Iden tifying Pockets of Poverty: Insights from Poverty Mapping Experiments in Andhra Pradesh, Orissa and West Bengal." *Indian Journal of Human Development* 4 (1): 5–28.

Gardner, K., and F. Osella. 2003. "Migration, Modernity and Social Trans formation in South Asia: An Overview." *Contributions to Indian Sociol ogy* 37 (1 & 2): 5–27.

GoI (Government of India, Planning Commission). 2009. *Report of the Expert Group to Review the Methodology for Estimation of Poverty*. http://planningcommission.nic.in/reports/genrep/rep_pov.pdf.

Henstchel, J., J. O. Lanjouw, P. Lanjouw, and J. Poggi. 2000. "Combining Census and Survey Data to Trace the Spatial Dimensions of Poverty: A Case Study of Ecuador." *World Bank Economic Review* 14 (1): 147–65.

Himanshu. 2007. "Recent Trends in Poverty and Inequality: Some Prelimi nary Results." *Economic and Political Weekly* 42 (6): 497–508.

————. 2009. "Estimate of Consumption Expenditure from National Accounts and Household Surveys." Manuscript, Jawaharlal Nehru University, New Delhi.

Jayaram, R., and P. Lanjouw. 1999. "The Evolution of Poverty in Indian Villages." *World Bank Research Observer* 14 (1): 1–30.

Jensen, R., and N. Miller. 2008. "Giffen Behavior and Subsistence Con sumption." *American Economic Review* 98 (4): 1553–77.

Jha, Raghbendra. 2000a. "Reducing Poverty and Inequality in India: Has Liberalization Helped?" Working Paper 204, World Institute of Develop ment Economics Research, Helsinki.

————. 2000b. "Growth, Inequality and Poverty in India: Spatial and Temporal Characteristics." *Economic and Political Weekly* 35 (March 11): 921–28.

Kapur, D., and J. Witsoe. 2008. "The Role of Spatial Mobility in India's 'Silent Revolution': A Case Study of Migration from Rural Bihar." Background paper prepared for India Poverty Assessment Report, Center for the Advanced Study of India, University of Pennsylvania, Philadelphia.

Kozel, V., and B. Parker. 2005. "Understanding Poverty and Vulnerability in India's Uttar Pradesh and Bihar: A Q-Squared Approach." Working Paper No. 9, October.

Krishna, A. 2004. "Escaping Poverty and Becoming Poor: Who Gains, Who Loses, and Why?" *World Development* 32 (1): 121–36.

————. 2006. "Pathways Out of and Into Poverty in 36 Villages of Andhra Pradesh, India." *World Development* 34 (2): 271–88.

Lanjouw. P., and R. Murgai. 2009. "Poverty Decline, Agricultural Wages, and Non-Farm Employment in India: 1983–2004." Policy Research Working Paper 4858, World Bank, Washington, DC.

Lewis, W. A. 1954. "Economic Development with Unlimited Supplies of Labour." *Manchester School* 28 (2): 139–91.

Munshi, K., and M. Rosenzweig. 2007. "Why Is Mobility in India So Low? Social Insurance, Inequality and Growth." International Policy Center Working Paper Series 68, University of Michigan, Ann Arbor.

Narayan, D., L. Pritchett, and S. Kapoor. 2009. *Moving Out of Poverty: Success from the Bottom Up*. New York: Palgrave Macmillan; Washington, DC: World Bank.

Patnaik, U. 2007. *The Republic of Hunger and Other Essays*. Gurgaon, India: Three Essays Collective.

Praxis. 1999. "Consultations with the Poor: India 1999." Background paper prepared for the *World Development Report 2000–01*, World Bank, Washington, DC.

Purfield, C. 2006. "Mind the Gap: Is Economic Growth in India Leaving Some States Behind?" IMF Working Paper 06/103, International Monetary Fund, Washington, DC.

Radhakrishna, R., K. H. Rao, C. Ravi, and B. S. Reddy. 2004. "Chronic Poverty and Malnutrition in the 1990s." *Economic and Political Weekly* 39 (28): 3121–30.

Rao, C. H. 2005. *Agriculture, Food Security, Poverty and Environment: Essays on Post-Reform India*. New Delhi: Oxford University Press.

Ravallion, M. 2000. "Should Poverty Measures Be Anchored to the National Accounts?" *Economic and Political Weekly* 34: 3245–52.

————. 2003. "Measuring Aggregate Economic Welfare in Developing Countries: How Well Do National Accounts and Surveys Agree?" *Review of Economics and Statistics* 85: 645–52.

———. 2008. "A Global Perspective on Poverty in India." *Economic and Political Weekly* 43 (October 25): 31–37.

Ravallion, M., S. Chen, and P. Sangraula. 2007. "New Evidence on the Urbanization of Global Poverty." *Population and Development Review* 33 (4): 667–702.

———. 2008. "Dollar a Day Revisited." Policy Research Working Paper 4620, World Bank, Washington, DC.

Ravallion, M., and G. Datt. 1996. "How Important to India's Poor Is the Sectoral Composition of Economic Growth?" *World Bank Economic Review* 10: 1–26.

Saith, A. 1981. "Production, Prices and Poverty in Rural India." *Journal of Development Studies* 19: 196–214.

Sen, A. 2005. "Estimates of Consumer Expenditure and Its Distribution. Statistical Priorities after the NSS 55th Round." In *The Great Indian Poverty Debate*, ed. A. Deaton and V. Kozel. New Delhi: Macmillan.

Sen, A., and Himanshu. 2004. "Poverty and Inequality in India 2: Widening Disparities during the 1990s." *Economic and Political Weekly* 39 (September 25): 4361–75.

Sen, P. 2005. "Of Calories and Things: Reflections on Nutritional Norms, Poverty Lines and Consumption Behaviour in India." *Economic and Political Weekly* 40 (43): 4611–18.

Sengupta, A., K. P. Kanan, and G. Raveendran. 2008. "India's Common People: Who Are They, How Many Are They, and How Do They Live?" *Economic and Political Weekly* 43 (11): 49–63.

Srinivasan, R. 2007. "A Decade of Economic Growth in India and China: Its Impact on Well-Being." Presentation, World Bank, Delhi, November.

Sundaram, K. 2007. "Employment and Poverty in India, 2000–2005." *Economic and Political Weekly* 42 (30): 3121–31.

Sundaram, K., and S. D. Tendulkar. 2001. "NAS–NSS Estimates of Private Consumption for Poverty Estimation: A Disaggregated Comparison for 1993–94." *Economic and Political Weekly* 42 (30): 119–29.

Swaminathan, M. 1995. "Aspects of Urban Poverty in Bombay." *Environment and Urbanization* 7 (1): 133–44.

Topalova, P. 2008. "India: Is the Rising Tide Lifting All Boats?" IMF Working Paper 08/54, International Monetary Fund, Washington, DC.

van de Walle, D. 1985. "Population Growth and Poverty: Another Look at the Indian Time Series Data." *Journal of Development Studies* 21: 429–39.

World Bank. 2009. *Moving Out of Poverty: The Promise of Empowerment and Democracy in India*. Washington, DC: World Bank.

2

Urban Growth and Poverty in Towns of Different Sizes

India's small towns rarely feature in discussions of the country's historical development experience. Nor do they figure prominently in forward-looking growth scenarios. That lack of attention merits revisiting. In his book *Butter Chicken in Ludhiana: Travels in Small Town India* (1995, 2006), Pankaj Mishra vividly documents the aggressive individualism and brash hunger for, and respect given to, wealth in India's small towns. He also bemoans the appalling infrastructural and civic conditions in the towns he visits. Much has been made of India's highly successful national cricket team, captained, in recent years, by such players as Mahindra Singh Dhoni. Dhoni hails from the small town of Ranchi, Jharkhand, and his aggressive style of play is often contrasted with the style of suave sporting heroes such as Kapil Dev, who come from more affluent, big-city backgrounds. India's small towns, it is increasingly argued, have been overlooked for too long. They are a potent source of dynamism and growth whose potential is waiting to be unleashed.

Introduction

This chapter examines the nature and dimensions of urban poverty, focusing in particular on small and medium-size conurbations in India, both as the urban subsector in which urban poverty is overwhelmingly concentrated and as a subsector that could potentially stimulate rural-based poverty reduction.

The analysis demonstrates that whereas poverty remains disproportionately rural at the aggregate level, urban poverty in India is growing in significance. In some states urban poverty rates are already judged to be greater than those in rural areas. Among urban areas, however, poverty rates in India's small towns are markedly higher than those in large metropolitan areas. Moreover, because a disproportionate share of India's urban population resides in small and medium-size cities, the urban poor are overwhelmingly to be found in these smaller places. Alongside the higher poverty rates, access to key services and institutions in small towns also lags behind the larger cities. These observations combine to indicate that efforts to address urban poverty should explicitly recognize its spatial distribution and the prominence of small towns in the picture.

This chapter examines more closely how city size and poverty might be related. Recent findings from the literature on economic geography (summarized in the 2009 *World Development Report*) emphasize potential positive spillovers from urban growth (often referred to as "agglomeration externalities") that may help to reduce poverty. The chapter attempts to distinguish such agglomeration externalities from other explanations for a poverty–city size gradient, such as policy biases (in infrastructure and service provision) in favor of large towns. It also investigates whether the observed poverty–city size relationship could arise out of a particular spatial distribution of cities, in which town size declines with distance from a dominant metropolitan area. In other words, the chapter asks whether the agglomeration externalities radiate only from a single dominant city or could be expected to arise also out of growth within individual towns and cities. The chapter finds evidence that agglomeration externalities do arise at the level of individual towns and cities. But it shows that inequalities in infrastructure access and proximity to a dominant metropolitan area can also play a role.

The chapter argues further that growth and poverty alleviation in India's small towns may also serve as an important entry point to *rural* poverty reduction. A small but growing literature points to a possible causal link from urban to rural poverty reduction, as also suggested by aggregate patterns of poverty reduction and growth (see chapter 1). Rural diversification into nonfarm activities (and resultant rural poverty reduction), for example, is found to occur more rapidly where consumption growth occurs in neighboring urban centers. Evidence suggests that the association is stronger if the urban center is a small town than if it is a large city. Such considerations suggest that an instrumental case may exist for special attention to small towns in urban poverty reduction efforts, alongside the strong normative case for such a focus.

Trends at the National and the State Level

A Slow but Persistent Urbanization of Poverty

Between 1983 and 2004–05, the incidence of poverty in India's urban population fell from 42.3 percent to 25.8 percent (table 2.1). This rate of decline in urban areas was broadly in line with the drop in the incidence of poverty from 46.5 percent to 28.1 percent recorded in rural areas during the same period. Similarly, as was also seen in rural areas, there is no evidence that the reduction of urban poverty accelerated between 1993–94 and 2004–05, compared to the preceding decade. Urban poverty fell seven percentage points between 1993–94 and 2004–05, a decline of 21 percent over the period. Between 1983 and 1993–94, urban poverty had fallen 9.5 points, a decline of 22 percent. The rate of poverty decline in urban areas thus remained roughly constant over the two decades.

Considering other summary measures of poverty, such as the poverty gap and the squared poverty gap, the overall picture on poverty trends remains unchanged (table 2.1). More striking, however, is that by 2004–05 these more distribution-sensitive measures of poverty suggest that urban poverty had come to exceed rural poverty. The poverty gap measure for 2004–05 takes a value of 5.9 for urban India, versus 5.5 in rural areas. Similarly the squared poverty gap measure takes a value of 2.0 in urban areas relative to 1.6 in rural

Table 2.1 Poverty in Urban India Tracks Rural Poverty

Indicators	1983	1993–94	2004–05
Headcount (%)			
Urban	42.3	32.8	25.8
Rural	46.5	36.8	28.1
Poverty gap (%)			
Urban	11.9	8.3	5.9
Rural	13.6	8.4	5.5
Squared poverty gap (%)			
Urban	4.9	3.0	2.0
Rural	5.8	2.8	1.6
Share of total population (%)			
Urban	23.3	25.7	27.8
Rural	76.7	74.3	72.2

Source: Authors' estimates based on respective NSS rounds.

Note: Based on population totals from the 1981, 1991, and 2001 censuses, respectively. Poverty rates based on official poverty lines and uniform recall period consumption measure.

areas. How to interpret these findings is somewhat unclear, however. As has already been noted in chapter 1, some controversy is associated with the comparison of India's official urban poverty lines to rural poverty lines. At the all-India level, these imply a cost of living in urban areas that is often 50 percent higher than in rural areas. It is clear that if this overstates the true cost-of-living difference between the two sectors, then urban poverty rates would be lowered relative to rural poverty rates.[1]

Setting aside possible doubts about implicit cost-of-living adjustments, the massively larger rural population in India means that in numbers of poor people, rural areas continue to claim the overwhelming share. At the time of the 1981 Population Census, 77 percent of India's population resided in rural areas. The proportion declined to 72 percent by the 2001 census.[2] Even with poverty rates that are roughly the same in rural and urban areas, therefore, out of every 100 poor people in India, only about 21 resided in urban areas in 1983, and only 26 did so in 2004–05.

As in the many other contexts considered in this book, all-India averages mask considerable geographic heterogeneity (table 2.2).

Table 2.2 At the State Level, There Is Some Stagnation and Some Dramatic Declines in Urban Poverty

percent

State	1983	1993–94	2004–05
Andhra Pradesh	38.0	38.8	27.4
Assam	22.1	7.9	3.6
Bihar	58.7	40.7	36.1
Gujarat	41.4	28.3	13.3
Haryana	28.1	16.5	14.5
Himachal Pradesh	12.6	9.3	3.2
Karnataka	43.0	39.9	32.6
Kerala	45.7	24.3	20.0
Madhya Pradesh	54.8	49.0	42.7
Maharashtra	41.0	35.0	32.1
Orissa	49.7	40.6	44.7
Punjab	23.5	10.9	6.3
Rajasthan	38.5	31.0	32.3
Tamil Nadu	50.8	39.9	22.5
Uttar Pradesh	52.4	36.1	30.1
West Bengal	33.4	22.9	13.5
Delhi	28.6	16.1	16.3
Others	22.8	11.4	7.1
All India	42.3	32.8	25.8

Source: Authors' estimates based on respective NSS rounds.

Although urban poverty declined steadily in India as a whole, it declined much more impressively in states such as Gujarat (from near the all-India average in 1983, to approximately half the average in 2004–05) and Punjab (from more than half the all-India average in 1983, to less than one-quarter in 2004–05). In Kerala and Tamil Nadu, urban poverty was higher than the all-India average in 1983 but had declined to well below the national average by 2004–05. In the former, progress was most rapid between 1983 and 1993–94, whereas in the latter the most impressive gains were achieved between 1993–94 and 2004–05.

Against such impressive performances, urban poverty reduction in Bihar, Madhya Pradesh, Maharashtra, Orissa, Rajasthan, and Uttar Pradesh was less encouraging. In Maharashtra urban poverty was approximately at the national average in 1983, but failed to decline in line with national trends, and in 2004–05 was some six percentage points higher than the all-India level. In Rajasthan, urban poverty was relatively low in 1983 but failed to decline appreciably over the survey period. In Orissa, an initially encouraging decline of nearly 10 percentage points between 1983 and 1993–94 was reversed to a certain extent after 1993–94, with the result that in 2004–05 urban poverty was highest in this state. In Bihar, Madhya Pradesh, and Uttar Pradesh urban poverty levels were already high in 1983 and fell only sluggishly over the survey period.

A recent study of global urban poverty by Ravallion, Chen, and Sangraula (2007) estimates that at the beginning of the present decade, roughly three quarters of the world's poor lived in rural areas. However, poverty is clearly becoming more urban over time (figure 2.1). In Latin America the process has advanced furthest, so that the majority of that region's poor now reside in urban areas. In East Asia the process is much less advanced, with less than 10 percent of the region's poor living in urban areas. As we have said, urbanization of poverty is also under way in India, although at a relatively slow rate. With the rural share of total poverty remaining at about 75 percent in 2004–05, India's situation is broadly in line with the global experience documented in Ravallion, Chen, and Sangraula (2007).

Poverty in Towns of Different Sizes

A relatively unnoticed feature of urban poverty throughout the developing world is that poverty rates can vary markedly across cities of different sizes, though it is far from a homogeneous phenomenon. Ferré, Ferreira, and Lanjouw (2009) drew on small-area poverty

Figure 2.1 A Slow but Persistent Urbanization of Poverty

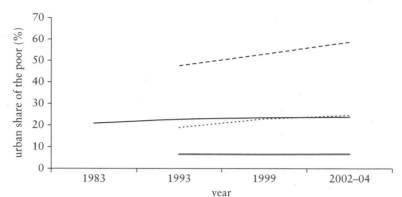

Sources: Ravallion, Chen, and Sangraula 2007, for regional estimates; authors' calculations from NSS data for Indian estimates.

estimation methods to investigate the relationship between poverty and city size in six developing countries (Albania, Brazil, Kazakhstan, Kenya, Morocco, and Sri Lanka). They found that in five of the six countries, poverty is clearly lowest and public service availability greatest in the largest cities—those where governments, middle classes, opinion makers, and airports are disproportionately located. They asked whether some kind of "metropolitan bias" might exist (including attention from policy makers) in the allocation of resources to larger cities, at the expense of the smaller towns where most of the poor live.[3] Alternatively, cities may attract better-educated, relatively affluent migrants, who are drawn to the more human-capital-intensive occupations that tend to cluster in larger cities and who are better able to withstand the cities' higher cost of living. Relatively less affluent migrants from rural areas may find the smaller towns more affordable. Rural communities that have grown and been reclassified as urban are also likelier to be classified initially as small urban centers. Given the relatively high incidence of poverty in rural areas, such communities may also be poorer than more established urban areas. The impetus behind the gradient between poverty and city size may also derive not so much from "neglect" of small towns as from the virtuous combination of factors that underpins economic and population growth in some urban centers.

In India, the higher incidence of poverty in small and medium-size towns has indeed been noticed and has been documented in several studies, notably Dubey, Gangopadhyay, and Wadhwa (2001); Kundu and Sarangi (2005); and Himanshu (2008). In his introductory chapter for the *India Urban Poverty Report* (UN 2009), Amitabh Kundu points to the comparatively high incidence of poverty in India's small towns (relative to metro cities) and argues that it is the consequence of a variety of factors that have favored large towns in recent decades. For example, he argues that globalization has facilitated the mobilization of resources by large cities by strengthening their internal resource base and enabling them to attract funds from global capital markets. Small towns, by contrast, have not seen similar opportunities arise. Kundu emphasizes further that small towns have fewer human and technical resources at their disposal and that consequently their capabilities for administration, planning, and implementation can be exceedingly weak (Kundu 2009).

BOTH SMALL AND MEDIUM-SIZE TOWNS AND LARGE CITIES HAVE EXPERIENCED SIGNIFICANT REDUCTION IN POVERTY LEVELS

Table 2.3 documents the heterogeneity in poverty rates across city size categories in all three survey years considered here. Although overall urban poverty in India was 42.3 percent in 1983, the rate in cities with populations of 1 million or more was only 29 percent. In towns with up to 50,000 inhabitants, the poverty rate at the same time was nearly 50 percent, higher even than rural poverty in that year. In 1993–94 and 2004–05, the same picture emerges: poverty in the large metropolitan centers is markedly lower than in the

Table 2.3 Poverty in Small Towns Approximates or Exceeds Rural Poverty

percent

Location	1983	1993–94	2004–05
Rural	46.5	36.8	28.1
Urban	42.3	32.8	25.8
Small town	49.7	43.4	30.0
Medium town	42.3	31.5	
Large town	29.0	20.2	14.7

Source: Authors' estimates based on respective NSS rounds.

Note: Poverty rates based on uniform recall period and official poverty lines. Town-size classifications based on population size: small (less than 50,000), medium (more than 50,000 and less than 1 million), and large (greater than or equal to 1 million). Small and medium classifications data are not possible for 2004–05 because of data considerations.

smaller urban centers. The National Sample Survey (NSS) data for 2004–05 do not lend themselves to a breakdown of the small and medium centers into separate categories. Nonetheless, even in that year it is clear that poverty in the large metro centers is considerably lower than in small and medium-size towns.[4] Despite different poverty levels in cities of different sizes, poverty trends indicate a broadly uniform rate of poverty decline. In proportional terms, the decline in the large cities was most significant (a 50 percent decline, from 29 percent to 14.7 percent), but that was not echoed in the absolute percentage point decline.

It is, of course, possible that poverty in metro centers is relatively low, but the overall distribution of the urban population is such that the bulk of the urban poor are to be found in the large cities. The empirical evidence does not bear that out, however.

SMALL AND MEDIUM-SIZE TOWNS CONTAIN ABOUT 70 PERCENT OF INDIA'S URBAN POPULATION AND, BECAUSE THEY ARE POORER, AN EVEN LARGER PROPORTION OF INDIA'S URBAN POOR, ABOUT 85 PERCENT

As depicted in table 2.4, in all three survey years considered here, small and medium-size towns accounted for between 73 percent and 81 percent of India's urban population. Combining the relatively high poverty rates in small and medium-size towns with their very large population share implies that the share of small and medium towns in urban poverty is overwhelming: 87 percent in 1983, declining only to 84.4 percent by 2004–05 (table 2.5).

Unsurprisingly, the aggregate picture reported in the tables masks a good deal of heterogeneity at the state and even the intrastate level

Table 2.4 Large Cities Account for a Small Share of the Urban Population

percent

Town size	1983	1993–94	2004–05
Small	34.3	31.3	72.6
Medium	46.9	47.4	
Large	18.9	21.3	27.4
Total	100	100	100

Source: Authors' estimates based on respective NSS rounds.

Note: Poverty rates based on uniform recall period and official poverty lines. Town-size classifications based on population size: small (less than 50,000), medium (more than 50,000 and less than 1 million), and large (greater than or equal to 1 million). Small and medium classifications data are not possible for 2004–05 because of data considerations.

Table 2.5 India's Urban Poor Are Overwhelmingly Found in Small and Medium-Size Towns

percent

Town size	1983	1993–94	2004–05
Small	40.3	41.4	84.5
Medium	46.8	45.5	
Large	12.9	13.1	15.6
Total	100	100	100

Source: Authors' estimates based on respective NSS rounds.

Note: Poverty rates based on uniform recall period and official poverty lines. Town-size classifications based on population size: small (less than 50,000), medium (more than 50,000 and less than 1 million), and large (greater than or equal to 1 million). Small and medium classifications data are not possible for 2004–05 because of data considerations.

(table 2.6). In states such as Gujarat, Karnataka, Maharashtra, and Uttar Pradesh, the basic pattern observed at the national level (table 2.3) is more or less replicated at the state level. In Andhra Pradesh, however, although the broad pattern holds, a more subtle trend appears over time: In 1983 poverty levels were high in all three size categories, even though poverty in the large towns was lowest. Between 1983 and 1993–94, poverty in the large size category declined sharply, whereas it actually rose in the two smaller size categories. Between 1993–94 and 2004–05 poverty in the smaller categories registered a significant decline, while poverty in the large towns did not appear to decline further. By the latter year, urban poverty overall was considerably lower than in 1983, but differences across size categories were again relatively muted. The evidence thus suggests something of a ratcheting process in poverty reduction across city size categories, perhaps as a result of varying policy stances vis-à-vis urban areas over time. A similar process appears for West Bengal where, although poverty is relatively low in the metro centers, an impressive reduction of poverty in the small and medium-size towns was achieved between 1993–94 and 2004–05.

In Bihar in the first two survey years a fairly strong gradient in poverty appears between the small and the medium size categories. In those two survey rounds no city in Bihar had more than 1 million inhabitants. By 2004–05, Patna had passed the million mark, and poverty in this center is clearly lower than in the other city size category. Unfortunately, the data do not permit us to assess whether the gradient between the small and medium-size towns was less once Patna was no longer counted among the medium-size towns.

The evidence for Rajasthan reminds us that although the NSS sample size for the quinquennial rounds is large, estimating poverty rates

Table 2.6 A Relatively Low Poverty Rate in Large Cities Is Also Reflected in State-Level Estimates

percent

State	1983				1993–94				2004–05		
	Small	Medium	Large	All	Small	Medium	Large	All	Small and medium	Large	All
Andhra Pradesh	39.1	37.7	36.4	38.0	45.1	39.0	19.6	38.8	28.4	22.7	27.4
Assam	26.9	14.5	n.a.	22.1	9.0	6.5	n.a.	7.9	3.6	n.a.	3.6
Bihar	67.8	52.2	n.a.	58.7	54.4	34.5	n.a.	40.7	42.0	12.9	36.1
Gujarat	50.0	42.1	26.7	41.4	36.5	24.5	25.4	28.3	16.7	8.6	13.3
Haryana	31.0	26.7	n.a.	28.1	12.6	17.9	n.a.	16.5	16.3	6.1	14.5
Himachal Pradesh	13.2	10.1	n.a.	12.6	11.1	2.0	n.a.	9.3	3.2	n.a.	3.2
Karnataka	49.0	46.9	26.9	43.0	52.2	39.8	17.2	39.9	41.7	7.9	32.6
Kerala	49.6	41.7	n.a.	45.7	28.8	18.7	n.a.	24.3	20.0	n.a.	20.0
Madhya Pradesh	61.1	50.5	n.a.	54.8	58.6	44.7	38.4	49.0	47.0	24.2	42.7
Maharashtra	55.2	51.3	24.6	41.0	59.0	44.3	17.0	35.0	48.5	16.5	32.1
Orissa	54.6	46.1	n.a.	49.7	44.7	37.5	n.a.	40.6	44.7	n.a.	44.7
Punjab	31.3	18.9	n.a.	23.5	14.9	11.5	3.1	10.9	7.0	3.4	6.3
Rajasthan	40.5	36.7	n.a.	38.5	38.1	29.7	17.7	31.0	29.8	42.3	32.3
Tamil Nadu	56.8	51.3	40.9	50.8	45.6	39.5	32.3	39.9	25.5	8.7	22.5
Uttar Pradesh	62.7	48.8	29.9	52.4	50.3	27.6	25.6	36.1	33.8	17.7	30.1
West Bengal	41.7	32.4	25.2	33.4	33.8	22.8	10.3	22.9	16.9	3.2	13.5
Delhi	n.a.	n.a.	28.6	28.6	n.a.	n.a.	16.1	16.1	23.4	14.9	16.3
Others	25.0	21.3	n.a.	22.8	11.5	11.3	n.a.	11.4	7.1	n.a.	7.1
All India	49.7	42.3	29.0	42.3	43.4	31.5	20.2	32.8	30.0	14.7	25.8

Source: Authors' estimates based on respective NSS rounds.

Note: Poverty rates based on uniform recall period and official poverty lines. Town-size classifications based on population size: small (less than 50,000, medium (more than 50,000 and less than 1 million), and large (greater than or equal to 1 million). Small and medium classifications data are not possible for 2004–05 because of data considerations. n.a. = not applicable.

across city size categories at the state level may at times be pushing the data too hard. Although the 1993–94 round indicates that the poverty rate in the large towns in Rajasthan was 17.7 percent, the rate for that category in 2004–05 is estimated to be 42.3 percent. Such a sharp rise is surprising, and the fact that the estimate for large cities is now markedly *higher* than that for small and medium-size towns presents a further puzzle. It is, of course, possible that push migration from rural areas to Rajasthan's largest cities has been dramatic between 1993–94 and 2004–05, leading to an extraordinary increase in poverty in the largest city size category. That such major migration flows took place, however, is difficult to imagine. The *India Urban Poverty Report* documents a relatively slow rate of rural-urban migration during recent decades, and it points to a muted role for the kind of push factors that are likely to result in a sharp increase in urban poverty following significant migration flows (UN 2009). Another possible explanation may be that in 2004–05 the NSS sample size for large-city Rajasthan was less than half that in 1993–94, and at 117 (clustered) observations, it may not provide a very robust estimate of urban poverty.

As was observed at the national level, the patterns of poverty across city size categories are such that at the state level, the disproportionate share of the poor are also generally to be found in smaller towns. The data in table 2.7 reveal that whereas in all the states the proportion of poor people in large cities is lower than in small and medium-size cities, states such as Gujarat, Maharashtra, and Rajasthan (although note the discussion above about poverty estimates in urban Rajasthan) have shares of poor people in their large metropolitan areas that are markedly higher than at the national level, indicating that the large urban centers in these states are particularly large in number or in size.

Small Towns Have Less Access to Services

As Pankaj Mishra observed in his travels through small-town India, and as Kundu notes explicitly in the *India Urban Poverty Report,* small towns differ from large cities not only in their higher poverty rates, but also in lower levels of access to public services. In their examination of six developing countries, Ferré, Ferreira, and Lanjouw (2009) document marked differences in per capita availability of a variety of public services across city size categories. For example, in Brazil 92 percent of the population in large metropolitan centers has access to waste removal services, but only 75 percent of the population in the smallest cities does. Similarly, in Morocco 84 percent of the population in the largest cities is connected to a networked water supply, and 87 percent has access to the electricity

Table 2.7 At the State Level, the Urban Poor Also Reside Overwhelmingly in Small Towns

percent

State	1983				1993–94				2004–05		
	Small	Medium	Large	All	Small	Medium	Large	All	Small and medium	Large	All
Andhra Pradesh	33.5	51.6	14.9	100	35.1	59.6	5.3	100	85.2	14.8	100
Assam	74.7	25.3	n.a.	100	63.8	36.2	n.a.	100	100.0	n.a.	100
Bihar	48.0	52.0	n.a.	100	41.8	58.2	n.a.	100	92.8	7.2	100
Gujarat	43.9	41.0	15.1	100	37.8	34.5	27.7	100	73.2	26.9	100
Haryana	36.2	63.8	n.a.	100	20.7	79.3	n.a.	100	92.4	7.6	100
Himachal Pradesh	86.0	14.0	n.a.	100	95.7	4.3	n.a.	100	100.0	n.a.	100
Karnataka	47.7	37.5	14.9	100	48.3	43.2	8.5	100	93.5	6.5	100
Kerala	55.4	44.6	n.a.	100	65.8	34.2	n.a.	100	100.0	n.a.	100
Madhya Pradesh	45.0	55.0	n.a.	100	46.7	39.7	13.6	100	89.5	10.6	100
Maharashtra	31.6	43.2	25.2	100	34.9	43.1	22.1	100	73.7	26.4	100
Orissa	46.1	53.9	n.a.	100	47.6	52.4	n.a.	100	100.0	n.a.	100
Punjab	49.3	50.7	n.a.	100	31.0	64.3	4.7	100	89.8	10.2	100
Rajasthan	50.2	49.8	n.a.	100	43.6	48.5	7.8	100	73.3	26.7	100
Tamil Nadu	35.6	47.2	17.2	100	36.6	46.6	16.9	100	93.0	7.1	100
Uttar Pradesh	45.8	49.2	5.0	100	53.5	38.9	7.6	100	86.7	13.3	100
West Bengal	33.8	50.8	15.5	100	35.1	55.9	9.0	100	94.0	6.0	100
Delhi	n.a.	n.a.	100.0	100	n.a.	n.a.	100.0	100	24.5	75.5	100
Other	45.5	54.6	n.a.	100	43.8	56.2	n.a.	100	100.0	n.a.	100
All India	40.3	46.8	12.9	100	41.4	45.5	13.1	100	84.4	15.6	100

Source: Authors' estimates based on respective NSS rounds.

Note: Poverty rates based on uniform recall period and official poverty lines. Town-size classifications based on population size: small (less than 50,000), medium (more than 50,000 and less than 1 million), and large (greater than or equal to 1 million). Small and medium classifications data are not possible for 2004–05 because of data considerations. n.a. = not applicable.

grid. In the small and medium-size Moroccan cities, access to such public services is roughly 10 percentage points lower (Ferré, Ferreira, and Lanjouw 2009).

NSS data for India do not provide much systematic evidence on access to public services. However, the information on access to electricity connections across city size classes suggests that the patterns observed elsewhere also apply in India (table 2.8). At the all-India level in 1983, 54 percent of the population in small towns used electricity as the chief source of lighting, and 66 percent in medium-size towns did so. In the largest cities in that year, access to electricity was markedly higher, at 77 percent. By 2004–05, access to electricity had improved across all urban areas. Nonetheless, whereas more than 96 percent of the population in metro centers used electricity for lighting, the figure for small and medium-size cities was still lagging, at about 90 percent. In some states differences in access are far more pronounced.

Whereas the broad pattern of higher poverty levels and less access to services in small towns is likely fairly robust in India, an important caveat to this assessment concerns health outcomes. Chattopadhyay and Roy (2005) drew on National Family Health Survey (NFHS) data for 1998–99 to demonstrate that a variety of indicators of child mortality are higher in large cities than in towns and medium-size cities. Interestingly, the analysis reveals that although infant mortality rates among the wealthiest classes in large cities are particularly low, the rates among the poorest classes are quite high, higher than among the poor in small and medium-size towns (table 2.9). These are suggestive findings and may be related to the particularly unhealthy living conditions in overcrowded slum areas of large cities.

Evidence on such health patterns remains scarce, however, and no broad consensus appears in the literature on the relatively higher health risks in large cities. For example, Kapadia-Kundu and Kanitkar (2002) argue, on the basis of evidence from microstudies in Maharashtra, that urban public health services generally place greater emphasis on megacities and metro centers, to the relative neglect of smaller cities and towns.[5]

Insights from Small-Area Estimation in West Bengal, Orissa, and Andhra Pradesh

As mentioned above, there are limits to how far one can push NSS survey data in an analysis of the patterns of poverty across city size classes. For example, sample size considerations prevent a city-by-city analysis of poverty. As was noted in chapter 1, poverty map

Table 2.8 Access to Electricity Is Generally Higher in Large Towns

percent

State	1983				1993–94				2004–05		
	Small	Medium	Large	All	Small	Medium	Large	All	Small and medium	Large	All
Andhra Pradesh	53.0	65.0	76.4	62.8	75.5	83.5	96.5	82.5	95.7	94.4	95.5
Assam	43.5	55.5	n.a.	48.1	69.5	81.3	n.a.	74.7	84.9	n.a.	84.9
Bihar	28.6	43.1	n.a.	37.1	37.0	70.3	n.a.	59.9	63.3	99.6	70.7
Gujarat	80.6	81.7	80.6	81.0	87.6	93.8	89.5	90.7	97.0	95.4	96.3
Haryana	75.0	89.8	n.a.	84.9	94.6	89.5	n.a.	90.9	95.6	97.3	95.9
Himachal Pradesh	91.0	97.4	n.a.	92.1	99.1	100.0	n.a.	99.3	91.4	n.a.	91.4
Karnataka	62.2	70.6	68.7	66.6	76.7	84.3	93.1	83.2	95.6	96.7	95.9
Kerala	56.3	66.2	n.a.	61.1	74.3	81.2	n.a.	77.4	93.5	n.a.	93.5
Madhya Pradesh	60.8	66.7	n.a.	64.3	86.1	92.9	95.5	90.7	96.1	98.9	96.6
Maharashtra	59.9	70.6	82.0	72.9	75.9	92.0	95.1	90.1	94.1	97.8	96.0
Orissa	37.3	56.5	n.a.	48.5	63.4	74.8	n.a.	69.9	81.5	n.a.	81.5
Punjab	84.1	88.3	n.a.	86.7	96.3	95.8	99.2	96.5	98.5	98.2	98.4
Rajasthan	53.5	73.4	n.a.	63.9	84.3	93.1	94.7	90.2	91.8	79.3	89.3
Tamil Nadu	58.4	67.9	68.6	65.0	81.5	82.5	81.4	81.9	94.3	96.4	94.7
Uttar Pradesh	36.2	64.2	64.9	53.5	53.6	86.7	85.8	73.9	78.7	97.5	83.0
West Bengal	32.0	52.8	76.4	52.0	55.9	71.3	88.3	71.0	83.9	93.5	86.3
Delhi	n.a.	n.a.	82.6	82.6	n.a.	0.0	97.9	97.9	99.9	98.6	98.8
Other	68.3	82.8	n.a.	76.8	89.6	90.9	n.a.	90.4	97.6	n.a.	97.6
All India	54.2	66.5	77.2	64.3	73.4	85.2	92.6	83.1	90.3	96.4	92.0

Source: Authors' estimates based on respective NSS rounds.

Note: Poverty rates based on uniform recall period and official poverty lines. Town-size classifications based on population size: small (less than 50,000), medium (more than 50,000 and less than 1 million), and large (greater than or equal to 1 million). Small and medium classifications data are not possible for 2004–05 because of data considerations. Data indicate share of population using electricity as primary source for lighting. n.a = not applicable.

Table 2.9 Urban Infant and Child Mortality Is Highest among the Poor in Large Cities

Standard of living	Infant mortality rate (%)	Neonatal mortality (%)	Post-neonatal mortality (%)	Child mortality (%)	Under-five mortality (%)	Child not anemic (%)
Large city						
Low	77	42	35	64	141	16
Medium	44	34	10	15	59	27
High	27	18	9	5	32	42
Medium city or town						
Low	66	39	27	35	101	24
Medium	56	36	19	19	75	32
High	31	23	8	5	36	37
Countryside						
Low	87	53	34	44	130	25
Medium	70	44	26	27	97	29
High	45	33	12	11	56	33

Source: Chattopadhyay and Roy 2005, 8 and 10, using National Family Health Survey - II 1998–99.

estimates are available for West Bengal, Orissa, and Andhra Pradesh. The poverty mapping pilot project from which these derive combined unit record data from the 2001 Population Census with NSS data from the 2004–05 round to estimate poverty and inequality at the *tehsil* and district levels. The procedure also makes it possible to estimate poverty at the level of individual towns and cities for urban areas and thereby offers an opportunity to further assess the relationship between poverty and city size in those three states. The three states included in the pilot project are interesting for the purpose of the analysis in this book because their profiles of urbanization vary appreciably. For example, West Bengal has one dominant metro center, Kolkata, whereas Andhra Pradesh has a few large cities and many small and medium-size cities. Orissa has no large metro center at all, but it, too, has many small and medium-size cities.

The basic patterns described in earlier sections also appear in small-area estimates for the three states (table 2.10). In West Bengal, Orissa, and Andhra Pradesh the incidence of poverty is systematically higher in the small towns than in the large cities. As those smaller urban settings also account for a disproportionate share of the urban population, the overwhelming share of the poor in all three states can be found in towns of 500,000 persons or less.

Figure 2.2 reveals that when poverty at the city level is regressed on its population, and allowance is made for some nonlinearity in the relationship between poverty and population, then for the states of Andhra Pradesh and Orissa an inverted U shape appears, in which poverty first rises and then falls with city size. In West Bengal the relationship is broadly linear. However, even in Andhra Pradesh and Orissa, the turning point in the U-shaped relationship occurs at 40,000 and 15,000 inhabitants, respectively, indicating that even in these states the broad relationship of lower poverty in larger towns and cities is quite robust.

Data from the *Census Town Directory* for 2001(GoI 2001) provide an opportunity to examine in somewhat greater detail the relationship between city size and access to certain key public services. Data for this purpose are available for West Bengal and Andhra Pradesh and are displayed in table 2.11. In these two states, the pattern appearing in table 2.8, of greater access to electricity for lighting in large towns, can be seen to extend also to other important infrastructure services, such as waterborne latrines, access to piped drinking water, and availability of hospital beds. The pattern of access can be readily understood when related to data on public revenues and expenditures across city size classes. *Census Town Directory* data on such revenues and expenditures reveal that the smallest towns in Andhra Pradesh and West Bengal raise fewer rupees per capita than

Table 2.10 Small-Area Estimates Reveal High Poverty in Small Towns in Three States

City size	West Bengal				Orissa				Andhra Pradesh			
	Number of towns	% of population	% of poor	Poverty rate (%)	Number of towns	% of population	% of poor	Poverty rate (%)	Number of towns	% of population	% of poor	Poverty rate (%)
Extra large	1	20	8	5	n.a.	n.a.	n.a.	n.a.	1	18	17	23
Large	1	5	4	12	2	21	20	34	3	13	7	14
Medium	54	48	46	13	6	22	19	31	37	39	37	24
Small	28	9	12	17	15	19	19	36	40	15	20	33
Extra small	298	18	31	23	121	38	42	39	104	15	18	31

Source: Authors' estimates from the poverty mapping pilot.
Note: City-size classifications based on population: Extra large > 1 million; Large: 500,000–1,000,000; Medium: 100,000–500,000; Small: 50,000–100,000; Extra small < 50,000. n.a. = not applicable.

Figure 2.2 In Andhra Pradesh and Orissa Poverty First Rises with Town Size, but Then Falls

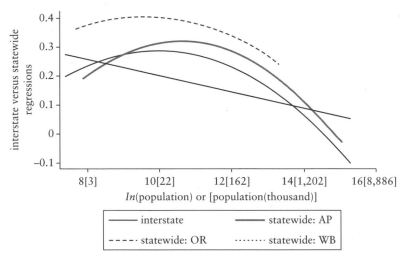

Source: Authors' estimates from the poverty mapping pilot.
Note: AP = Andhra Pradesh, OR = Orissa, and WB = West Bengal.

do larger urban centers.[6] To some extent, the imbalance appears to be compensated for by higher per capita receipts from government grants in the small towns. However, the imbalance remains when total expenditures per capita are considered, with the smallest towns spending considerably less per person than medium-size and larger towns. If the per capita cost of public service provision is higher in small towns relative to large cities (because of, say, significant fixed costs), then these patterns of expenditures understate the imbalance in service delivery across city size classes. Given our specific interest in poverty, perhaps the most worrying feature of the data on public funding in table 2.11 is that per capita spending on public works projects is markedly lower in the small towns, despite evidence that poverty is particularly pronounced in such towns.

Urban Agglomeration and Poverty Reduction

Combining small-area estimates of poverty at the individual town level with data from the Population Census and from the *Census Town Directory* provides an opportunity to probe the links between urbanization and poverty in greater depth. The "new economic geography" literature and also the recent *World Development Report,*

Table 2.11 Differential Access to Services in Andhra Pradesh and West Bengal Mirrors Per Capita Spending across City Size Classes

Town class (population in 2000s)	Number per 1,000 population			Piped water as primary source of drinking water (% towns)	Rs per capita			
	Latrines (waterborne)	Domestic electricity connections	Hospital beds		Total revenues	Government grants	Total expenditures	Public works
< 50	99.5	125.2	0.88	48.5	461.6	285.2	430.2	80.0
50–100	96.0	135.9	2.40	76.5	577.5	272.0	509.0	113.6
100–500	90.5	126.4	1.78	76.5	638.1	248.4	552.4	119.4
> 500	145.0	186.0	2.04	100	677.2	164.5	522.2	166.6
All	98.1	127.6	1.25	57.7	509.7	275.8	462.6	92.3

Source: Census 2001.

titled *Reshaping Economic Geography*, devote considerable attention to the mechanisms through which concentration of population and economic activities can generate various kinds of externalities (for example, Krugman 1999; Henderson, Shalizi, and Venables 2001; World Bank 2009). The literature shows that urban agglomeration can be associated with positive externalities for productivity and economic growth but can also cause negative externalities once agglomeration has surpassed a certain threshold.[7]

An empirical literature exists that examines the links between urban agglomeration and productivity (see, for example, Lall et al. 2004; Deichmann et al. 2004; Lall, Schroeder, and Schmidt 2008), but empirical analysis of links between poverty and urbanization, particularly urban agglomeration, is still limited. This chapter attempts to fill that gap, treating population of cities and towns as a key proxy of urban agglomeration. However, it is important to recognize that the association between urban poverty and city population need not represent solely an urban agglomeration effect. As we have seen above, large cities often have better access to infrastructure and other public services. Residents in large cities also may be affluent because the city in which they reside happens to be located near a dominant metropolitan area (with its own agglomeration externalities), and not because of agglomeration effects within their city of residence. Because the distinction between the three factors is critical for urban planning, it is not sufficient simply to associate urban poverty and city size (as shown in tables 2.3, 2.6, and 2.10 and in figure 2.2). In this section we try to distinguish among the three factors of agglomeration, public service access, and proximity to other urban centers.

Using data from the India poverty mapping pilot for Andhra Pradesh, Orissa, and West Bengal, we estimate a model of poverty on city size, also controlling for access to infrastructure services and distance to the nearest large town. As described above, this latter effect also seems potentially important, as in all three states a positive relationship appears between poverty in a given urban center and distance from the nearest city of 100,000 (1 lakh) inhabitants or more (figure 2.3). This relationship is sharpest when examined using data from all three states combined ("interstate" regression).

Table 2.12 presents the results of the regression analysis. Four sets of models are estimated—one in which all towns and cities in West Bengal, Orissa, and Andhra Pradesh are combined and three that consider each state in turn. Within each set of models, the relationship among poverty, city size (proxied by population), and distance to the nearest large city is estimated, once controlling for a wide set of variables proxying access to infrastructure services and once

Figure 2.3 Poverty in a Town Is Higher the Farther the Town Is from a Large City

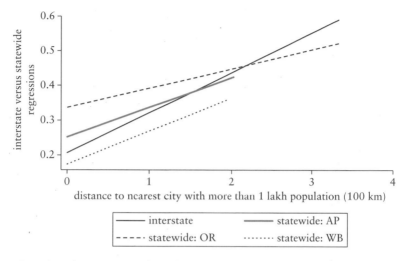

Source: Authors' estimates from the poverty mapping pilot.
Note: AP = Andhra Pradesh, OR = Orissa, and WB = West Bengal.

without conditioning on such infrastructure variables. For reasons of space, the models in table 2.12 do not report coefficients on the set of infrastructure variables, but these include such variables as per capita electricity connections, per capita health facilities, per capita school facilities, presence of a railway station, and the like. Multicollinearity across these variables implies that many of the parameter estimates are not estimated with precision. Moreover, endogeneity associated with placement effects implies that parameter estimates on several of the variables do not always accord with intuition (for example, in some of the models a positive correlation appears between poverty and the number of elementary schools). What is clear, though, is that inclusion of these infrastructure variables contributes significantly to the overall explanatory power of the models.

Urban Agglomeration Translates to Lower Urban Poverty, Independent of the Effect of Access to Infrastructure

In the models reported in table 2.12, poverty is found to decline with city size. In the combined state sample, in Andhra Pradesh, and (weakly so) in Orissa, some curvature appears in the relationship: poverty first rises, but then it falls with population size. However, the turning point in all three cases occurs at a rather small town size, such that the basic comparison of poverty in

Table 2.12 Poverty Is Lower in Large Towns and Cities, Even After Controlling for Infrastructure Access and Distance to Metropolitan Areas

Variables	Interstate		Andhra Pradesh		Orissa		West Bengal	
	Conditional	Unconditional	Conditional	Unconditional	Conditional	Unconditional	Conditional	Unconditional
Log (population)	0.099 [0.049]*	0.272 [0.057]**	0.4 [0.109]**	0.369 [0.092]**	0.009 [0.130]	0.23 [0.138]+	-0.033 [0.005]**	-0.028 [0.005]**
Log (squared population)	-0.006 [0.002]*	-0.014 [0.003]**	-0.018 [0.005]**	-0.017 [0.004]**	0 [0.006]	-0.012 [0.007]+		
Distance to the nearest large city (100 km)	0.093 [0.009]**	0.115 [0.009]**	0.082 [0.024]**	0.085 [0.021]**	0.062 [0.012]**	0.056 [0.012]**	0.111 [0.015]**	0.096 [0.016]**

Source: Authors' estimates based on data from the India poverty mapping pilot.
Note: Standard errors in brackets; + significant at 10 percent level; * significant at 5 percent level; ** significant at 1 percent level.

medium-size and large cities (above 100,000 inhabitants, for example) versus small towns (with less than 100,000) points unambiguously to higher poverty in the smaller towns. In the case of West Bengal, the data suggest a linear relationship and also point resolutely to higher poverty in smaller agglomerations. This relationship is robust to inclusion of infrastructure variables. In fact, comparing the conditional versus the unconditional models, respectively, in the four sets of models indicates that the parameter representing the broad relationship between poverty and city size is largely unchanged in the cases of Andhra Pradesh and West Bengal. Only in the case of Orissa is the relationship different in size, and no longer significant, after conditioning for access to infrastructure variables. Table 2.12 thus suggests that urban agglomeration does indeed translate to lower urban poverty, independent of the effect of access to infrastructure.[8]

More Remote Urban Centers Tend to Be Poorer

Table 2.12 further confirms that distance to the nearest large city also exerts an independent and significant effect on urban poverty. Although agglomeration effects are playing a role, the results also indicate a separate and significant influence on poverty of proximity to a large urban center. The data for West Bengal can be scrutinized in somewhat greater detail on this point because our dataset includes distance to Kolkata as a separate variable for each of 120 cities in West Bengal. Distance to Kolkata can thus be separately controlled for in the models reported in table 2.12. It shows that city size and distance to Kolkata are very strongly and negatively correlated within a radius of roughly 100–200 kilometers from Kolkata. Beyond that range, however, the relationship between city size and distance to Kolkata largely vanishes (figure 2.4).

After some experimentation, it was found that a model of poverty on city size in West Bengal can be usefully estimated on three subsets of the full dataset. Table 2.13 shows that when towns are split into three groups—within a 100-kilometer radius of Kolkata, in a radius of 100–200 kilometers, and more than 200 kilometers from Kolkata—poverty sharply rises with distance from Kolkata when the towns are within a 100-kilometer radius. This relationship is weaker in the second group, and completely absent in the third, most distant group. In the first group, no separate influence of city size appears, indicating that the agglomeration effect that really matters is the one generated by Kolkata. However, in the second group, and even more strongly so in the third group, a separate agglomeration effect (as proxied by city size) is discernible,

Figure 2.4 Only within a 100–200 km "Catchment Area" around Kolkata Does City Size Decline with Distance from Kolkata

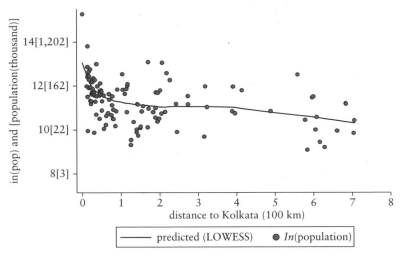

Source: Authors' estimates based on data from the India poverty mapping pilot.

Table 2.13 Proximity to Kolkata Is a Key Correlate of Urban Poverty in West Bengal, but Only within a Relatively Narrow "Catchment Area" around That City

Distance to Kolkata	< 100 km	100 km–200 km	> 200 km
Log (population)	0.003	−0.029	−0.056
	[0.011]	[0.014]*	[0.019]**
Distance to Kolkata	0.156	0.100	−0.008
	[0.041]**	[0.040]*	[0.011]
Distance to the closest large city[a]	0.098	−0.015	0.002
	[0.032]**	[0.041]	[0.030]
Observations	59	29	32
R^2	0.47	0.55	0.64

Source: Authors' estimates based on data from the India poverty mapping pilot.

Note: Standard errors in brackets; * significant at 5 percent level; ** significant at 1 percent level; controls include infrastructure variables, but no district fixed effects.

a. Distance to the closest city with more than 1 lakh population.

independent of the influence of distance to Kolkata. In other words, in areas of West Bengal that are distant from Kolkata, it is growth of the particular town that should be looked to for impetus in reducing urban poverty in that town, not the agglomeration effects deriving from Kolkata.

Urban Growth Is a Source of Rural Poverty Reduction

As described in chapter 1, a study by Datt and Ravallion (2009) draws on India's long series of household surveys, spanning roughly 55 years since 1951, to point to a noticeable change in the relative importance of urban versus rural economic growth. An earlier study by the same authors had found that urban growth had an impact on urban poverty but no discernible impact on rural poverty (Datt and Ravallion 1996). But after 1991 that picture appears to have changed markedly in India. Although it is unquestionable that rural growth remains vital for rural poverty reduction, Datt and Ravallion (2009) also highlight evidence of a growing link between urban economic growth and reduction of rural (and therefore also aggregate) poverty.

A recent study by Cali and Menon (2009) presents further evidence that urban growth is an important determinant of rural poverty reduction. Cali and Menon found multiple mechanisms that can account for this link. They distinguish, first, the obvious, first-round effects of population movements from rural to urban areas. For example, urban growth may induce migration of poor people from rural areas to urban areas. Rural areas may also grow in size over time and become classified as urban. If the formerly rural areas have significant concentrations of poor people, rural poverty may register a decline as a result of such reclassifications. Cali and Menon then point to numerous possible second-round paths of transmission. Growth in urban areas may translate into a growing demand for rural goods, and if those are perishable, such a demand will most likely be met through growing trade with surrounding rural areas (see, for example, Fafchamps and Shilpi 2003, on Nepal). Diversification out of agriculture in rural areas may take place via increased daily commuting to work in growing urban centers, greater specialization of rural households in certain economic activities (accompanied by a greater reliance on the market for other consumption and input needs), and increased marketing and transport activities associated with agricultural trade. Cali and Menon point further to remittance incomes from urban to rural areas that may rise as a result of urban growth, agricultural wages in rural areas that may rise as rural labor markets tighten (as a result of nonfarm diversification), and a rise in rural land prices as a consequence of demand to shift land from agricultural uses to residential use. Finally, the authors note that consumer prices for a variety of goods and services may fall (or rise less rapidly) as a result of urban growth and greater competition, and that can also benefit rural households in the surrounding areas.

In their study, Cali and Menon attempt to disentangle the first-round effects (those relating to the movement of poor people to urban areas) from the second-round effects. They argue that by estimating a district-level model of rural poverty on urban population as well as urban poverty (controlling, in addition, for rural population and population characteristics and also for agricultural productivity), the parameter estimate on urban population can be considered as largely purged of the first-round effect of population movement (migration) on rural poverty.[9] The study reveals a strong, robust effect of urban population growth in reducing rural poverty. This applies for various measures of rural poverty, as well as for numbers of rural poor people. According to the Cali and Menon study, the incidence of rural poverty in a district decreases by about 2 percent to 3 percent with an increase of 200,000 urban residents in the district. As noted, the authors argue that this is attributable to the second-round effects discussed above, rather than to migration into urban areas by the district's rural poor.[10]

A recent study by Lanjouw and Murgai (2009) found support for the suggestion in Cali and Menon (2009) that urban growth can promote rural nonfarm diversification. Drawing on a region-level panel dataset constructed from multiple rounds of NSS data, the study indicates that growth in per capita consumption in urban areas is associated with growth in rural nonfarm employment, particularly salaried and self-employment activities (not casual wage labor). Lanjouw and Murgai (2009) further show that growth in rural nonfarm employment is associated with rising agricultural wages and falling rural poverty (see also chapter 3).

Evidence Indicates That Small Towns Have a Closer Link with Rural Poverty

Does the relationship among urbanization, rural nonfarm employment, and rural poverty vary by city size? The small-area estimates of poverty and inequality for West Bengal, Orissa, and Andhra Pradesh provide some clues. Table 2.14 indicates that in West Bengal and Andhra Pradesh the share of the *tehsil*-level rural workforce employed in nonfarm activities is positively and significantly related to the proportion of urban centers in the district to which the *tehsil* belongs that are classified as small. This relationship holds whether or not the correlation between nonfarm employment and small town share also controls for a wide range of infrastructure and other, demographic, characteristics. In Orissa the relationship is not so

Table 2.14 Rural Nonfarm Employment Is Higher in Districts with More Small Towns and with Lower Urban Poverty

percent

Variable	Andhra Pradesh		Orissa		West Bengal	
	Unconditional	Conditional	Unconditional	Conditional	Unconditional	Conditional
Urban headcount	0.117	−0.356	−0.759	−0.246	−0.359	−0.501
	[0.042]***	[0.086]***	[0.112]***	[0.185]	[0.131]**	[0.201]***
Fraction of small towns	0.085	0.236	−0.012	−0.155	−0.230	1.370
in the district	[0.023]***	[0.045]***	[0.035]	[0.058]	[161]	[0.343]***
R^2	0.01	0.4	0.13	0.57	0.08	0.59

Source: Authors' estimates based on data from the India poverty mapping pilot.
Note: Standard errors in brackets; *** significant at 1 percert level, ** significant at 5 percent.

clear-cut, with the evidence in that state pointing to a negative relationship in the model with infrastructure controls. However, as noted above, there are very few large towns in Orissa. What the models for all three states also demonstrate is that, controlling for the share of small towns in the district, the overall level of urban poverty in the district is strongly and negatively associated with the fraction of the rural workforce employed in the nonfarm sector. Thus, rural nonfarm employment tends to be positively related to urban growth (poverty reduction), and that appears to be the case particularly if the urban growth occurs in small towns.

Not Only Would Poverty Reduction in Small Towns Target Most of India's Urban Poor, but Evidence Indicates That It Would Have a Larger, Spillover Effect on Rural Poverty

Table 2.15 indicates that for the three states the overall elasticity of rural, *tehsil*-level poverty with respect to urban poverty (calculated across towns and cities in the district in which the *tehsil* is located) is 0.44 for small towns (less than 100,000 inhabitants) and 0.26 for large towns. These estimates control for overall population in the district, as well as the share of the district population that is urban.

Table 2.15 The Elasticity between Rural and Urban Poverty Rates Is Greater for Small Towns

Variable		
Log incidence of poverty in small towns (in district)	0.435 [3.47]	0.400 [3.30]
Log incidence of poverty in large towns (in district)	0.263 [2.77]	0.262 [2.76]
Total population in district	−0.272 [−5.40]	−0.279 [−5.59]
Share of district population that is urban	0.059 [1.11]	
State dummy: Andhra Pradesh	−1.72 [−19.02]	−1.705 [−29.23]
State dummy: Orissa	−0.400 [−3.52]	−0.372 [−3.35]
Adjusted R^2	0.336	0.336

Source: Authors' estimates based on data from the India poverty mapping pilot.

Note: West Bengal, Orissa, and Andhra Pradesh combined. Standard errors in brackets. Dependent variable is log of rural poverty at the *tehsil* level.

The evidence is consistent with the notion that rural poverty is more sensitive to changes in poverty in small towns than in large cities. However, it is important to acknowledge that in all of the models presented the direction of causality between, say, rural poverty and urban poverty, or rural nonfarm employment and urban poverty, could be running both ways (and quite possibly causal effects may be running both ways at once). The findings reported here can thus at best be regarded as suggestive.

Implications for Policy

In this chapter we have provided an update to the year 2004–05 on the extent of urban poverty in India and on progress in reducing urban poverty (nationally and at the state level) during the two decades leading up to 2004–05. Poverty in India is urbanizing, albeit at a rate that at present is still moderate. Details of measurement methodology have a bearing on conclusions regarding the speed of the process, but it seems safe to say that looking forward, urban poverty is going to loom ever larger on the radar of Indian policy makers.

We have argued that it is important to appreciate that urban areas are far from homogeneous and that one important way in which one can document heterogeneity is by distinguishing among small, medium-size, and large cities. Both nationally and at the state level, there exists a fairly consistent relationship between the extent of urban poverty and the size of the urban center. Poverty rates are uniformly higher in smaller towns than in the large cities of India. In addition, in terms of sheer numbers, small towns account for a disproportionate share of the urban poor. This is readily understood in light of the high poverty rates in such towns, as well as the number of such towns in the country as a whole, so that they represent a dominant share of the entire urban population. The patterns observed in India are consistent with those also observed in other developing countries.

How one thinks about this empirical regularity from a policy perspective is not entirely clear. One point of departure is to argue that poverty in small towns is higher than in large cities as a result of neglect of small towns by policy makers. One could point to evidence of lower public service provision and access in small towns in favor of this perspective. However, other plausible departure points exist. Migration flows and the factors influencing migration destinations may operate in such a way that poor migrants from rural areas are more likely to settle in small towns than to make the wholesale shift from their rural origins to large metropolitan areas. At the same time, educated and relatively affluent migrants may be drawn to the large cities from both rural areas and small towns, attracted by the skill-intensive occupations that tend to cluster in the larger cities. Reclassification of rural areas as urban areas is also occurring as a result of population growth. Formerly rural communities become classified as urban as their populations grow. Initially they are likely to be classified as small urban settlements. These rural communities may also harbor larger concentrations of poor people than are generally found among the incumbent urban population. In this way, small urban settlements naturally come to be seen as homes to the urban poor. One can also frame the observation of lower poverty levels in large cities as a story of particularly successful development in these large conurbations. The question then comes to be whether, and how, policy makers can anticipate, and possibly assist in, the acceleration of such virtuous development processes in other towns.

"Agglomeration externalities" are a widely noted feature of successful large cities. We have attempted in this chapter to distinguish the role of such agglomeration externalities from other explanations for a poverty–city size gradient, such as policy biases (in infrastructure and service provision) in favor of large towns. We have also investigated whether agglomeration externalities radiate only from a single dominant city or could be expected to arise also out of growth within individual towns and cities. We have uncovered evidence that a single, dominant metropolitan area can indeed exert considerable "pull" on urban poverty rates but that agglomeration externalities arise also at the level of individual towns and cities. Differences in infrastructure access across city size categories also reveal an independent association with poverty.

Irrespective of the normative view one takes of the relatively high poverty in small towns, we argue here that the empirical regularity cannot be ignored. It raises important questions that require additional investigation. A clear priority is to uncover the determinants of growth in India's towns and cities and to delineate the role that policy makers can play. More work is also needed to understand better the role of migration in the dynamics of urban growth and the spatial distribution of urban poverty. How does the cost of providing public goods and services vary across city size categories? How are the challenges of urban administration and city management best confronted, in light of significant shortages of skilled and experienced administrators? With urban poverty only likely to loom larger on the horizon, these are important questions that call for urgent attention.

The chapter closes with the conjecture that a good strategy of urban development and poverty reduction may also make excellent sense from a rural poverty perspective. We have argued that rural nonfarm diversification (and resultant rural poverty reduction), for example, is found to occur more rapidly where consumption is growing in neighboring urban centers. We point to evidence suggesting that the association is stronger if the urban center is a small town than if it is a large city. Galvanizing the urban sector, particularly small towns, may thus be an important pillar of a strategy to combat rural poverty.

Notes

1. It is clear that assessment of poverty levels and poverty trends is sensitive to the choice of poverty lines underpinning the estimates. The *Report of the Expert Group to Review the Methodology for Estimation of Poverty* (GoI 2009) proposes an alternative, as yet not officially endorsed, set of poverty estimates for 1993 and 2004–05. The revised poverty lines proposed by the Expert Group indicate that urban-rural price differences may be less than in the current official poverty lines. State-level urban poverty rates are thus correspondingly lower than rural poverty rates in all states. At the national level, the rate of poverty decline between 1993–94 and 2004–05 is somewhat lower according to these estimates than is reflected in the official statistics. However, in contrast to the official statistics, the new estimates suggest that the percentage decline in poverty has been somewhat more rapid in urban than in rural areas between 1993–94 and 2004–05. For further discussion of the alternative poverty estimates for India, see chapter 1.

2. As was noted in chapter 1, NSS and Population Census data indicate that rural-urban migration in India is relatively slow. However, this evidence does not command a universal consensus. Certain commentators draw on village study evidence to argue that seasonal migration and short-duration migration are not well captured in large-scale survey data (Kapur and Witsoe 2008; Gardner and Osella 2003).

3. Ferré, Ferreira, and Lanjouw (2009) suggest that although "urban bias" was a much-discussed concern during the 1970s and 1980s, following Lipton (1977), the idea of a "metropolitan bias" has not been widely emphasized in the poverty measurement literature. That is likely attributable, at least in part, to scant availability of data on living standards across finely defined city size categories.

4. A potentially important objection to poverty comparisons across city size classes is that the use of a single set of urban poverty lines fails to allow for cost-of-living variation across city size categories. Palmer-Jones

and Dubey (2007) investigated such cost of living differences in India and found that the cost of living in cities is indeed higher than in other urban areas. However, the differences they documented are unlikely to suffice to overturn the conclusion that poverty in small towns exceeds that in large metro centers. Ferré, Ferreira, and Lanjouw (2009) undertook a similar analysis in Brazil and found that correcting for price variation across city size categories somewhat attenuates the gradient between poverty and city size but is far from sufficient to negate or overturn the broad finding that in Brazil, the incidence of poverty in the smallest towns is roughly three times higher than in metro centers.

5. Lanjouw and Rascon (2010) scrutinized the incidence of stunting among children up to five years of age across city size categories in Mexico and found a clear pattern of lower stunting rates in larger towns and cities.

6. The quality of these data on public revenues and expenditures is not easily assessed. We point here simply to some patterns across city size classes, without subjecting them to particularly close scrutiny.

7. The threshold is likely to be highly context specific; no fixed "optimal city size" exists. Tokyo is a city that arguably works well with a population of 40 million; other cities with a fraction of Tokyo's population barely function at all.

8. For the specific case of Andhra Pradesh, where there is a relatively high frequency of multiple towns and cities per district, we were able to experiment with a district-level fixed-effects specification, in addition to controlling for infrastructure access at the city level and distance to nearest large city. The basic finding of a (nonlinear) negative relationship between poverty and city size is robust to this specification.

9. Cali and Menon (2009) also apply instrumental variables to control for direction of causality between urbanization (urban population growth) and rural poverty. They use the number of migrants from other states to the urban areas of the district as an instrument.

10. In contrast to Datt and Ravallion (2009), the Cali and Menon study indicates that the sensitivity of rural poverty to urbanization is in fact greatest in the period prior to 1993. The results in Cali and Menon (2009) also show that rural poverty is significantly associated with urban poverty. A 10 percent fall in the incidence of poverty in urban areas is associated with a 3–4 percent fall in rural poverty.

References

Cali, M., and C. Menon. 2009. "Does Urbanization Affect Rural Poverty? Evidence from Indian Districts." Spatial Economics Research Center Discussion Paper 14, London School of Economics, London, U.K.

Chattopadhyay, A., and T. K. Roy. 2005. "Are Urban Poor Doing Better Than Their Rural Counterpart in India? A Study of Fertility, Family Planning and Health." *Demography India* 34 (2): 299–312.

Datt, G., and M. Ravallion. 1996. "India's Checkered History in the Fight against Poverty: Are There Lessons for the Future?" *Economic and Political Weekly* 31: 2479–86.

———. 2009. "Has Poverty in India Become Less Responsive to Economic Growth?" Background paper prepared for *India Poverty Assessment Report*, World Bank, Washington, DC.

Deichmann, U., M. Fay, K. Jun, and S. V. Lall. 2004. "Economic Structure, Productivity, and Infrastructure Quality in Southern Mexico." *Annals of Regional Science* 38: 361–85.

Dubey, A., S. Gangopadhyay, and W. Wadhwa. 2001. "Occupational Structure and Incidence of Poverty in Indian Towns of Different Sizes." *Review of Development Economics* 5: 49–59.

Fafchamps, M., and F. Shilpi. 2003. "The Spatial Division of Labour in Nepal." *Journal of Development Studies* 39 (6): 23–66.

Ferré, C., F. H. G. Ferreira, and P. Lanjouw. 2009. "Is There a Metropolitan Bias? Urban Poverty and Access to Services by City Size in Six Developing Countries." Draft, World Bank, Washington, DC.

Gardner, K., and F. Osella, eds. 2003. "Migration, Modernity and Social Transformation in South Asia: An Overview and Contributions to Indian Sociology." *Contributions to Indian Sociology* 37 (1–2) : 109–39.

GoI (Government of India). 2001. *Census Town Directory*. New Delhi: Office of the Registrar General.

———. 2009. *Report of the Expert Group to Review the Methodology for Estimation of Poverty.* New Delhi: Government of India, Planning Commission.

Henderson, J. V., Z. Shalizi, and A. J. Venables. 2001. "Geography and Development." *Journal of Economic Geography* 1: 81–105.

Himanshu. 2008. "Agriculture and Non-Farm Employment: Exploring the Inter-linkages in Rural India." Draft, Jawaharlal Nehru University, New Delhi.

Kapadia-Kundu, N., and T. Kanitkar. 2002. "Primary Healthcare in Urban Slums." *Economic and Political Weekly* 37: 5086–89.

Kapur, D., and J. Witsoe. 2008. "The Role of Spatial Mobility in India's 'Silent Revolution': A Case Study of Migration from Rural Bihar." Background paper prepared for *India Poverty Assessment Report,* Center for the Advanced Study of India, University of Pennsylvania, Philadelphia.

Krugman, Paul. 1999. "The Role of Geography in Development." *International Regional Science Review* 22 (2): 142–61.

Kundu, A.. 2009. "Elite Capture and Marginalization of the Poor in Participatory Urban Governance. A Case of Resident Welfare Associations in Metro Cities." In *India Urban Poverty Report 2009*. New Delhi: Oxford University Press.

Kundu, A., and N. Sarangi. 2005. "Employment Guarantee in India: The Issue of Urban Exclusion." *Economic and Political Weekly* 40: 3642–46.

Lall, S. V., U. Deichmann, M. K. A. Lundberg, and N. Chaudhury. 2004. "Tenure, Diversity, and Commitment: Community Participation for Urban Services Provision." *Journal of Development Studies* 40: 1–26.

Lall, S. V., E. Schroeder, and E. Schmidt. 2008. "Geographically Prioritizing Infrastructure Improvements to Accelerate Growth in Uganda." Background paper for 2009 *World Development Report: Reshaping Economic Geography*, World Bank, Washington, DC.

Lanjouw, P., and R. Murgai. 2009. "Poverty Decline, Agricultural Wages, and Nonfarm Employment in Rural India: 1983–2004." *Agricultural Economics* 40 (2): 243–64.

Lanjouw, P., and E. Rascon. 2010. "Child Malnutrition and City Size in Urban Mexico." Draft, Development Economics Research Group, World Bank, Washington, DC.

Lipton, M. 1977. *Why Poor People Stay Poor: Urban Bias and World Development*. London: Temple Smith.

Mishra, P. 2006. *Butter Chicken in Ludhiana. Travels in Small Town India*. London: Picador.

Palmer-Jones, R., and A. Dubey. 2007. "Poverty Measurement, Poverty Lines and Consumer Price Indexes in India: A Critique." Presentation at the "International Seminar on Revisiting the Poverty Issue: Measurement, Identification and Eradication," A. N. Sinha Institute, Patna, July 20–22.

Ravallion, M., S. Chen, and P. Sangraula. 2007. "New Evidence on the Urbanization of Global Poverty." *Population and Development Review* 33 (4): 667–702.

World Bank. 2009. *World Development Report 2009: Reshaping Economic Geography*. Washington, DC: World Bank.

UN (United Nations). 2009. *India Urban Poverty Report, 2009*. New Delhi: Oxford University Press.

3

A Casual Transformation: The Growing Rural Nonfarm Sector

Rural India is home to 75 percent of the country's population and about the same proportion of its poor. Seventy percent of the rural workforce is in agriculture, a sector whose growth has lagged others in the economy. Although the need to galvanize agriculture is inescapable, it is also clear that India needs to manage a transition of people out of agriculture. The gap between the number of new rural workers and the number of new agricultural jobs is growing; advances in agriculture alone will not meet the rural employment challenge. Migration to urban areas will be important, but the nonfarm rural economy will also have to produce many new jobs. Chapter 1 alludes to a growing importance of the nonfarm sector. This chapter asks whether the growth of the nonfarm sector has played a role in reducing rural poverty. In particular, it brings together various National Sample Survey (NSS) employment surveys that enable us to track changes in the nonfarm sector over the last 20 years.[1]

The chapter begins by looking at the transformation of India's countryside that is currently under way, a transformation in the economic basis of ordinary people's lives. Individuals and households are migrating from rural to urban areas, and an increasing number of those staying behind are moving into the nonfarm sector—30 percent in 2004–05, up from 20 percent in 1983. In the last 10 years, nonfarm employment has been growing about four times as fast as farm employment, and in rural areas more new jobs have been created off-farm than on. Though the growth of nonfarm employment is accelerating, it remains slow when compared to rates in China and other successful Asian countries.

Nonfarm employment is of many different types and in many different sectors. Contrary to popular perception, most nonfarm jobs are in the service sector. The manufacturing sector now provides less than a third of nonfarm jobs. Construction is the fastest-growing rural nonfarm sector and provides almost 20 percent of nonfarm employment, up from 10 percent only a decade ago. The employment growth rates of the different sectors show tremendous variation. Growth in all sectors accelerated in the 1990s, compared to the 1980s, except for social services and public administration, where growth fell to zero. Rural manufacturing employment has been growing at an annual average rate of 3 percent since 1994, other services (largely transportation, trade, and communications, largely dominated by the private sector) at 5.5 percent, and construction at almost 10 percent.

The changing composition of nonfarm employment has had major implications for the types of employment on offer. About 50 percent of participants in the nonfarm sector are self-employed, a ratio that has stayed fairly constant over time. Although growth in all types of nonfarm employment accelerated after 1993, the fastest growth was in casual employment, and the share of casual employment in the total rose from 24 percent in 1983 to 29 percent in 2004. In addition, the gap in wages between regular and casual employment has narrowed, especially when measured in terms of the median, and a dual wage structure is emerging in the regular employment category: well-paid regular employees have seen a growth in their average wage, whereas poorly paid regular employees have seen little growth in the average wage and more growth in numbers. This is all consistent with the large increases in government pay of 1999–2000, which led to a fiscal crisis and resultant contraction in government employment. An expansion in private activity occurred, offering a mix of lower-paid jobs, a large amount of casual work, and opportunities for self-employment. In sum, a trend emerged toward the "casualization" of the nonfarm sector.

Thus, the picture is mixed. The number of workers moving into nonfarm employment is growing, but the quality of nonfarm employment is declining. It is difficult to say much about total nonfarm earnings inasmuch as data on the earnings of half of the nonfarm workforce, namely, the self-employed, are unavailable. However, if we restrict our attention to the employed group within the rural nonfarm sector and look at the nonfarm wage bill, which includes the effects of changes in participation and compensation, we find it growing very steadily through the two-decade period, at about 6 percent.

What sort of impact is this expansion of the nonfarm employment sector having on rural poverty in India? Further on in the chapter we look at the characteristics of those individuals who obtain nonfarm jobs and what sort of jobs they get. It is mainly men who obtain nonfarm jobs, primarily young men. Women of all ages, as well as older men, are much more likely to be locked into agriculture. Not surprisingly, the better-educated are more likely to obtain regular employment. They are also more likely to become self-employed, as are socially advantaged groups. In the casual segment of the nonfarm sector, however, the education barriers are lower, and the socially disadvantaged have participated in the expansion of the nonfarm sector as much as any other group. In the last decade fewer high-paying government jobs have been available, but the poor were less likely to obtain those jobs in any case. Casual jobs have seen the fastest growth, and they are precisely the jobs that the poor are more likely to obtain (because they are more likely to be uneducated and socially disadvantaged). Given that casual nonfarm employment, though worth considerably less than regular employment, still pays considerably better than agriculture (the wage premium is about 45 percent), the direct impact of nonfarm growth on the poor is likely to have been positive.

Such a household-level analysis can only take us so far. Ultimately, an aggregate analysis of the impact of nonfarm employment on rural poverty is required to take account of indirect effects, such as the upward pressure exerted by nonfarm employment growth on rural wages. The regression analysis described later in this chapter finds a positive impact, with nonfarm employment reducing poverty both directly and through upward pressure on the agricultural wage rate. Agricultural wages have been growing at a decelerating rate in rural India; the analysis shows that in the absence of labor market tightening due to the nonfarm sector, agricultural wage growth would have been even slower.

It is clear from our findings that expansion of the nonfarm sector will further the reduction of rural poverty in India. But what can be done to accelerate such an expansion? Later in the chapter we take advantage of the variations in the nonfarm sector across the country to explore the determinants of its growth. Although the data available do not permit investigation in depth, the analysis suggests that expansion of the nonfarm sector in recent years has been more closely linked with urban than with agricultural growth. The nonfarm sector is also expanding more rapidly in areas of the country where education levels are higher. Of course, state and local factors are also important, but without more information on the rural investment climate, we cannot be certain what they are picking up.

Three main policy conclusions follow from this analysis. First, promoting nonfarm employment is an important poverty reduction strategy. Nonfarm jobs are now responsible for almost 50 percent of rural household incomes. Even casual nonfarm jobs pay significantly more than agriculture, and nonfarm employment puts upward pressure on agricultural wages. All that said, not enough nonfarm employment exists to displace agriculture as an important determinant of rural poverty in India today. Efforts to improve agricultural productivity will still be essential, even as the agricultural workforce continues its transition out of agriculture into rural (and urban) nonfarm jobs. Second, nonfarm rural growth may be accelerated by faster urban growth. Third, improving access to education will improve the access of the poor to all forms of nonfarm employment, but especially the better-paying regular jobs.

India's Rural Transformation: In Slow Motion but Picking Up Speed

Rural Nonfarm Employment Is Expanding

After a long period during which the share of agriculture in the labor force remained constant, its share started declining in the mid-1970s, a trend that continues to this day. The share of the rural nonfarm sector (all rural employment activities other than agriculture and its associated enterprises) has been increasing ever since, and it now employs nearly 30 percent of India's rural workforce (figure 3.1). That amounts to about 100 million people who spend most of the year working in nonfarm activities.[2]

The Rate of Expansion Is Accelerating. Since 1993, Most New Rural Jobs Have Been in the Nonfarm Sector

In fits and starts (with a slowdown immediately following the reforms in the early 1990s) the pace of diversification away from agriculture picked up in the decade 1993–2004, especially after 1999.[3] Over the first period, 1983 to 1993–94, the average annual growth in nonfarm jobs was just over 2 percent. Between 1993–94 and 1998–99, growth increased to 3 percent, and from 1999 to 2004–05, it increased again to 4 percent. In the 1980s, of the nearly 40 million additional rural jobs generated, 6 out of every 10 were in the farm sector. But more recently, between 1993 and 2004, nonfarm employment growth has outstripped agriculture: of the 56 million new rural jobs created over that period, 6 out of every 10 were in the nonfarm sector (figure 3.2).

Figure 3.1 The Rural Nonfarm Sector Is Expanding at a
Slow, but Accelerating, Pace

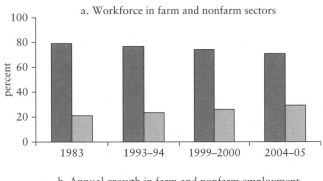

a. Workforce in farm and nonfarm sectors

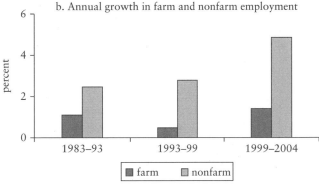

b. Annual growth in farm and nonfarm employment

Source: Authors' estimates based on employment and unemployment surveys of
respective NSS rounds.

Note: Employment defined on the basis of principal-cum-subsidiary (usual) status.
Farm versus nonfarm assignment is based on workers' reported industry, occupation,
and employment status. The numbers of farm and nonfarm workers are calculated
using (a) estimated proportions from unit-level data and (b) total rural workforce as
in Sundaram 2007.

Nearly One-Half of Rural Incomes Are Now from Nonfarm Earnings

Data on rural nonfarm income are not available over time. But,
according to the 2004 India Human Development Survey by the
National Council of Applied Economic Research and the University
of Maryland, nearly one-half (48 percent) of the income of the average rural household comes from nonfarm earnings (Dubey 2008).
This is true also if we look specifically at farming households, whose
income from nonagricultural activities (46 percent) matches the
share from agriculture (Cai, de Janvry, and Sadoulet 2008).

Figure 3.2 Rural Nonfarm Sector Is the Source of Most
New Jobs

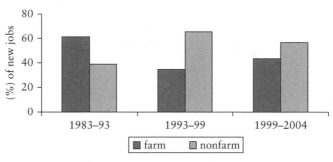

Source: Authors' estimates based on employment and unemployment surveys of
respective NSS rounds.

Note: Employment defined on the basis of principal-cum-subsidiary (usual) status.
Farm versus nonfarm assignment is based on workers' reported industry, occupation,
and employment status. The numbers of farm and nonfarm workers are calculated
using (a) estimated proportions from unit-level data and (b) total rural workforce as
in Sundaram 2007.

India's Rural Transformation Is Nevertheless Slow and Is Unusual by International Standards

India's transformation in employment has been slow compared to
those in fast-growing East Asian countries (Ghose 2004). In China,
the percentage of the labor force engaged in agriculture fell sharply
from 70 percent in 1979 to 47 percent in 1999. India, by contrast,
witnessed only a nine percentage point decline in the agricultural
labor force over roughly the same 21-year period, despite a sharp
decline in the contribution of agriculture to national income since the
early 1980s. At that time agriculture accounted for nearly two-fifths
of gross domestic product (GDP), whereas it accounted for half that
by 2004. Much of the rural labor force, especially women, as we will
see, remains locked into agriculture. The nature of India's rural transformation—described in the next section—is also in marked contrast
to that of other developing countries, especially in East Asia, where
manufacturing, not services and construction, has been the major
source of employment for workers moving out of agriculture.

The Casualization of Nonfarm Work

Rural nonfarm employment displays enormous heterogeneity in
terms of both sector and type of employment. The analysis of this

section points to a growing, but increasingly casualized, rural non-farm sector. The casualization of nonfarm work is evident in the sectors where jobs are being created as well as the types of jobs.

Rural Nonfarm Work Is Mainly, and Increasingly, in Services and Construction, Rather Than Manufacturing

Although manufacturing activities are often the first that come to mind in discussions of the nonfarm sector, services, in fact, now provide employment for just over half of rural nonfarm workers (figure 3.3). Only one-third of jobs are in manufacturing; the remaining one-sixth are in construction. These shares have changed significantly over time. Particularly notable is the rapid rise of construction over the last decade, from only 11 percent of rural nonfarm employment in 1993 to 18 percent in 2004–05. The share of social services (actually public administration and community services, as well as health and education) shows a corresponding decline over the period, from 26 percent to 18 percent.

Employment in Construction is Booming; That in Social Services Stagnating

All sectors saw a pickup in their employment growth rate in the 1990s, except for social services, which did not grow at all. The evident stagnation is likely due to the tight restrictions on government hiring following the fiscal crisis of the late 1990s (World Bank 2005). Construction was the sector that grew fastest since the mid-1980s. It saw the biggest jump in growth after the mid-1990s, when the rural construction labor force grew by an average of about 8.5 percent a year. The more than doubling of the rural construction labor force needs further investigation. Are those workers commuting to urban areas to work? Or is a rural construction boom occurring? Employment growth was also rapid after the mid-1990s in the private sector–dominated service areas of trade, transportation, and communication, at more than 5 percent a year. Manufacturing employment increased by 3 percent.

New Nonfarm Jobs Are Increasingly in Construction, Trade, Transportation, and Communications

Half of new jobs were in these sectors between 1983 and 2003–04. But with the collapse of social services and the boom in construction,

Figure 3.3 Rural Nonfarm Sector Includes Not Only
Manufacturing but Also Services and Construction

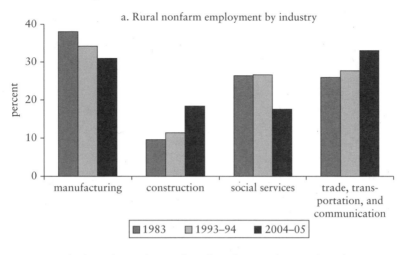

a. Rural nonfarm employment by industry

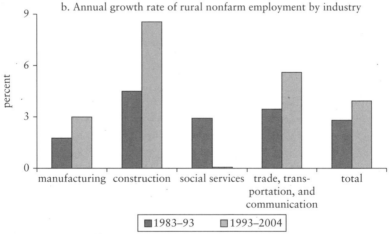

b. Annual growth rate of rural nonfarm employment by industry

Source: Authors' estimates based on employment and unemployment surveys of
respective NSS rounds.

Note: Social services include public administration, defense, education, health,
community, and other personal or household services. Trade, transportation, and
communication include wholesale and retail trade, hotels, restaurants, transportation,
storage and warehousing, and communication. See figure 3.1.

three-quarters of new nonfarm jobs created since 1993–94 were
in construction and trade, transportation, and communications
(figure 3.4). Some of the services in trade and transport may well
be related to the development of agriculture value chains, reflecting
positive links with agriculture.

Figure 3.4 New Nonfarm Jobs Are Increasingly Available
in Construction, Trade, Transportation, and Communication

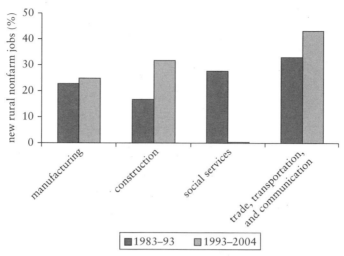

Source: Authors' estimates based on employment and unemployment surveys of
respective NSS rounds.

Note: Employment defined on the basis of principal-cum-subsidiary (usual) status.
Farm versus nonfarm assignment is based on workers' reported industry, occupation,
and employment status. The numbers of farm and nonfarm workers are calculated
using (a) estimated proportions from unit-level data and (b) total rural workforce as
in Sundaram 2007. See figure 3.3.

These Sharp Shifts in Sectoral Composition Suggest Fundamental Changes in the Nature of Nonfarm Work

Jobs in manufacturing and in social services are likely to be better
paid and more secure because the employer is more likely to be
either the government or a large company. Jobs in construction and
in areas such as retail and transportation are more likely to involve
casual labor and self-employment. This casualization of the nonfarm
sector is exactly what we find when we analyze the rural nonfarm
sector in these terms.

The Terms and Conditions of Rural Nonfarm Jobs Vary Enormously, but Self-employment Is the Dominant Form

Nonfarm activities can be crudely divided into three subsectors representing very different types of employment: *regular salaried
employment,* in which the worker has a long-term contract that does
not require daily, weekly, or monthly renewal; *casual wage labor*

that entails a daily or periodic renewal of the work contract; and *self-employment*, in which the worker operates her own business.

Regular nonfarm employment is typically highly sought after and most clearly associated with relatively high and stable incomes. But only 6 percent of rural workers, or 22 percent of the nonfarm workforce, hold regular salaried jobs. Casual laborers make up 28 percent of the rural nonfarm workforce. Although it is generally thought to be less demeaning to a worker than agricultural wage labor, and it pays better, casual work may be both physically demanding and hazardous (construction, rickshaw pulling, industrial workshops, and so forth). The other half of the nonfarm rural workforce is self-employed. Nonfarm self-employment activities can be residual, last-resort options (such as unpaid family labor or wage work concealed as self-employment under different forms of contracting), as well as high-return activities. Whether they are the former or the latter generally depends on the skills and capital available for deployment.

Growth of All Three Types of Nonfarm Employment Has Accelerated, but Casual Employment Has Grown Most Quickly

As shown in figure 3.5, the share of the self-employed has remained at roughly 50 percent, while casual employment grew from 24 percent in 1983 to 29 percent in 2004. The share of regular employment has fallen slowly but consistently, from 24 percent to 22 percent. In absolute terms, between 1983 and 2004–05, the number of self-employed rose by 23 million, the number in regular employment by 10 million, and the number in casual employment by 16 million.

The declining share of regular employment is surprising, since in the normal course of development one would expect the share of regular jobs to increase. The slower growth of jobs in the regular sector since 1993 would seem to be linked to the absence of growth in social services employment, in which regular jobs would be more common, and the very rapid growth of construction and other services, in which casual jobs would predominate.

Indeed, the puzzle becomes why growth in regular jobs has gone up rather than down in recent years. The contraction of jobs in the public sector, which has historically been the primary source of salaried work in rural areas, has been offset by a growth in private sector jobs. Public sector jobs are highly coveted for the job security and the wage premium they provide. As we will see, private sector jobs fail to share those characteristics.[4]

Figure 3.5 Growth of All Three Types of Nonfarm Jobs, Particularly Casual Jobs, Has Accelerated

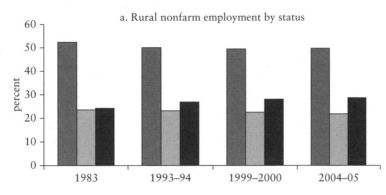

a. Rural nonfarm employment by status

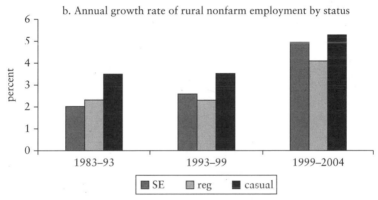

b. Annual growth rate of rural nonfarm employment by status

■ SE   ▨ reg   ■ casual

Source: Authors' estimates based on employment and unemployment surveys of respective NSS rounds.

Note: SE = self-employment; reg = regular salaried employee. See figure 3.1.

Nonfarm Regular Jobs Pay Much Better Than Casual Ones, Though the Distinction between the Two Is Becoming Blurred

Unfortunately, the NSS does not collect data on income from self-employment. Since the self-employed make up 50 percent of the rural nonfarm workforce, that makes it impossible to analyze changes in the income of the nonfarm workforce. Our discussion is perforce restricted to the employed nonfarm workforce.

Although regular jobs are still much better paid than casual ones, with the casualization of the nonfarm sector the gap between the two is narrowing. Figure 3.6 shows the gap over four of the surveys,

Figure 3.6 The Declining Premium of Regular Wages
Compared with Casual Nonfarm Wages

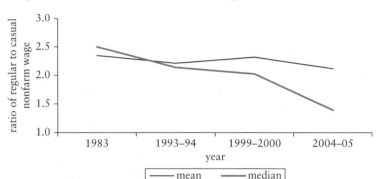

Source: Authors' estimates based on employment and unemployment surveys of respective NSS rounds.
Note: Mean and median daily wages are in Rs and are calculated for 19 major states of India.

using both the mean and the median to compare wages in regular and casual nonfarm employment. Both ratios show a declining trend, much stronger with respect to the median than the mean, in the first 10 and last five years.

Figure 3.7 compares the distribution of casual and regular non-farm wages over time. The emerging dualism in salaried employment since 1993–94 is notable. By 2004–05, a significant share of salaried jobs are relatively poorly paid and are comparable to casual jobs. One reason is the contraction of the public sector, which pays a high premium over the private sector to employees who have similar skills and characteristics (Desai et al. 2008). Another reason might be the rising informalization of work, as noted by the National Commission for Enterprises in the Unorganized Sector (NCEUS 2007). An increasing number of regular salaried workers have jobs without employment benefits (no protection against arbitrary dismissal), work security (no protection against accidents and illnesses at the workplace), or social security benefits (no pension or health care, and so forth). The commission reports that *all* of the growth in regular jobs since 1999–2000 has been in employment of this informal nature.

Casual Nonfarm Employment Pays about 45 Percent More Than Agricultural Wage Labor

The premium embedded in the casual nonfarm wage over the agri-cultural wage rose from around 25 percent to 30 percent in 1983

Figure 3.7 Emerging Dualism in Salaried Employment

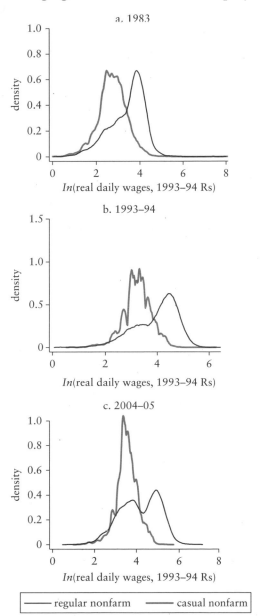

Source: Authors' estimates based on employment and unemployment surveys of respective NSS rounds.

Note: Distributions of log of real daily wages are in 1993–94 Rs and are corrected for inflation using state consumer price indexes for agricultural labor.

Figure 3.8 The Increasing Premium of Casual Nonfarm Wages Compared with Agricultural Wages

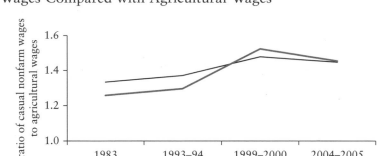

Source: Authors' estimates based on employment and unemployment surveys of respective NSS rounds.

Note: Employment defined on the basis of principal-cum-subsidiary (usual) status. Farm versus nonfarm assignment is based on workers' reported industry, occupation, and employment status. Mean and median daily wages are in Rs and are calculated for 19 major states of India.

(depending on whether it is based on a comparison of means or medians), to about 45 percent in 2004–05 (figure 3.8). The premium is evident not only in a higher mean but across the distribution (figure 3.9).

Village-Level Studies Confirm That Nonfarm Jobs in Government and Business Are Highly Desirable

These results from large-sample survey datasets conform with findings from detailed village studies, which point both to the great desire for nonfarm occupations, especially among youth, and to the obstacles to entry into nonfarm jobs (box 3.1).

Nonfarm Wage Growth May Have Slowed

Comparing the 1980s and the 1990s, a slowdown in regular nonfarm wage growth has taken place, one that is much more rapid if measured by the median than by the mean (table 3.1). This is consistent with wage growth at the top of the regular pay scale, but more rapid entry of new workers at the bottom end of the scale. The slowdown is particularly marked in the period 1999 to 2004 and extends to the nonfarm casual sector. The median regular

Figure 3.9 Casual Nonfarm Jobs Pay Better Than
Agricultural Wage Labor across the Distribution

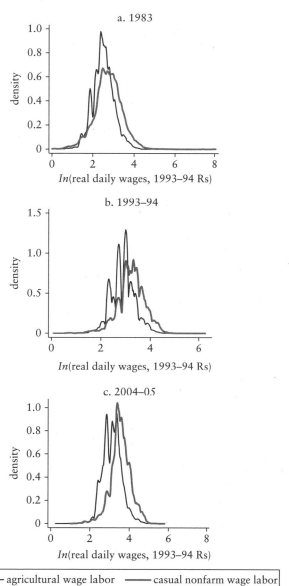

Source: Authors' estimates based on employment and unemployment surveys of
respective NSS rounds.

Note: Distributions of log of real daily wages are in 1993–94 Rs and are corrected
for inflation using state consumer price indexes for agricultural labor.

wage fell by an annual average of more than 5 percent between 1999 and 2004. This surely reflects the large public service pay increases associated with the Fifth Pay Commission, the public sector hiring freeze that followed, and the rapid growth in low-paid regular jobs.

Box 3.1 The Great Desire for Nonfarm Jobs

Kathalbari is a pseudonymous village in the district of Jalpaiguri, in West Bengal. Visited for the World Bank's study *Moving Out of Poverty*, the village is among several in the state that have benefited from the government's land reform program. A majority of families in Kathalbari practice agriculture and cultivate rice, vegetables, and jute, but for many, their plots are too small to reap anything beyond food for home consumption. Nearly a third of the households are landless people who work as daily wage labor or farmhands or do odd jobs such as carpentry. It is unsurprising that most families in Kathalbari look at strategies to diversify beyond farming. A discussion with youths in the village revealed their aspirations to move away from agriculture—a finding confirmed in a youth survey undertaken for all 80 villages visited in the state for the study. The survey data suggest that about 82 percent of youth want to be employed in the nonfarm sector—40 percent want to have their own business, 36 percent want a government job, and another 6 percent want a private job.

Young men and women in Assam also dream of branching out of agriculture. Nearly 40 percent of youth (15–25 years) interviewed as part of the same study want to own a business enterprise by the age of 30. Another 44 percent aspire to government jobs, and only 7 percent want to engage in farming, a familial occupation for most.

The desire exists, but so do obstacles to entry into nonfarm occupations. For most, the obstacles are financial. Loans, though available, come at a significant additional cost. "Even if you apply for a bank loan, you have to pay sums of Rs 10 and 20 at various places," says Dinesh, a young man in the village of Deharkuchi. "Otherwise your file will rot in some office behind a table." Bribes paid in some cases are estimated to be two-fifths of the original loan amount applied for. Every little step in the process—from getting a license to start a business to getting a form or a signature—requires paying up. Lack of money to pay up, compounded by the inability to mortgage any assets as collateral or furnish any reference or guarantee, leads to denial of loans to youth from poor families. Most people in Kathalbari admit that permanent jobs—more so government jobs—while desirable are

(continued next page)

virtually impossible to get. Only 3 percent of households in the village are in government service. A discussion group of women in the village rues, "All people cannot get government jobs as they have to give bribes. And all people do not have the money."

Another common refrain is lack of proper infrastructure to do business. In the village of Leteku Gaon, young men complain, "It is hard for anyone to set up business here because there is no good market. To bring anything to the village or supply anything outside, we have to spend 5 rupees instead of 1 rupee, only because of bad roads."

Still, 75 percent are completely or fairly sure of being able to fulfill their dreams. Eighteen-year-old Purnima, in Leteku Gaon, sums up why: "There is nothing impossible if there is a will."

Source: Based on interviews carried out for the World Bank's study *Moving Out of Poverty* (Narayan, Pritchett, and Kapur 2009).
Note: All villages are identified by pseudonyms.

Table 3.1 Annual Average Growth in Real Wage

	1983–93	1993–99	1999–2004	1993–2004
Growth in mean wage (% per year)				
Agricultural wage	3.2	2.8	1.7	2.3
Nonfarm regular	2.9	4.9	−0.5	2.4
Nonfarm casual	3.5	4.1	1.3	2.8
Growth in median wage (% per year)				
Agricultural wage	4.1	1.0	2.9	1.9
Nonfarm regular	2.9	2.8	−5.4	−1.0
Nonfarm casual	4.4	3.8	1.9	2.9

Source: Authors' estimates based on employment and unemployment surveys of respective NSS rounds.
Note: Nominal daily wages (Rs) for respective periods in 19 major states are converted to 1993–94 prices using deflators implicit in the official poverty lines.

Self-employed Rural Workers Show the Greatest Diversity of All and Are Spread Evenly through the Rural Income Distribution

A lack of data makes it difficult to comment on the average earnings of the self-employed or to assess whether the growth in their ranks is a symptom of agrarian distress or a sign of upward mobility. But it is clear that they are a diverse group. As evident from figure 3.10, in the next section, nonfarm self-employment activities tend to be spread evenly over the income distribution, indicating that both rich and poor households are involved in such work.

The majority of rural nonfarm enterprises tend to be very small, reliant largely on family labor, and operated with very little capital investment. In 2004–05, only 6 percent of self-employed workers were running enterprises that employed more than five workers. Many others are disguised wage workers, who work at home producing goods using raw materials supplied to them by agents or firms that purchase the outputs (NCEUS 2007). The location of these enterprises is indicative of the small amounts of capital in many nonfarm businesses: In 2004–05, 41 percent of self-employed workers worked out of their own dwelling, 12 percent had no fixed location, and another 10 percent worked on the street. Further, only one-fourth received a regular monthly or weekly payment, with the vast majority relying on irregular daily or piece rate modes of payment. Benefits such as social security or paid leave were virtually nonexistent.

Perceptions of remuneration of the self-employed also suggest the relatively low earnings from a large share of self-employment activities.[5] About half of nonfarm workers regard their earnings from self-employment as remunerative. When asked what amount they would regard as remunerative, about 40 percent of males and nearly 80 percent of rural females said that their income of less than Rs 2,000 per month was remuneration enough.

Of course, not all self-employment enterprises are small and poorly remunerative. In some industries, earnings of self-employed workers are better than those of salaried workers (Glinskaya and Jalan 2005). Such enterprises, as well as multiple occupations within households, would explain the presence of self-employed workers at the top of the income distribution.

With the Conflicting Trend of a Growing, but Casualizing, Nonfarm Sector and without Data on the Earnings of the Self-employed Over Time, It Is Difficult to Reach a Verdict on the Rate of Expansion of the Rural Nonfarm Sector in Value Terms

Available data point to a steady increase in the nonfarm wage bill of about 6 percent a year over the last 20-plus years (table 3.2). Broadly speaking, employment growth in the nonfarm wage sector has accelerated over the years, while the growth in average earnings has slowed. These two trends have canceled each other out, and growth in total earnings has been constant for the last two decades at about 6 percent, with earnings in the casual segment growing slightly faster than those in the regular sector.

Table 3.2 Annual Growth in Nonfarm Wage Bill
percent

Type of work	1983–93	1993–2004	1983–2004
Nonfarm employment	5.9	6.2	6.0
Nonfarm regular	5.3	5.6	5.5
Nonfarm casual	7.1	7.2	7.2

Source: Authors' estimates based on employment and unemployment surveys of respective NSS rounds.

Note: Nominal daily wages (Rs) for respective periods in 19 major states are converted to 1993–94 prices using deflators implicit in the official poverty lines.

Who Gets What Job? Does Nonfarm Employment Reach the Poor?

Obtaining a regular nonfarm job is the surest way for rural people to avoid poverty. Regular salaried jobs are the most desirable form of employment from the point of view of earnings, stability of employment, and availability of some social security. Regular non-farm employment is regressively distributed across the rural population: the richer you are, the more likely you are to enjoy such employment (figure 3.10).

Casual Nonfarm Employees Are Much Better Off Than Agricultural Laborers but Are Still Relatively Concentrated Among the Poor

Because casual wages have consistently exceeded agricultural wages, a shift away from agricultural labor to casual nonfarm labor is not necessarily distress driven. Casual nonfarm employees are much less likely to be poor than agricultural laborers. Three-quarters of agricultural laborers are in the bottom two quintiles, but only one-quarter of casual nonfarm workers are. Nevertheless, casual employment is not a reliable route out of poverty. Casual workers tend not to have year-round employment and to make ends meet by working at several jobs, often combining agricultural and nonfarm activities. In 2004–05, 55 percent of casual nonfarm workers reported that they were without work for one or more months in the year, compared to 8 percent of salaried workers and 12 percent of the self-employed. Among casual nonfarm workers, 14 percent reported that they were seeking, or available for, additional employment even when working.

Figure 3.10 Regular Nonfarm Workers Are More Likely to
Be Found at the Top End of the Rural Income Distribution

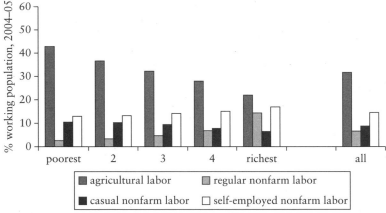

Source: World Bank staff estimates based on employment and unemployment surveys of respective NSS rounds.

Note: Employment defined on the basis of principal-cum-subsidiary (usual) status. Farm versus nonfarm assignment is based on workers' reported industry, occupation, and employment status.

The Self-employed Are Spread through the Income Distribution

The most recent survey round shows a slight tendency for self-employment to be concentrated among richer rural households. However the tendency is nothing like as marked as it is for regular employment, and it is not evident in the earlier surveys, which show a flatter distribution of self-employment through the income distribution. This is consistent with the heterogeneity of this type of employment.

Given the close links between earnings and consumption, average incidence analysis is of limited use when we want to understand whether nonfarm jobs reach the poor. For example, was a regular salaried employee drawn from the ranks of the rich? Or was she in the poorest quintile, catapulted into the richest quintile on the basis of her regular salaried job? To understand who obtains what jobs, we asked whether gender, age, social status, education level, and landholding—characteristics that are associated with poverty but that, unlike consumption, will not change once a household member moves out of the farm economy—make it more or less likely that individuals will take up some form of nonfarm work.

Women Are Barely Transitioning into the Nonfarm Sector

The percentage of males working primarily in nonfarm activities increased from 25 percent in 1983 to 35 percent in 2004–05, but for women the increase over the same period has been only from 15 percent to 19 percent (figure 3.11). In growth terms, the number of rural men working off-farm doubled between 1983 and 2004–05; for women the number increased by 73 percent.

Women's share in nonfarm employment declined from 26 percent in 1983 to 23 percent in 2004–05. The only category in which an improvement in gender equity occurred is regular employment, where the share of jobs held by women increased from 14 percent to 19 percent. However, regular jobs still employ less than 4 percent of working rural women (8 percent for men), and many salaried rural women work only part time (Unni and Raveendran 2007).

Young Men Are the Group Likely to Exit Agriculture. Older Men and All Women Are Locked into Agriculture

Figure 3.12 shows a cohort analysis tracing the same age groups of men and women through the three NSS rounds of surveys. Of the eight cohorts shown—four male, four female—only one, the group

Figure 3.11 Women Are Barely Transitioning into the Nonfarm Sector

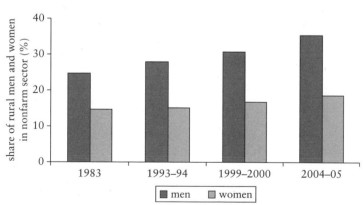

Source: Authors' estimates based on employment and unemployment surveys of respective NSS rounds.

Note: Employment defined on the basis of principal-cum-subsidiary (usual) status. Farm versus nonfarm assignment is based on workers' reported industry, occupation, and employment status.

Figure 3.12 Young Men Are the Group Most Likely to Enter the Nonfarm Sector

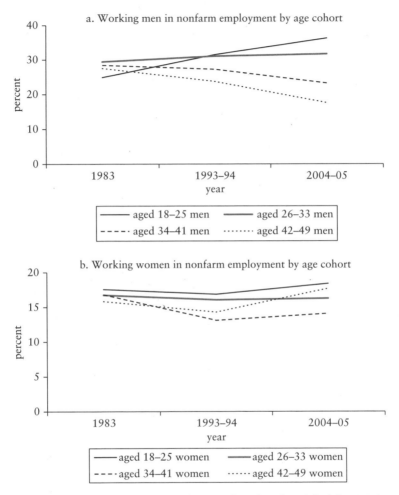

a. Working men in nonfarm employment by age cohort

——— aged 18–25 men   ——— aged 26–33 men
- - - - aged 34–41 men   ········ aged 42–49 men

b. Working women in nonfarm employment by age cohort

——— aged 18–25 women   ——— aged 26–33 women
- - - aged 34–41 women   ······ aged 42–49 women

Source: Tabulations provided by Wilima Wadhwa based on Schedule 10.0 data from respective NSS rounds.

Note: Data based on daily status of the individual derived from data on the weekly disposition of time.

of men aged 18–25 in 1983, shows any shift out of agriculture. Older men show a move back into agriculture, as they exit nonfarm occupations. Women of all the cohorts show little shift. The only (weak) force, therefore, that is (modestly) driving up the rate of female participation in nonfarm employment is the slightly higher (but constant) nonfarm participation rates of the younger female relative to the older female cohorts.

The Participation of Disadvantaged Groups in the Nonfarm Sector Is Growing

On average, the farm sector takes a higher proportion of its labor force than the nonfarm sector from individuals belonging to a scheduled caste or tribe (SC/ST). However, the picture is changing over time, as figure 3.13 demonstrates. At the margin, an increasing number of new workers entering the nonfarm sector are from an SC/ST background. This is especially the case for casual nonfarm work and since 1994. After 1994, 34 percent of the new jobs in the nonfarm sector went to SC/STs, which is precisely their share in the rural workforce. Hence, in an expanding sector SC/STs are just as likely to get a nonfarm job as others. The distribution is notable: members of scheduled castes or tribes are less likely to get a regular job (only 24 percent), as likely to get a self-employed job (34 percent), and much more likely to get a casual job (51 percent).

Figure 3.13 Participation of Scheduled Castes and Scheduled Tribes in the Nonfarm Sector Is Growing

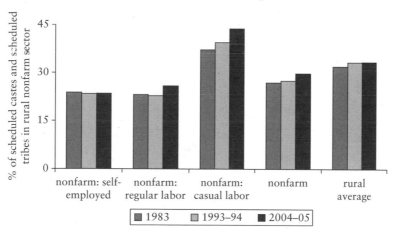

Source: Authors' estimates based on employment and unemployment surveys of respective NSS rounds.

Note: Employment defined on the basis of principal-cum-subsidiary (usual) status. Farm versus nonfarm assignment is based on workers' reported industry, occupation, and employment status. The numbers of farm and nonfarm workers are calculated using (a) estimated proportions from unit-level data and (b) total rural workforce as in Sundaram 2007.

Literacy Helps People Exit from Agriculture

Of the farm workforce, 50 percent are illiterate; 60 percent of agricultural laborers are illiterate (figure 3.14). By contrast, only 30 percent of the nonfarm workforce is illiterate. Secondary and tertiary

Figure 3.14 Literacy Helps Exit Agriculture

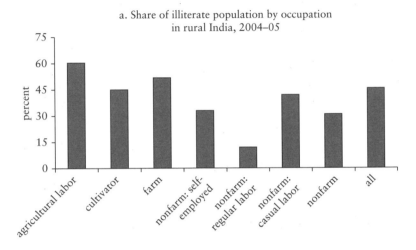

a. Share of illiterate population by occupation
in rural India, 2004–05

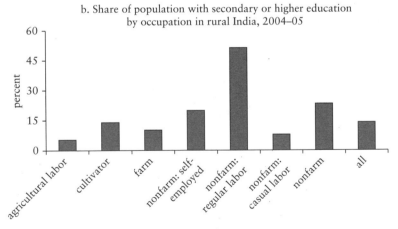

b. Share of population with secondary or higher education
by occupation in rural India, 2004–05

Source: Authors' estimates based on employment and unemployment surveys of respective NSS rounds.

Note: Employment defined on the basis of principal-cum-subsidiary (usual) status. Farm versus nonfarm assignment is based on workers' reported industry, occupation, and employment status. The numbers of farm and nonfarm workers are calculated using (a) estimated proportions from unit-level data and (b) total rural workforce as in Sundaram 2007.

qualifications only make a large difference for regular employment. Beyond attainment of basic literacy skills, going on to complete secondary or even tertiary education hugely increases a worker's probability of obtaining regular nonfarm employment but has little effect on obtaining other types of nonfarm employment.

Workers in the Nonfarm Sector Have a Similar Landownership Profile to Agricultural Laborers, though the Salaried Sector Contains More Large Landowners

Within the farm sector, cultivators and agricultural laborers have very different landholding profiles (figure 3.15). Among agricultural laborers, 70 percent own less than 0.4 hectare. More than 50 percent of owner-cultivators own more than one hectare. Nonfarm workers are much more similar to agricultural laborers, except that nonfarm regular workers tend to have slightly greater landholdings. In which direction the causality runs is unclear: the greater landholdings may reflect the greater prosperity of salaried workers, or these asset holdings might help family members obtain access to the formal sector.

Figure 3.15 Landownership Profile of Rural Workforce

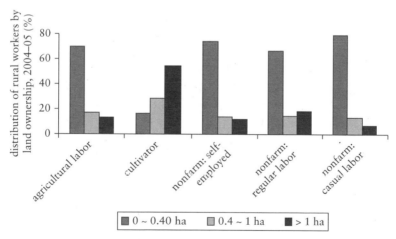

Source: Authors' estimates based on employment and unemployment surveys of respective NSS rounds.

Note: Employment defined on the basis of principal-cum-subsidiary (usual) status. Farm versus nonfarm assignment is based on workers' reported industry, occupation, and employment status. The numbers of farm and nonfarm workers are calculated using (a) estimated proportions from unit-level data and (b) total rural workforce as in Sundaram 2007.

*Regression Analysis of Occupational Choice Confirms
That Education, Wealth, and Social Networks Shape
Access to Nonfarm Jobs—and Often Hold Back
Participation by the Poor*

The analyses presented above are simple bivariate correlations. But
the same patterns are confirmed in more systematic regression
analysis that examines the relationship between occupational
choice and household characteristics (see Lanjouw and Murgai
2009). In all four NSS survey rounds, and in line with the results
shown above and with much other work on access to nonfarm
occupations, education emerges as an important determinant. Even
a small amount of education (achieving literacy) improves prospects of finding nonfarm employment, and with higher levels of
education, the odds of employment in well-paid, regular nonfarm
occupations improve.

The regression analysis also shows that individuals from scheduled castes and tribes are markedly more likely to be employed as
agricultural laborers than in nonfarm activities, even controlling for
education and land (see also Thorat and Sabharwal 2005). This
effect is weakest for nonfarm casual employment (and in fact insignificant for the last survey round) and strongest for nonfarm self-
employment.

Finally, the regression analysis shows that those in the nonfarm
sector own more land, on average, than agricultural laborers, except
for those in casual nonfarm employment, who, on average, own
significantly less.

*Village-level Studies Confirm the Importance of
Both Social Status and Wealth for Getting a Regular
Nonfarm Job*

Our analysis suggests that caste is important for getting a regular
nonfarm job. The finding that large landowners are disproportionately represented among households with rural salaried workers
might simply reflect that such households are rich (and therefore
buy land). But it might equally represent that households with land,
like households of high social status, are more likely to have the
personal connections and the financial capacity required to obtain a
regular job. The village study of Drèze, Lanjouw, and Sharma (1998)
is one of a number to suggest that finding a regular nonfarm job
often requires both the ability to pay a bribe and personal connections. That analysis suggests that regular nonfarm jobs "cluster"
around a small number of establishments that some village resident

succeeded in entering and then helped others to enter. Those who follow are frequently of the same caste as, or are otherwise related to, the initial entrant.[6]

Does an Expansion of Nonfarm Employment Reach the Poor?

Potential entrants into casual nonfarm labor appear similar to agricultural laborers in social status and landholdings, but even this pool is much more likely to be literate, and so will not contain as many of the poor as the pool of agricultural laborers. Entrants into other types of nonfarm labor are better educated and less socially disadvantaged than the farm workforce. In general, expansion of the nonfarm sector tends to bypass women and older workers. Encouragingly, an increasing share of the nonfarm sector is drawn from the ranks of the socially disadvantaged.[7] This suggests that at the margin, an expansion of nonfarm jobs will be progressive. And the part of the nonfarm sector that is growing the fastest is the part in which participation by the socially disadvantaged and illiterate is greatest. Given that casual nonfarm employment, though worth considerably less than regular employment, still pays considerably better than agriculture (the wage premium is about 45 percent), the direct impact of recent nonfarm growth on the poor is likely to have been positive.

In the end, however, this analysis of the extent to which an expansion of the nonfarm sector will reach India's poor, while suggestive, is both inconclusive and incomplete. In particular, it takes no account of general equilibrium effects, for example, that the exit of some, even nonpoor, from the farm sector could put upward pressure on agricultural wages, which would benefit the poorest (figure 3.15). It is also possible that the presence of nonfarm opportunities could increase demand for education, which over time would itself reduce poverty. To allow for the possibility of such indirect effects, a more aggregate analysis is needed. We turn to that in the next section.

The Impact of the Nonfarm Sector on Rural Poverty: A Regression Analysis

Views are divided as to the impact of the nonfarm sector on rural poverty. A large empirical literature in India has documented the association of poverty with agricultural and nonagricultural output growth and with agricultural wages (Himanshu 2005, 2008;

Lal 1976; Singh 1990; Lanjouw and Stern 1998; Sharma 2001; Sundaram 2001). Some analysis has pointed to the role of the non-farm sector, primarily through the pressure it puts on agricultural wages. Himanshu (2008) and Dev and Ravi (2007) speculate that nonfarm growth may have been a key factor behind the decline in poverty during the 1990s. Foster and Rosenzweig (2004) argue that not only has nonfarm expansion been the prime driver of rural incomes, but its growth has been especially pro-poor.

But historical evidence also suggests that poverty reduction has been closely tied to agricultural growth. Fears have been expressed about whether the growth in nonfarm employment can be sustained, about the accompanying deceleration in wage growth, and about the quality of the jobs being created, leading some to refer to the growth of employment as an "illusion of inclusiveness" (Unni and Raveendran 2007).

Aggregate Trends in Poverty, Wages, and Nonfarm Growth Suggest a Complex Relationship

In the two decades between 1983 and 2004–05, real agricultural wages grew at the rate of 2.8 percent per year. The rate of growth was higher in the first decade—1983 to 1993–94—but slowed down appreciably in the next decade, to 2.3 percent per year, and much more drastically to 1.7 percent per year in the five years between 1999–2000 and 2004–05 (table 3.3).

But the rate of rural poverty reduction has not declined along with agricultural wage growth (and agricultural GDP). The decline of rural poverty has been remarkably consistent over the last 20 years at an average rate of just over 2 percent a year. Whether the accelerating growth of nonfarm employment also seen in table 3.3 has helped to offset the impact of slower agricultural wage growth on the rate of rural poverty reduction requires closer investigation.

Regression Analysis Can Help us Better Understand the Relationship among Nonfarm Expansion, Poverty, and Agricultural Wages

We use a region-level panel dataset constructed from the 1983, 1993–94, and 2004–05 surveys of the NSS. The three surveys span a period of over 20 years, and given that the major states of India comprise some 60 regions, they also reflect considerable spatial heterogeneity. The analysis asked whether regions where the non-farm sector grew were also the ones where poverty declined (or

Table 3.3 Trends in Rural Poverty, GDP, and Agricultural
Wages
annualized rates of growth (%)

Year	Rural poverty	Agricultural wage	Nonfarm employment	GDP	Nonfarm GDP	Agriculture GDP
1983–2004	–2.3	3.2	3.3	5.8	7.1	2.6
1983–93	–2.2	3.2	2.5	5.2	6.4	2.9
1993–2004	–2.4	2.3	3.7	6.3	7.7	2.4
1999–2004	–	1.7	4.8	6.0	7.2	1.8

Sources: Eswaran et al. 2009; poverty rates, agricultural wages, and nonfarm employment estimated by authors based on NSS data.

Note: GDP at factor cost at 1993–94 prices. Agriculture GDP originating in agriculture, forestry, and fishing. Nonfarm GDP defined as a residual. Poverty rates based on official poverty lines. 1999–2004 change in rural poverty was not reported because 1999–00 NSS consumption data are not comparable to other rounds.

agricultural wages grew), net of trends in other determinants of poverty or wages (see Lanjouw and Murgai 2009).

Agricultural Productivity Growth, Rising Agricultural Wages, and Urban Growth All Emerge as Important Factors in Reducing Rural Poverty

Various econometric specifications were used and are reported in table 3.4. All the specifications confirm that higher yields are associated with declining rural poverty and that agricultural wage growth exerts a strong and negative impact on rural poverty. Growth in urban per capita expenditures is also strongly associated with lower rural poverty, echoing results reported in earlier chapters of the external stimulus that urban development can provide for raising rural incomes.

Nonfarm Employment Is Higher in Poorer Regions, Consistent with Nonfarm Employment as a Sign of Distress or of Enterprises Seeking Out Low-Wage Areas

When state fixed effects are used, nonfarm employment is positively associated with rural poverty. This pattern is consistent with the notion put forward by Foster and Rosenzweig (2004) that nonfarm enterprises producing tradable goods (the rural factory sector) locate in settings where reservation wages are lower. If the rural factory sector seeks out low-wage areas, factory growth will be largest in those areas that have not experienced local agricultural productivity growth. It is also consistent with distress-induced

Table 3.1 Correlates of Rural Poverty and Agricultural Wages

	ln regional poverty rate		ln real agricultural wage (Rs per day)		
Variables	(1)	(2)	(3)	(4)	(5)
ln(real agricultural wages)	−1.09 (8.02)***	−0.7 (3.88)***	—	—	—
ln(yield)	−0.45 (3.36)***	−0.62 (2.81)***	0.35 (4.68)***	0.14 (1.14)	0.14 (1.21)
ln(real urban mean per capita expenditure)	−0.31 (1.98)**	−0.41 (1.98)*	0.06 (0.66)	−0.04 (0.40)	−0.08 (0.76)
ln(land per capita)	−0.14 (2.53)**	−0.11 (1.66)*	0.03 (0.90)	0.02 (0.45)	0.01 (0.38)
1993–94 dummy	0.22 (3.02)***	0.16 (1.58)	0.28 (7.54)***	0.35 (7.85)***	0.34 (7.60)***
2004–05 dummy	0.25 (2.40)**	0.19 (1.11)	0.45 (9.54)***	0.58 (8.26)***	0.57 (7.41)***
Nonfarm variables					
ln(nonfarm employment per adult)	0.74 (2.07)**	−3.4 (2.27)**			1.37 (1.72)*
ln(nonfarm employment share)*% with below primary education	−0.7 (1.78)*	3.87 (2.31)**			−1.52 (1.69)*
Constant	4.61 (4.55)***	4.1 (2.90)***	1.66 (3.14)***	2.63 (3.89)***	2.98 (4.21)***
Fixed effects	State	Region	State	Region	Region
R^2	0.81	0.89	0.87	0.94	0.94

Source: Lanjouw and Murgai 2009.

Note: Absolute value of *t*-statistics in parentheses. * significant at 10 percent level; ** significant at 5 percent level; *** significant at 1 percent level.

recourse to nonfarm employment. Both these hypotheses are explored further below.

Expanding Nonfarm Employment Provides an Escape from Poverty, with Greater Efficacy when Education Levels Are Higher

When the same model is estimated with region-level fixed effects (column 2 of table 3.4), however, the relationship is overturned: expansion of nonfarm employment is associated with a reduction in poverty, and the effect is stronger the smaller the share of the working population with low education levels.[8] Thus, when we focus specifically on changes over time and sweep away cross-sectional variation across regions, poverty decline is observed to occur most rapidly in regions where the nonfarm sector has grown.

An Important Indirect Route by Which Nonfarm Expansion Affects Poverty Is through Placing Pressure on Agricultural Wages; in the Absence of Nonfarm Growth, Agricultural Wage Growth Would Have Decelerated Further in the 1990s

No decline occurred—until the most recent period of 1999–2000 to 2004–05—in the share of the adult population whose primary occupation was agricultural wage labor.[9] Agricultural wages can be viewed not only as useful proxies of poverty but also as indicators of poverty in their own right insofar as they capture the reservation wages of the rural labor force.

Column 3 of table 3.4, which reports state-level fixed effects estimates for the log of real agricultural wage rates, indicates that regions with higher growth in agricultural yields also have rising agricultural wages. However, once fixed factors at the NSS region level are swept out (column 4), the correlation between agricultural yields and wages becomes smaller and insignificant. That could reflect attenuation bias due to measurement error in our measure of yields as a proxy for true physical agricultural productivity over time.[10]

Regression estimates are consistent with labor-tightening effects of employment opportunities outside agriculture. In both columns 3 and 4, the time dummy variables show that net of yield improvement, agricultural wages were highest in 2004–05 and lowest in 1983. This suggests that the observed deceleration of agricultural wage growth between the two decades can be attributed to declining agricultural productivity growth. Agricultural wages would have declined even further if other employment opportunities, which raise labor costs and draw labor out of agriculture, had been absent.

Suggestive evidence of the impact of nonfarm employment opportunities on labor market tightening is reported in column 5, in which nonfarm employment per adult and its interaction with education levels are added to the regression. Coefficient estimates on these variables suggest that, contrary to the aggregate picture reported above, within regions, nonfarm employment growth is associated with rising agricultural wages. This association is weakened if education levels are particularly low. Presumably low education levels prevent agricultural workers from accessing non-farm jobs (see the discussion in the previous section), and expansion of that sector then results in less tightening of the agricultural wage market.

The econometric analysis thus suggests that expansion of the non-farm sector is associated with falling poverty via two routes: a direct impact on poverty independent of the effect that nonfarm growth may have on the agricultural sector, and an indirect impact attributable to the positive effect of nonfarm employment growth on agricultural wages.

Going further to try to establish the relative importance of the farm and nonfarm sectors for rural poverty reduction is difficult. Previous studies have reported sharply contrasting results. A recent study by Eswaran et al. (2008) asked how much of the increase in agricultural wages can be attributed to nonfarm sector growth. By constructing a counterfactual scenario of what would have happened if nonfarm productivity was held constant, they estimated that the contribution of the nonfarm sector (between 1983 and 1999–2000) is likely to have been no greater than a quarter; rising agricultural productivity is the primary driver of agricultural wages. Thus, in their judgment, although the nonfarm sector has indeed contributed to a tightening of labor markets, its success has been relatively modest. Contrasting results are reported by Foster and Rosenzweig (2004) who, using different methods and data, suggest that rural nonfarm incomes have grown substantially and that nonfarm growth has been especially pro-poor. They found that in contrast to agricultural productivity growth, which largely benefits landowners, growth of the rural factory sector tends to have a greater proportional impact on unskilled labor.

Continued debate about the appropriate sectoral focus for poverty reduction efforts is warranted. Promoting nonfarm growth is an important poverty reduction strategy. At the same time, agriculture is still the employer of too many of India's poor (especially the female and the elderly poor) to be ignored.

Why Isn't the Nonfarm Sector Growing Faster?

We have shown above that the nonfarm sector is growing, but not rapidly compared to China and other successful Asian countries. By the analysis of the last two sections, faster growth in the nonfarm sector would lead to greater poverty reduction. This section explores why the nonfarm sector is not growing faster.

The Indian Literature Has Been Dominated by Two Debates about the Determinants of the Size and Growth of the Rural Nonfarm Sector

First, is the growth of rural nonfarm activities a positive development, or is it a response to slow agricultural growth (see Himanshu 2008)? Do "push factors" into the nonfarm sector dominate—such as the need to manage income risk in agriculture via income diversification, to cope with short-term shocks such as drought and to compensate for long-term constraints such as access to farmland—or are the "pull factors" more important, such as lower risk or higher returns in the nonfarm sector? Second, to the extent that pull factors are important, is the growth of the rural nonfarm sector driven by the internal dynamism of the rural economy, particularly growth in agricultural productivity, or by exogenous factors, such as the agency of the state or growing demand for nonfarm goods and services from urban areas?

Regional and Temporal Variations in Nonfarm Growth in India, While Not Showing Any Obvious Patterns, Can Be Used to Address These Questions

Employment shares in nonfarm activities have grown since 1983 in nearly all states, but with large differences in sector sizes and in how fast they have grown (figure 3.16). In Kerala, the share of nonfarm employment in total rural employment was as high as 69 percent in 2004–05. In other states, such as Madhya Pradesh and Chhattisgarh, the sector has still to make its presence felt. In Tamil Nadu, nonfarm employment grew by 1.7 percent a year, well below the 6.5 percent growth in Himachal Pradesh between 1983 and 2004–05. No straightforward relationship exists between state incomes and the size of the nonfarm sector (in terms of employment). Relatively high-income states, such as Maharashtra and Gujarat, have small nonfarm sectors, with less than one-fourth of the rural workforce employed in nonfarm activities. Nor is a clear relationship seen between the initial size of the sector and its growth.

Regression of National Sample Survey Region-level, Nonfarm Employment Growth on Changes in Agricultural Yield, Urban Consumption Levels, and Education Levels Sheds Some Light on the Drivers of Nonfarm Growth

Correlation with yield allows us to examine the links between agricultural productivity growth and nonfarm development. Average per capita urban consumption per region is included as a proxy for

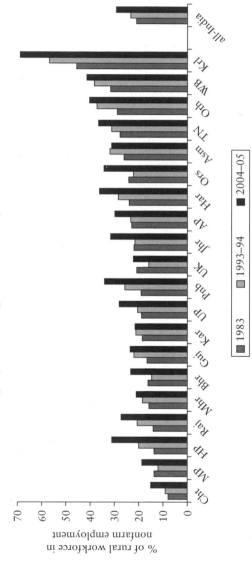

Figure 3.16 Growth in Nonfarm Employment Is Spread Unevenly

Source: Authors' estimates based on employment and unemployment surveys of respective NSS rounds.

Note: Employment defined on the basis of principal-cum-subsidiary (usual) status. Farm versus nonfarm assignment is based on workers' reported industry, occupation, and employment status. The numbers of farm and nonfarm workers are calculated using (a) estimated proportions from unit-level data and (b) total rural workforce as in Sundaram 2007. Regions are: AP = Andhra Pradesh, Asm = Assam, Bhr = Bihar, Cht = Chhattisgarh, Guj = Gujarat, Har = Haryana, HP = Himachal Pradesh, Jhr = Jharkhand, Kar = Karnataka, Krl = Kerala, Mhr = Maharashtra, MP = Madhya Pradesh, Ors = Orissa, Oth = Other states, Pnb = Punjab, Raj = Rajasthan, TN = Tamil Nadu, UK = Uttarakhand, UP = Uttar Pradesh, WB = West Bengal.

the size of the market for rural nonfarm products and services. In addition, the regressions control for land abundance, casual non-farm wages (as a proxy for reservation wages), education levels (to capture the extent to which low education levels in rural areas may impede rural nonfarm employment growth), and secular time trends. Regressions are estimated with either state-level or NSS region-level fixed effects. Given that there is more spatial than temporal variation in the data, parameter estimates from state-level fixed-effects regressions are driven largely by cross-sectional variation. Region-level fixed-effects regressions control for unobserved characteristics within regions, and variation arises largely from region-level changes over time. A number of interesting findings emerge about the patterns of nonfarm employment growth (see Lanjouw and Murgai 2009).

A Dynamic of Production and Consumption Linkages with Agriculture Has Not Been the Primary Driver of Nonfarm Sector Growth. Rather, the Nonfarm Sector Has Expanded in Regions Where Agriculture Is in Decline or Agricultural Wages Are Low

Very little evidence appears to suggest that nonfarm employment growth in the past two decades has been driven by a rural dynamic of production and consumption links with the agricultural sector. Whereas regression results indicate that regions with high agricultural productivity growth tend to have high nonfarm employment growth, the parameter estimates become insignificant once control variables other than yield are added to the specifications. In addition, *within* regions the analysis shows that nonfarm employment, and self-employment in particular, expanded when agricultural productivity declined. This suggests that self-employment activities may serve as a safety net, acting to absorb labor when agriculture is in decline, rather than being promoted by growth in the agricultural sector. A negative relationship between agricultural productivity growth and nonfarm diversification is also consistent with the findings of Foster and Rosenzweig (2003, 2004) that nonfarm diversification tends to be more rapid and extensive in places where agricultural wages are lower and where agricultural productivity growth has been less marked.

Growth in Urban Areas Appears to Be Important

During the two periods of analysis, 1983 to 1993–94 and 1993–94 to 2004–05, regression estimates suggest, nonfarm employment increased more in regions where urban incomes also grew. If one disaggregates the analysis by different types of nonfarm employment, the results show regular salaried jobs and self-employment activities to be the most strongly and positively correlated with urban growth; casual nonfarm employment is not correlated with urban growth. This evidence from regressions that control for state-level fixed effects must be tempered with the finding that the urban parameter estimates become insignificant when changes in nonfarm employment over time *within* regions are examined.

Since the seminal work of Lewis (1954), theories of growth have emphasized the role played by population shifts from the traditional rural to the modern urban sector. Later work has also emphasized other channels through which the fortunes of rural and urban areas are linked (see previous chapter). The results presented here show that one such channel is the external (to the rural economy) stimulus that urban development can provide to the development of the non-farm sector.[11]

Average Education Levels Also Matter

Nonfarm employment growth tends to be lower in regions with lower average levels of education. This is consistent with the household analysis previously described, which found higher education levels among those in nonfarm employment, especially in regular jobs.

Important State- and Local-level Effects Are Driving Diversification Out of Agriculture

Both state and local fixed effects are significant. We cannot be certain what these are picking up. The three NSS rounds used for the regression analysis did not collect data on the constraints faced by rural entrepreneurs, and only sporadic information is available from other sources. However, rural investment climate surveys in Bangladesh, Pakistan, and Sri Lanka, which collect information on rural nonfarm enterprises and perceptions of the main hurdles to their operation, reveal that the chief constraints to investment include poor access to credit and its high cost, inadequate supplies of electricity, and poor-quality roads.

It is possible that fixed effects are picking up differences in infrastructure provision: basic infrastructure, such as power and roads, is largely the responsibility of the states. States are also responsible for the regulation of rural credit cooperatives. Sen (1996) has argued that expansion of government expenditures in rural areas played a pivotal role in the growth of nonfarm employment in the 1980s, and the state fixed effects might also be picking up a demand-side effect.

What the local-level effects are picking up is less clear, but they are clearly important because the explanatory power of the regressions improves when region-level fixed effects are added. Tremendous variation in the regional dynamism of the Indian economy is well documented. For the same reasons that economic activities cluster in urban areas, it is not surprising to find that even outside of the urban areas concentrations of nonfarm economic activity occur.

Notes

1. Most of the analysis is based on four "thick" rounds of the NSS—1983, 1993–94, 1999–2000, and 2004–05. We do not report data from the 1987–88 thick rounds because the unit record data do not produce wage rates that are comparable to wage estimates for that year published by the NSS itself. In addition, because of well-known comparability problems of the 1999–2000 consumption aggregate with other rounds, in regression analysis of impacts on poverty we exclude the 1999–2000 survey round. Sections of this chapter summarize findings in Lanjouw and Murgai (2009).

2. Unless mentioned otherwise, the NSS-based employment data presented in this chapter refer to the Usual Principal and Subsidiary workers ("usual status") definition of employment. A worker's principal status is determined by the activity the worker spent most of his time doing in the year preceding the survey. Principal status workers are those who spent most of their time either employed or looking for jobs. Any activity other than the principal status constitutes a worker's subsidiary status. Usual status workers include principal status workers and subsidiary workers who spent part of their time working or looking for jobs in the year preceding the survey.

3. Lanjouw and Murgai 2009; Himanshu 2008; Eswaran et al. 2009. Sen and Jha (2005) contend that no acceleration occurred in the first half of the 1990s because of a decline in public expenditures in large parts of rural India in the postreform period. Accelerated diversification of the rural workforce toward nonfarm activities is mainly due to recovery in the sector since 1999–2000.

4. Using the Additional Rural Incomes Survey and Rural Economic and Demographic Survey (ARIS-REDS) panel dataset (1969–99), Foster and Rosenzweig (2003, 2004) reported very rapid growth in rural factory employment. In their data, rural factory employment increased 10-fold between 1980 and 1999. About half the villages in their sample were located near a factory, and in those villages 10 percent of the male labor was employed in a factory. NSS data over the same period do not show any such growth, although they do confirm the importance of manufacturing as the next-most-important source of salaried jobs after the public sector.

5. The NSS does not collect data on earnings of the self-employed, but as a first effort, information on perceptions of remuneration of the self-employed was collected in the 2004–05 survey round.

6. Munshi and Rosenzweig's work (2006) also suggests that because access to blue-collar jobs is typically through networks (possibly a reflection of information and enforcement problems), the result is occupational persistence among subcastes, locking generations into the same types of jobs even as returns to other occupations may well be greater.

7. For more discussion of trends and patterns of labor force participation by scheduled castes, see chapter 6.

8. The size and significance of parameter estimates remain similar if a measure of regular salaried nonfarm employment—on the grounds that it is more rationed than other forms of nonfarm employment—is used instead of overall nonfarm employment.

9. Prior to 1999, the reduction in the share of farms in total rural employment was driven by a reduction in the share of cultivators, with the share of agricultural laborers staying constant.

10. Some component of the spatial and temporal variation in the measure reflects input-use variations.

11. The positive role of urbanization in stimulating nonfarm diversification in India has previously been noted by a number of scholars, including Bhalla (1997); Papola (1992); Jayaraj (1994); and Eapen (1994). Evidence from other countries, such as Nepal and Bangladesh, also clearly demonstrates that better-paid nonfarm activities tend to cluster around urban areas (see, for example, Fafchamps and Shilpi 2008).

References

Bhalla, S. 1997. "Trends in Poverty, Wages and Employment in India." *Indian Journal of Labour Economics* 40 (2): 213–22.

Cai, J., A. de Janvry, and E. Sadoulet. 2008. "Rural Households in India: Sources of Income and Incidence of Burden of Rising Prices." Background paper prepared for India Poverty Assessment Report, Agriculture and Resource Economics, University of California–Berkeley, Berkeley.

Desai. S., A. Dubey, B. L. Joshi, M. Sen, A. Shariff, and R Vanneman. 2008. *India Human Development Report: Challenges for a Society in Transitions.* New Delhi: National Council for Applied Economic Research and College Park: University of Maryland.

Dev, M., and C. Ravi. 2007. "Poverty and Inequality: All-India and States, 1983–2005." *Economic and Political Weekly* 42 (6): 509–21.

Drèze, J., P. Lanjouw, and N. Sharma. 1998. "Economic Development 1957–93." In *Economic Development in Palanpur over Five Decades,* ed. P. Lanjouw and N. H. Stern. New Delhi and Oxford: Oxford University Press.

Dubey, A. 2008. "Consumption, Income and Inequality in India." Background paper prepared for India Poverty Assessment Report, National Council of Applied Economic Research, New Delhi.

Eapen, M. 1994. "Rural Non-agricultural Employment in Kerala—Some Emerging Tendencies." *Economic and Political Weekly* 29 (21): 1285–89.

Eswaran, M., A. Kotwal, B. Ramaswami, and W. Wadhwa. 2008. "How Does Poverty Decline: Suggestive Evidence from India, 1983–1999." Bureau for Research and Economic Analysis of Development (BREAD) Policy Paper No. 14.

———. 2009. "Sectoral Labour Flows and Agricultural Wages in India, 1983–2004: Has Growth Trickled Down?" *Economic and Political Weekly* 44 (2): 46–55.

Fafchamps, M., and F. Shilpi. 2008. "Isolation and Subjective Welfare: Evidence from South Asia." Policy Research Working Paper 4535, World Bank, Washington, DC.

Foster, A., and M. Rosenzweig. 2003. "Agricultural Development, Industrialization and Rural Inequality." Unpublished manuscript, Brown University and Harvard University, Providence, RI.

———. 2004. "Agricultural Productivity Growth, Rural Economic Diversity, and Economic Reforms: India, 1970–2000." *Economic Development and Cultural Changes* 52: 509–42.

Ghose, A. K. 2004. "The Employment Challenge in India." *Economic and Political Weekly* 39 (48): 5106–16.

Glinskaya, E., and J. Jalan. 2005. "Quality of Informal Jobs in India." Background paper prepared for draft World Bank report, "India's Employment Challenge: Creating Jobs, Helping Workers," World Bank, New Delhi.

Himanshu. 2005. "Wages in Rural India." *Indian Journal of Labour Economics* 48 (2): 375–406.

———. 2008. "Agriculture and Nonfarm Employment: Exploring the Interlinkages in Rural India." Background paper prepared for India Poverty Assessment Report, Jawaharlal Nehru University, New Delhi.

Jayaraj, D. 1994. "Determinants of Rural Non-Agricultural Employment." In *Non-agricultural Employment in India: Trends and Prospects,* ed. P. Visaria and R. Basant. New Delhi: Sage Publications.

Lal, D. 1976. "Agricultural Growth, Real Wages and the Rural Poor in India." *Economic and Political Weekly* 11 (26): A47–A61.

Lanjouw. P., and R. Murgai. 2009. "Poverty Decline, Agricultural Wages, and Nonfarm Employment in India: 1983–2004." Policy Research Working Paper 4858, World Bank, Washington, DC.

Lanjouw, P., and N. H. Stern, eds. 1998. *Economic Development in Palanpur over Five Decades.* New Delhi and Oxford: Oxford University Press.

Lewis, W. A. 1954. "Economic Development with Unlimited Supplies of Labour." *Manchester School* 28 (2): 139–91.

Munshi, K., and M. Rosenzweig. 2006. "Traditional Institutions Meet the Modern World: Caste, Gender, and Schooling Choice in a Globalizing Economy." *American Economic Review* 96 (4): 1225–52.

Narayan, D., L. Pritchett, and S. Kapoor. 2009. *Moving Out of Poverty: Success from the Bottom Up.* New York: Palgrave Macmillan; Washington, DC: World Bank.

NCEUS (National Commission for Enterprises in the Unorganised Sector). 2007. *Report on Conditions of Work and Promotions of Livelihoods in the Unorganised Sector.* New Delhi: Government of India.

Papola, T. S. 1992. "Rural Nonfarm Employment: An Assessment of Recent Trends." *Indian Journal of Labour Economics* 35 (3): 238–45.

Sen, A. 1996. "Economic Reforms, Employment and Poverty: Trends and Options." *Economic and Political Weekly* 31 (35–37): 2459–77.

Sen, A., and P. Jha. 2005. "Rural Employment: Patterns and Trends from National Sample Survey." In *Rural Transformation in India—The Role of the Nonfarm Sector,* ed. Rohini Nayyar and A. N. Sharma. New Delhi: Institute for Human Development.

Sharma, H. R. 2001. "Employment and Wage Earnings of Agricultural Labourers: A State-wise Analysis." *Indian Journal of Labour Economics* 44 (1): 27–38.

Singh, I. 1990. *The Great Ascent: The Rural Poor in South Asia.* Washington, DC: Johns Hopkins University Press.

Sundaram, K. 2001. "Employment and Poverty in the 1990s: Further Results from NSS 55th Round Employment-Unemployment Survey, 1999–2000." *Economic and Political Weekly* 36 (11): 931–40.

———. 2007. "Employment and Poverty in India: 2000–2005." Working Paper 155, Center for Development Economics, Delhi.

Thorat, S., and N. S. Sabharwal. 2005. "Rural Nonfarm Employment and Scheduled Castes: Activities, Education and Poverty Inter-linkages." In *Rural Transformation in India—The Role of the Nonfarm Sector,* ed. Rohini Nayyar and A. N. Sharma. New Delhi: Institute for Human Development.

Unni, J., and G. Raveendran. 2007. "Growth of Employment (1993–94 to 2004–05): Illusion of Inclusiveness?" *Economic and Political Weekly* 42 (3): 196–99.

World Bank. 2005. *State Fiscal Reforms in India: Progress and Prospects.* New Delhi: World Bank and Macmillan India.

4

Beyond Consumption Poverty: Nutrition, Health, and Education

As the preceding chapters demonstrate, India has steadily reduced consumption poverty since the 1970s. This chapter examines whether that process has been accompanied by improvements in the quality of the lives of the poor in other dimensions—as seen in their nutrition, health, and education outcomes. The expansion of these basic aspects of human capabilities allows the poor to participate in the development process—as seen, for example, in the key role of education in households' participation in the growing nonfarm sector (chapter 3)—and is also intrinsically valuable in improving quality of life (Drèze and Sen 2002). When communities are asked what it means to be poor, they make it clear that consumption captures only one aspect of being poor (see chapter 1).

The evidence is that in contrast to the steady reduction in poverty, India's record in improving human development indicators is mixed. Several health outcomes have improved over the last three decades. Elementary school attendance has improved substantially in the last decade. Education equity has improved as a result, as has the mobility of each generation over that of its predecessors. Literacy rates are expected to rise more rapidly.

In other dimensions, however, particularly in the area of child nutrition, the pace of progress has been slow, much slower than would be expected given the pace of growth of India's gross domestic product (GDP). India's undernutrition figures are among the highest in the world, making the slow progress all the more troubling. Infant and child mortality rates have also declined slowly, and progress in child immunization has stalled in rural areas. In education, success in bringing more children into school has brought the challenge of improving learning outcomes to the fore. Learning outcomes for a large share of children are poor, and inequalities in learning are high.

Disaggregating outcomes between the poor and others shows that outcomes are worse for the poor. But the burden of undernutrition, for example, is not confined to the poor. Rates of undernutrition among India's children (as measured by percentages underweight and stunted) are nearly one-and-a-half times the percentage of the population that is below the official poverty line.

From the vantage point of this book, two points are key: First, improving human development outcomes for the poor remains a key challenge for India. Based on the recent record, it is simply not the case that continued rapid economic growth will automatically translate to commensurate improvements in those outcomes. Second, some problems, such as undernutrition and poor learning outcomes, are endemic and not confined to the poor.

These challenges have stimulated a vast debate about what actions are needed to improve the delivery of services (see, for example, Peters et al. 2002; FOCUS 2006; World Bank 2006). Although that debate is beyond the scope of the book, it is clear from the findings reported in this chapter that improving human development outcomes is not merely, or even primarily, a matter of better targeting of existing programs and services to the poor. Larger—and systemic— service delivery challenges remain.

Nutrition Outcomes: Short, Thin, and Wasted

Viewed Through the Prism of Anthropometric Outcomes, Indians Are Not Doing Well

Undernutrition, particularly child undernutrition, has remained stubbornly high, despite recent rapid growth and the reduction of poverty (see figure 4.1), leading to India's being categorized as "an economic powerhouse and a nutritional weakling" (Haddad 2009, 1). In general, South Asian countries perform worse than Sub-Saharan African countries with respect to nutrition, despite better performance on other measures, such as economic growth and reduction in infant and child mortality.[1] Even within South Asia, however, India performs badly, with only Bangladesh and Nepal having a higher proportion of underweight children.

Indian adults are also among the world's most undernourished. In the mid-2000s, more than half of adult women in India were anemic, and a third of all adults (men and women) were underweight (defined

Figure 4.1 Child Undernutrition Is Persistently High in India: An International Comparison

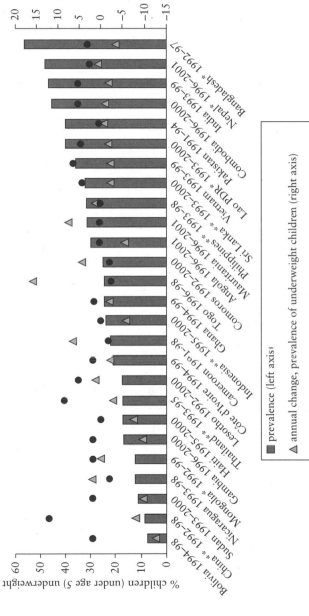

Source: Gragnolati et al., 2006, figure 1.4.

Note: Countries chosen for this table are either in Asia or comparable to India in terms of per capita GDP at PPP (1995 constant international dollars), i.e., in the range $1,333–$2,333, where India's per capita GDP was $1,833 in 1995. Countries in Asia with somewhat lower per capita GDP (<$1333) are denoted by * and with higher per capita GDP (>$2333) by **.

Figure 4.2 South Asian Women Are among the Shortest Women in the Developing World

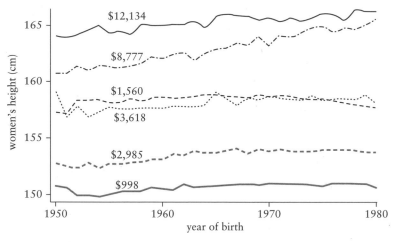

Source: Deaton 2007, Figure 1; Data based on Demographic and Health Surveys (DHS) from 43 countries between 1993 and 2004.

Note: Data are simple unweighted averages of country data within regions. The dollar figures are real 1996 international prices. GDP per capita in 1970 (chained) is from the Penn World table, version 6.1.

by low body mass index or BMI).[2] Those numbers compare unfavorably to about 16 percent of women underweight in 23 African countries (Deaton and Drèze 2009). In his investigation of adult heights, Deaton (2007) shows that South Asian women are among the shortest in the developing world and attain adult height at a later age than women in contemporary rich countries (figure 4.2). The population-weighted average of women's heights in Bangladesh, Nepal, and India (countries for which Demographic and Health Survey data are available) is 151.2 centimeters, compared to 155.0 for Latin America and the Caribbean, 156.9 for Central Asian countries, and 157.8 centimeters for African countries. It is argued that adult height is a marker of childhood insults; early childhood insults translate over time into a significant disadvantage in later life.

A large proportion of Indian children are *short, thin,* and *wasted.*[3] In 2005–06, 43 percent of Indian children (aged less than five years) were underweight, 48 percent were stunted, and 20 percent were wasted; about 70 percent were anemic (IIPS and Macro International 2007).[4] Undernutrition happens very early in life. Nearly a third of Indian infants had low birth weight in 2005–06, and most of the damage, largely irreversible, is done before the child turns two (see, for example, Gragnolati et al. 2006; Swaminathan 2009; FOCUS 2006).

In the Area of Nutrition, as with Consumption Poverty, Data Inconsistencies Make the Detection of Clear Trends Difficult. but Even Assuming That the More Optimistic Data Are Correct, the Pace of Improvement in Nutrition Has Been Slow Relative to the Pace of Growth of India's Gross Domestic Product

Although nutrition status has improved over the long term, progress has been slow, and recent trends suggest a possible stalling of progress. In the three decades since 1975, the proportion of severely undernourished children (weight- or height-for-age) declined by 50 percent (table 4.1). Similarly, the proportions of underweight men and women declined by 41 percent and 31 percent between 1970 and the mid-2000s. Although those long-term trends are reasonably clear, more recent trends since the late 1990s are unclear and depend on the anthropometric indicator and the data source—the National Nutritional Monitoring Bureau (NNMB) or the National Family Health Surveys (NFHS). NNMB data suggest a continuation of the decline in the proportion of children underweight and wasted, with some increase in stunting. In contrast, NFHS data indicate almost no decline in the proportion of underweight children, a significant decline in stunting, and some rise in wasting. This apparent stalling of nutritional status, as suggested by the most recent round of the NFHS, is worrying, but the source of the discrepancy between data sources and indicators is not clear, raising the critical need for better statistics to monitor nutritional outcomes (see box 4.1).

Regardless of data source, the pace of improvement has been slow and stands in sharp contrast to India's performance on economic growth. For instance, the 1.5 percent annual reduction in the prevalence of underweight children lags far behind the reductions achieved by countries with similar economic growth rates (Gragnolati et al. 2006; see also figure 4.1). Cross-country data suggest that the rate of decline in the proportion of underweight children tends to be about half the rate of growth of GDP per capita (Haddad et al. 2003). That would predict a decline of 38 percent in India between

Table 4.1 Slow Pace of Improvement in Undernutrition

	NNMB % undernourished children (below five years)					NFHS % undernourished children (below three years)		
	1975–79	1988–90	1996–97	2000–01	2004–05	1992–93	1998–99	2005–06
Weight-for-age (underweight)								
Below 2 SD	77	69	62	60	55	52	47	46
Below 3 SD	37	27	23	21	18	20	18	—
Height-for-age (stunting)								
Below 2 SD	79	65	58	49	52	—	46	38
Below 3 SD	53	37	29	26	25	—	23	—
Weight-for-height (wasting)								
Below 2 SD	18	20	19	23	15	—	16	19
Below 3 SD	2.9	2.4	2.5	3.1	2.4	—	3	—
% undernourished adults								
% low BMI (men)	56	49	46	37	33	—	—	—
% low BMI (women)	52	49	48	39	36	—	36.2	33.0

Source: Deaton and Drèze 2009.

Note: NNMB refers to the National Nutritional Monitoring Bureau data covering children below five years of age in rural areas of nine states; NFHS refers to the National Family and Health Survey data for children below three years of age in rural and urban areas across India. For comparability with NNMB data, NFHS estimates based on NCHS standards have been reported. See end-of-chapter notes 3 and 4 for definitions of indicators and standards. BMI = body mass index; SD = standard deviation; — = not available.

Box 4.1 Tracking Nutrition, Health, and Education

It is difficult to track nutrition indicators accurately in India, especially child nutrition status. Nutrition data are weak and are collected infrequently. Different data sources disagree, and on occasion, different anthropometric indicators do as well. Important differences exist between the two main data sources with respect to scope and methodology that may influence data quality. The National Nutritional Monitoring Bureau (NNMB) surveys are conducted annually (since 1975–79) in primarily rural areas of nine (mostly southern) states. These data are collected by trained, regular staff, using standardized anthropometric assessments. In contrast, the National Family Health Surveys (NFHS) are conducted once every five years (since 1992–93) in a nationwide sample, using survey investigators. Some concerns also exist about the comparability of the last two rounds of National Family Health Surveys, for example, with respect to trends in child nutrition, adult heights, and school attendance.

Similarly, the burden of illness in India is hard to assess because data on morbidity patterns are scarce. The two national surveys, the National Sample Surveys (NSS) and the National Family Health Surveys, provide information on self-reported morbidity only. The usefulness of these estimates as comparative measures of health outcomes is limited, as the self-reported information is likely to be highly correlated with the respondent's level of health awareness, the availability of health care facilities, and the standard of living. Cultural and linguistic variations in responses may also be occurring, making comparisons across states problematic. Serious limitations are also present in the mortality data. The Registrar General has attempted to address these through periodic compilation of cause-specific mortality data, using verbal autopsy techniques.

Tracking education participation in public and recognized private schools has become easier in recent years through the District Information System for Education. However, the current state of knowledge regarding learning achievement in India is hampered by a lack of coordination and systematization of testing tools and of sampling and reporting protocols. The most concerted effort to generate consistent statistics on learning achievement over time has been by India's National Council of Educational Research and Training and the organization Pratham (through the Annual Survey of Education Reports). However, no internationally comparable measures of achievement exist, except for mathematics achievement in secondary schools in two of the Indian states.

Sources: Deaton and Drèze 2009; Drèze and Sen 2002; Das et al. 2006; World Bank 2009b.

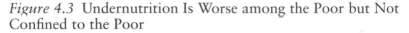

Figure 4.3 Undernutrition Is Worse among the Poor but Not Confined to the Poor

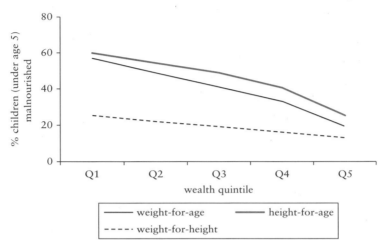

Source: NFHS III report.

Note: Measures of moderate malnutrition reported in asset index–based quintiles of the population.

1980 and 2005, compared to the actual decline of 29 percent. The actual decline since 1990 was only 20 percent (10 percent based on NFHS data), compared to the predicted decline of 27 percent. Similarly, the rate of growth in average adult height in India (with the exception of Kerala) has been much slower than has been the case in several European countries in the past and in China in recent decades (Deaton and Drèze 2009).[5]

Though undernutrition is endemic in India, it is far more widespread among the poor (figure 4.3).[6] Children from the poorest wealth quintile (based on an asset index) are three times more likely to be underweight or stunted, compared to children in the richest quintile. The contrasts between wealth groups on weight-for-height (wasting) are less sharp. But the problem is emphatically not one only of the poor. Tarozzi (2008) reports that even among children from privileged households (defined in terms of wealth, as well as urban residence, better sanitation, and educated parents), 22 percent are stunted, although there is no evidence of wasting.

Both the level and pace of improvements in undernutrition vary significantly across states (see, for example, Radhakrishna et al. 2004; Deaton and Drèze 2009). In general, poorer states tend to have higher prevalence of undernourished women and children (see figure 4.4).[7] Four states—Bihar, Madhya Pradesh, Rajasthan, and Uttar Pradesh—accounted for 43 percent of India's underweight children in 1998–99

Figure 4.4 Nutrition Is Worse in Poorer States

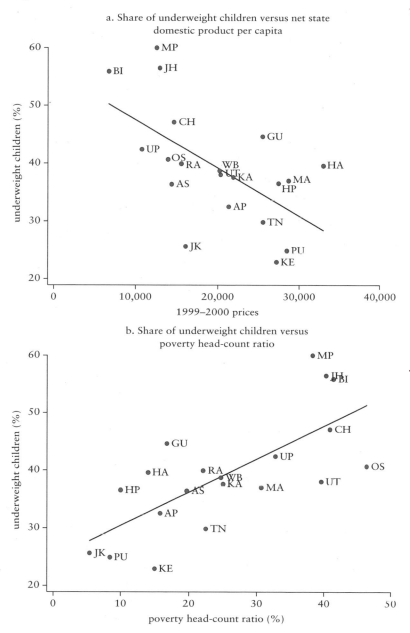

a. Share of underweight children versus net state
domestic product per capita

b. Share of underweight children versus
poverty head-count ratio

Source: Authors' estimates based on NFHS-III, 2005–06, data for percentage of
underweight children (below 5 years, using WHO standards); NSSO, 2004–05, data
for poverty incidence by state; and RBI, 2005–06, data on per capita net state domestic product at factor cost (in constant 1999–2000 prices).

(Gragnolati et al. 2006). Various factors could drive these interstate differences, including, among others, differences in income, social context (for example, the status of women), institutions, and political will (for example, the quality of the delivery of services that affect nutrition, the electoral balance of power, and so forth) (see, for example, Walton 2009; Hariss and Kohli 2009; FOCUS 2006). Of concern is the widening of these interstate, rural-urban, class, and social group disparities during the 1990s (Gragnolati et al. 2006; Hariss and Kohli 2009). The pace of improvement during the 2000s also varies significantly across states, though recent comparisons are made difficult by the possible lack of comparability between the more recent NFHS rounds (see box 4.1 above).[8]

The current slow (perhaps stalled) pace of improvement is disturbing, especially as, by preventing children from reaching their development potential, undernutrition can itself become a critical factor in perpetuating poverty. The evidence unambiguously suggests that childhood deprivation is associated with poorer childhood development, results in significant long-term impairment in later life, and may also adversely affect future generations.[9] Child undernutrition leads to growth retardation and shorter stature in adulthood, greater susceptibility to disease, and higher mortality.[10] Undernutrition in childhood is also associated with lower cognitive and motor development, leading to less schooling and lower human capital acquisition and hence lower earnings in adulthood. Maternal undernutrition, besides being associated with greater morbidity and mortality, also translates to lower birth weight of offspring, who then start life at a disadvantage.

Health Outcomes: Better but Not Well

Health outcomes in India are poor but have improved slowly over the last three decades. By the mid-2000s, life expectancy in India had increased to about 62 years, and fertility rates decreased to 2.9 per 1,000 population. India lies on the Preston curve that correlates health outcomes (as measured by life expectancy) with income per capita across countries (see Deaton 2006).[11] But it lags other countries, such as Brazil and Mexico, and the pace of improvement in health outcomes (as measured by life expectancy and child and infant mortality rates) in India has been slower since 1990 relative to earlier periods of slower economic growth (Deaton 2006). Infant mortality rate, a widely accepted indicator of the general health of the population and the quality of health care services available, declined from 134 to 58 per 1,000 live births between the early 1970s and the mid-2000s. Rural health outcomes steadily improved during the period, leading to narrowing rural-urban differentials (table 4.2).

Nevertheless, that the pace of improvement has reversed for key indicators such as child immunization, and remains very slow for others, such as infant and child mortality, is cause for serious concern (see table 4.2). India has the lowest child immunization rates in South Asia. The decline in infant and child mortality was slower during the 1990s, a period of rapid economic growth, than in previous decades (Deaton 2006, Peters et al. 2002). India continues to have a high burden of disease, potentially taking a significant toll on her productive capabilities.[12] In addition, public health outcomes, such as access to sanitation and safe drinking water, remain poor. Though access to drinking water has improved over time, considerable variation across states remains, and issues of quantity and regularity, as well as quality, remain of concern. Basic sanitation remains a challenge with three-quarters of rural households reporting no toilet facilities even in 2005–06. These conditions can result in poor health outcomes.

As with nutrition, poor households tend to have much worse health outcomes compared to the nonpoor (figure 4.5). Infants in the poorest two quintiles are twice as likely to die before their first birthday compared to infants in the richest quintile.[13] Such differences are also evident in indicators of health care utilization. For instance, in 1998–99, only about two-thirds of poor children in urban areas were fully immunized, compared to nearly all children belonging to the richest quintile. In addition, certain groups may be especially vulnerable to ill health, such as urban slum dwellers and those engaged in hazardous occupations (Sen 2008; Frank and Mustard 1994, cited in Peters et al. 2002). The variability of health status across the population is high—India ranked 153rd among 191 countries in estimates

Table 4.2 Health Status Has Improved Overall, but There Have Been Reversals in Some Key Indicators

Indicators	1992/93		1998/99		2005/06	
	Rural	Urban	Rural	Urban	Rural	Urban
Life expectancy at birth (years)	59.0	65.9	61.0	67.6	61.8	68.5
Infant mortality rate	85.0	56.1	73.3	47.0	62.2	41.5
Child mortality rate	119.4	74.6	103.7	63.1	82.0	51.7
Total fertility rate	3.7	2.7	3.1	2.3	3.0	2.1
% Children fully immunized	30.9	50.7	36.6	60.5	38.6	57.6

Sources: Life expectancy from Registrar General of India; all other information from NFHS II and III reports.

Note: Total fertility rate for the 1- to 36-months period preceding the survey.

Figure 4.5 Health Outcomes Are Substantially Worse among the Poor

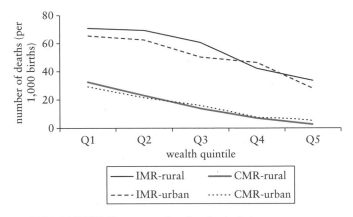

Source: 2005–06 NFHS III report and authors' calculations.

Note: CMR = child mortality rate; IMR = infant mortality rate; Q1–Q5 = asset index–based quintiles of population.

of variability of child mortality (Peters et al. 2002, based on WHO statistics).[14]

Place of residence is an important correlate of health status in India (see figure 4.6). Southern states, especially Kerala and Tamil Nadu, have health outcomes comparable with those of middle-income countries, whereas states such as Bihar, Madhya Pradesh, Orissa, and Uttar Pradesh consistently do poorly.[15] At the same time, however, some of the states that are otherwise lagging (including Bihar, Chhattisgarh, and Madhya Pradesh) showed impressive gains in immunization coverage in recent years, while the most pronounced declines were in richer or otherwise better-performing states (such as Punjab, Maharashtra, and Tamil Nadu) (Sen 2008).

Contrary to what one might expect, sick people in India visit doctors often, doing so at least as much, if not more often, compared to several South Asian and even developed countries in some cases. For example, the proportion of survey respondents who took their children to a health care facility for acute respiratory infection was almost three times as great as in Bangladesh or Nepal (and much higher than in Sub-Saharan African countries). Even the poor seek medical care at least as much as the nonpoor.[16] However, many of these visits are for small, sporadic episodes of sickness, whereas hospitalizations and institutional delivery care remain more common among better-off households. NSS data indicate that in 2004, hospitalization rates were nearly 4 percent among households in the top expenditure quintile in both rural and urban areas. In the

Figure 4.6 Health Indicators Vary Significantly across States and Are Weakly Correlated with Poverty

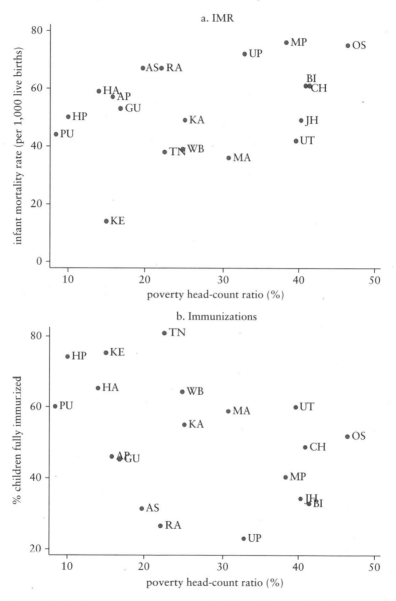

Source: Authors' estimates. See notes to table 4.2 and figure 4.4 for data sources.

poorest quintile, rates were about 1 percent among households in rural areas and 2 percent in urban areas. In addition, critical differences exist in medical care received by poor and nonpoor women during childbirth.

Poor health outcomes are not just a loss for the people concerned; health shocks can be a catastrophe for families and a significant cause of impoverishment. Household surveys from several states suggest that health shocks are the single most important source of idiosyncratic risk in India (see, for example, World Bank 2011). For households, ill health implies expenditure on treatment, potential loss of work, and often indebtedness. The poor in particular have little access to formal insurance, and informal networks have only a limited ability to protect against health risks (Das et al. 2006).[17] As a result, health care spending constitutes about 5 percent of total household expenditures (Gupta 2009), but the expenditure is likely to be lumpy, especially in the case of hospitalization. In 2005, out-of-pocket expenditure in India was as high as 76 percent of total health expenditures; this is among the highest in developing countries (as reported by Berman, Ahuja, and Bhandari 2010, using WHO 2008 statistics; see also GoI 2005). This expenditure imposes a considerable financial burden on households and may even push households into poverty. Estimates of the impoverishing effect of out-of-pocket expenditure on health care in India range from an overall poverty increase of 3.5 percent to 6.6 percent in rural areas, and 2.5 percent to 5 percent in urban areas, depending on the methodology and survey data used (see Garg and Karan 2008; Gupta 2009; and Berman, Ahuja, and Bhandari 2010).[18]

Education Outcomes: In School, but Not Learning Very Much

The inability to send children to school is often cited by communities as a marker of poverty (Krishna 2004, 2006; World Bank 2009a). Better education and more learning confer a range of advantages on the individual, including better labor market opportunities and income and better health outcomes, as well as substantially better education and health outcomes for the next generation. For women, better education also translates to more autonomy and decision-making power; education has value as a tool for social affirmation and political participation. Though it is an end in itself, education now is also playing a greater instrumental role in people's lives. As discussed in earlier chapters, the returns to education have risen in both rural and urban areas. That fits exactly with a story of accelerating urban growth and a growing rural nonfarm sector, as the less the economy is dominated by agriculture, the more important education is. Education of quality is critical if the poor are to share in the growth process.

Elementary School Attendance Has Increased Substantially in the Last Decade. Literacy, Educational Equity, and Intergenerational Mobility in Education Outcomes Have Improved as a Result

Almost all children, even poor children, are now enrolled in elementary school.[19] School attendance also rose substantially during the previous decade (see table 4.3).[20] The increase in school attendance was particularly large among children of primary and middle school age and slightly less among those of secondary school age. The recent surge in educational aspirations and the expansion of elementary school facilities are likely drivers of the increase in school participation.[21]

In addition, education equity has improved significantly at the elementary school level. The most rapid increases in attendance have occurred among children from poor households—80 percent of poor children age 6 to 14 were attending school in 2004–05, double the proportion two decades ago (figure 4.7). Elementary school attendance has increased faster for groups that were educationally disadvantaged to start with, including girls, scheduled caste and Muslim children, children from rural areas, and those from educationally backward states.[22] Many children are first-generation learners. Nearly half of the poorest children come from households with no educated household member, in contrast to only 5 percent of the richest children (Sankar 2008).

However, poor children remain far less likely than the nonpoor to attend school beyond the elementary level. Secondary school attendance is twice as high among children from nonpoor households, relative to children from poor households; children from the richest quintile are *14 times* more likely to attend tertiary school (Azam and Blom 2008; World Bank 2009b; see also figure 4.8). In general, disparities by location, class, social group, and gender are more pronounced at higher age groups and education levels. Many of these disparities have narrowed in the last decade, especially in urban areas. Of concern is the widening of gaps in tertiary enrollment between nonpoor and poor children (figure 4.8). Regression analysis suggests that some of the inequalities at the tertiary level (between poor and nonpoor children, girls and boys, rural and urban areas) are driven primarily by inequalities in enrollment and completion at the secondary school level (Azam and Blom 2008).

Table 4.3 Attendance Increased Substantially in the Past Decade, Particularly in Elementary Schools

percent

| | 1993/94 | | | | 2004/05 | | | |
| | Rural | | Urban | | Rural | | Urban | |
Age group	Male	Female	Male	Female	Male	Female	Male	Female
Age 5–29 years	45.4	30.5	47.7	34.9	53.2	43.6	54.1	51.9
Age 3–5 years	17.2	15.0	35.5	32.3	30.6	29.0	49.0	47.9
Age 6–14 years	74.5	58.2	87.0	82.4	86.9	79.5	91.0	89.5
Age 6–10 years	74.0	60.4	87.5	83.8	87.6	83.2	88.7	85.0
Age 11–14 years	75.3	54.5	86.4	80.6	85.8	74.1	88.4	86.9
Age 15–18 years	43.0	22.3	59.1	52.0	49.4	36.0	61.0	59.3
Age 19–29 years	8.0	2.4	16.8	9.9	8.6	3.9	17.4	12.3

Source: Authors' estimates based on NSS data.

Note: Table reports percentage of age group currently attending school.

Figure 4.7 More Poor Children Are Attending Elementary School

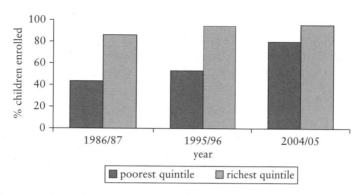

Source: Sankar 2008.
Note: Data are age-specific attendance rates among students aged 6 to 14 years.

Figure 4.8 Poor Children Are Less Likely to Attend Post-elementary School

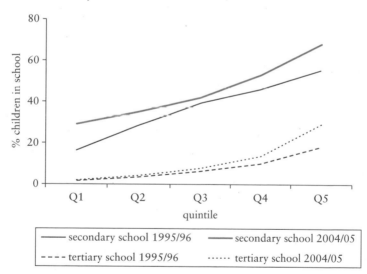

Source: Authors' estimates from NSS 50th and 61st rounds.
Note: Quintiles based on distribution of per capita expenditure.

Significant improvements in literacy and educational attainment have been achieved in recent decades. Literacy rates increased rapidly from about 52 percent in 1991 to 75 percent in 2001. An increase is also noticeable in mean years of schooling across successive generations, for men and women in both rural and urban areas

(Jalan and Murgai 2008; Sankar 2008). Mobility in education has improved significantly across generations for all major social groups and wealth classes.[23] In fact, in sharp contrast to its image of low social mobility, Jalan and Murgai (2008) show India to have average, or above average, mobility compared to estimates from similar studies of other countries. Despite these recent improvements, outcomes for the poor remain low. More than half the poor are illiterate, compared to a quarter of the nonpoor. Secondary school completion is six times as high among nonpoor children relative to poor; tertiary school completion is 23 times higher.

Because enrollment expansion is relatively recent, adult literacy in India is still poor in a global context. Adult literacy (among those 15 years and above) is on par with that in Sub-Saharan African countries.[24] Adult literacy in China in the early 2000s was near-universal and nearly 30 percentage points ahead of India's level (Drèze and Sen 2002; Kingdon 2007; see figure 4.9). A comparison of educational attainment in the two countries suggests that educational outcomes in India are below what China achieved 30 years ago (figure 4.9). Comparing current outcomes, China has nearly three times the proportion of secondary school graduates relative to India.

Children Are Learning Little in School, and Inequalities in Learning Outcomes Are Very High

A major concern is that children are learning little in school. Since the mid-1990s, three national and several state-specific studies testing

Figure 4.9 India's Educational Attainment Is below China 30 Years Ago

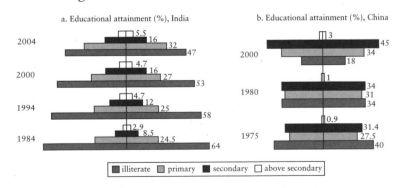

Source: Riboud, Savchenko, and Tan 2007.
Note: Educational attainment among the population aged 15 and older. Illiterate includes both the illiterate and below-primary-educated populations.

learning achievement of children at the terminal grades of primary school have been undertaken (see Das et al. 2006 for a summary). Differences in test content, test administration, and study samples render precise comparisons across studies and over time difficult (see box 4.1), but all studies agree that overall learning levels are low and children typically know little, both relative to their curriculum and relative to what they need to know to function in society. Considerably less agreement exists on household-level determinants of learning achievement. The discussion below focuses on elementary education and, to a lesser extent, secondary education, as much of the available evidence is for that level.

The most recent National Council of Educational Research and Training (NCERT) national midterm achievement survey for Class V students found average scores of 48 percent and 60 percent on curriculum-based mathematics and language tests (NCERT 2009). The Annual Survey of Education Report (ASER) surveys, carried out by the nongovernmental organization Pratham, suggest that a large proportion of children remain functionally illiterate and innumerate even after spending several years in school. The ASER 2009 survey found that 9 percent of children in grade 5 could not identify numbers up to 100, 44 percent could not read a short paragraph at grade 2 difficulty, and 29 percent were unable to divide or subtract (figure 4.10). Although achievement levels improve at higher grades,

Figure 4.10 Children Learn Little Even after Spending 5 Years in School

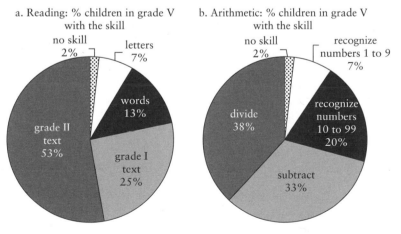

a. Reading: % children in grade V with the skill

b. Arithmetic: % children in grade V with the skill

Source: Pratham 2010.

Note: The panels are to be interpreted as follows: 7 percent of children in grade V can only recognize letters, 13 percent can recognize both letters and words, and so on.

even by the end of the upper primary, 18 percent of grade 8 children could not read a grade 2 text, and 11 percent could not subtract or divide (Pratham 2010). Results from other, state-specific surveys suggest similarly low levels of cognitive achievement (for example, Pandey, Goyal, and Sundararaman 2008; Goyal 2007). Not only have children not learned very much after even four or more years in school, but performance gains across grade cohorts are also low, implying low levels of incremental learning in each grade (Banerjee et al. 2007; Goyal 2007; Pandey, Goyal, and Sundararaman 2008).

National assessments of learning achievement in secondary school are not available.[25] Findings from a study on mathematical achievement among grade 9 students in two states (Orissa and Rajasthan), using internationally comparable testing methodologies, indicate that learning levels in secondary school are also low (Das and Zajonc 2009; World Bank 2009b). The data suggest that the median enrolled ninth grader in those two states fails to meet a basic, international low benchmark of mathematical knowledge. It is likely that the average cognitive achievement level would be even lower if the large numbers of children not currently enrolled in secondary school were included in the testing.

The learning distribution shows a high degree of inequality, one dimension of which is differences across states (NCERT 2009; Pratham 2010). For example, learning levels, assessed using the minimum learning framework as a benchmark, are low in Madhya Pradesh and Uttar Pradesh and relatively higher in Karnataka (Pandey, Goyal, and Sundararaman 2008). Several studies point to variations across schools, presumably capturing dimensions of school quality (see Das et al. 2006; Goyal 2007; Pratham 2009; Pandey, Goyal, and Sundararaman 2008; Muralidharan and Kremer 2008). An emerging body of research is engaged in identifying the links between school quality and learning outcomes. Several studies also point to a large dispersion in test scores within schools. It is not clear to what extent student characteristics and the socioeconomic characteristics of their families determine learning achievement. In fact, little consensus exists on the nature and extent of sociodemographic variation in achievement levels: Some studies report better learning outcomes for richer and more educated families, for boys, and for students from upper castes, whereas in others no gender or caste differences appear (see Das et al. 2006 and Pandey, Goyal, and Sundararaman 2008 for a discussion).

The distribution of mathematics test scores at the secondary school level, depicted in figure 4.11, shows a spread in achievement among ninth graders in Orissa and Rajasthan second only to that in South Africa among the 51 countries in the sample. In fact, this

Figure 4.11 Highly Unequal Distribution of Cognitive
Achievement in Secondary School in Two Indian States

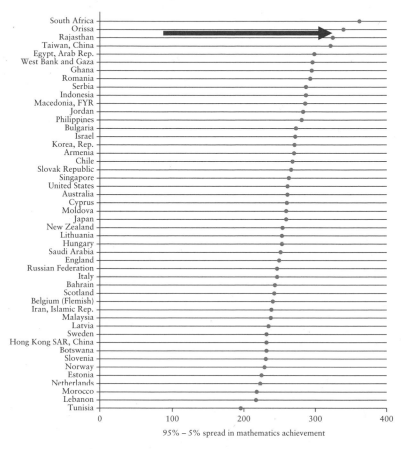

95% − 5% spread in mathematics achievement

Source: Das and Zajonc, 2009.

Note: Data are math achievements for grade IX students. Findings are for the two
Indian states—Orissa and Rajasthan—that can be placed in an international league
table and do not represent the country as a whole.

analysis provides some support for two contrasting views: that
average learning levels are low, *but* that Indians also form a substantial fraction of the top performers worldwide (Das and Zajonc
2009). That is to say, a crude extrapolation of these findings for
India as a whole implies that approximately 80 percent of 14-year-olds
either are not in school or cannot pass the lowest international
benchmark. At the same time, however, the top 5 percent of ninth
graders in these states score much higher than those in several other
low-income countries and are comparable to students in some high-
income countries.

The Need for Systemic Reform

Improving Human Development Outcomes for the Poor, but Not Just the Poor, Remains a Key Challenge in India

These challenges have led to a vast debate about what actions are needed to improve the delivery of services (see, for example, FOCUS 2006; World Bank 2006; Peters et al. 2002). Although that debate is beyond the scope of the book, we summarize its broad contours.

The World Bank's most recent development policy review (World Bank 2006) describes the current state of service delivery and argues that the capability of the public sector, in its current configuration, has not kept pace with the services that citizens demand and need. Health service provision in India is dominated by the private sector. By 2004, about 58 percent of all hospitalization cases and 78 percent of all outpatient visits for health care in rural areas used private providers. In urban areas the figures were 62 percent and 81 percent private providers. Moreover, the poor use the private system nearly as much as the nonpoor, including substantial private use of hospitals (figure 4.12). The public sector remains the dominant provider and financier of schooling. In 2004–05, 88 percent of students in urban areas and 71 percent in rural areas attended public schools (including private schools receiving government aid). Nonetheless, patterns and trends based on NSS data also suggest that the share of private schooling is much higher when such alternatives exist—as they do in urban areas—and the private share is growing among all but the poorest

Figure 4.12 The Poor Rely on Private Healthcare Providers Almost as Much as the Nonpoor

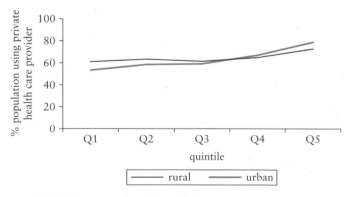

Sources: NFHS III report and authors' calculations.
Note: Q1–Q5 = asset index–based quintiles of population.

Figure 4.13 The Public Sector Is the Dominant Provider of Schooling but Private School's Share Is Growing

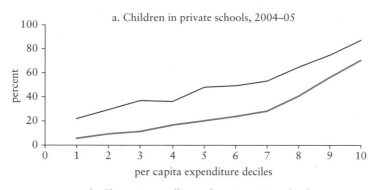

a. Children in private schools, 2004–05

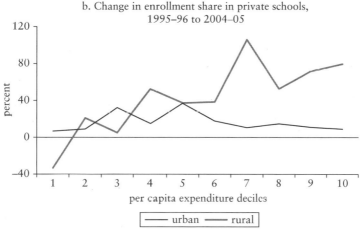

b. Change in enrollment share in private schools, 1995–96 to 2004–05

Source: Authors' estimates from NSS 52nd and 61st round.

Note: Private schools refer to privately managed schools (including aided and unaided).

(figure 4.13). Moreover, recent increases in secondary school enrollment have been in private schools for the richest three quintiles, while children from the poorest quintile have been enrolled in public schools. In secondary education, public schools typically serve households that either cannot afford private schooling or do not have physical access to a private secondary school (World Bank 2009b).

Growing reliance on private delivery of services is not the result of an announced public policy to reduce services but rather a strategy to deal with the failure of the public sector to provide services adequately. Specific conditions that add up to low service quality range among absenteeism by service providers, incompetence, indifference and corruption of staff, and underutilization and poor maintenance of assets

(World Bank 2006). Much careful research has shown that these are not problems particular only to the public sector.

Better service delivery will require improvements in both the public and private sectors. Few would argue that the state is not responsible for improving nutrition, health, and education services. The debates are around whether those responsibilities are best discharged through direct production of services by the state or by other modes. The debate has also shifted fundamentally from measuring success based on inputs to measuring outcomes. The goal of physical access (to a clinic, to a school) is within reach but creates the challenge to deliver better-quality services. The World Bank's development policy review (2006) argues that systemic reform is needed and that many routes to reform are possible. It discusses how three broad types of reforms—internal and administrative reforms, decentralization or devolution, and alternative modes of engagement with nonstate providers—can be successful in addressing the need.

Systemic reform aside, a growing body of research is also evaluating specific small-scale interventions and piloting experiments. The focus of those efforts is on revealing "market failures" (for example, lack of information) that the poor face in the social sectors. It is also increasingly recognized that attempts to improve service delivery will not make much headway without much better performance by "human inputs" which dominate health care and education expenditure, both public and private. Recent experiments with incentives to improve teacher and health service provider performance, for example, show that incentives matter but may not be sufficient on their own (Muralidharan and Sundararaman 2009; Banerjee et al. 2007; Banerjee et al. 2008; Pandey, Goyal, and Sundararaman 2008). These evaluations are still in their infancy, but they are useful to highlight channels to the conditions under which programs may work or may fail to do so.

Notes

1. For instance, more than 50 percent of South Asian children are underweight, compared to just over 30 percent of African children, as Ramalingaswami, Jonsson, and Rhode (1996) have pointed out. Those authors also offer some explanations for the apparent "(South) Asian enigma," including the roles played by low birth weight (in turn a reflection of poor maternal health and nutrition), feeding practices, hygiene and sanitation standards, and disease prevalence. Some of the underlying factors, such as women's status and autonomy, are deeply rooted in the social context of South Asia; these are explored more fully in chapter 6.

2. BMI (body mass index) is the weight in kilograms divided by the height in meters squared. A BMI of less than 18.5 kg/m^2 indicates chronic energy deficiency.

3. Anthropometric indicators for children include stunting (low height-for-age), wasting (low weight-for-height), and underweight (low weight-for-age). The common reference standard defining what is meant by "low" for the three indicators is the median minus two or three standard deviations, based on a well-nourished reference population. The first threshold measures moderate undernutrition; the second, severe. Additional measures of undernutrition include deficiencies of essential micronutrients.

4. These estimates are based on 2006 World Health Organization (WHO) standards and cover all children in the surveyed households (not just those born to women interviewed in the survey, as in previous National Family Health Survey rounds). The corresponding estimates for 2005–06 that are comparable with previous National Nutritional Monitoring Bureau (based on the U.S. National Center for Health Statistics standards) and National Family and Health Survey rounds (for children under three years born to interviewed women) are given in table 4.1.

5. In addition, although Indians are getting taller over time, men's height has grown at more than three times the rate of women's (Deaton 2008).

6. Significant disparities also exist across social groups and between men and women with respect to nutrition, as well as health and mortality, indicators (see chapter 6 for a detailed discussion). Some evidence has also appeared of widening disparities by class, caste, and gender during the 1990s (Gragnolati et al. 2006).

7. A high correlation appears between indicators of undernutrition and monetary indicators of poverty (using either the consumption head-count ratio from the NSS, or the proportion of asset-poor households per the NFHS). The correlation is relatively lower between poverty headcount and anemia among children, with even relatively rich states such as Punjab performing poorly.

8. The correlation between pace of improvement and prevalence levels is weak, with some reversal of trends between the three NFHS rounds. States such as Andhra Pradesh, Karnataka, Punjab, and Tamil Nadu continued to show an above-average reduction in the prevalence of underweight children between 1992–93 and 2005–06. During the 1990s, the reduction in the prevalence of underweight was among the lowest in high-prevalence states such as Bihar, Madhya Pradesh, and Uttar Pradesh. Data from the 2005–06 NFHS suggest that underweight prevalence actually rose in some high-prevalence states such as Bihar and Madhya Pradesh during the early 2000s, while Orissa and Rajasthan showed impressive reductions. Even Kerala showed a marginal increase in the prevalence of underweight children during the early 2000s.

9. See, for example, Black, Allen, and Zulfigar 2008 for a review of short-term consequences of maternal and child undernutrition in low- and middle-income countries; see Victoria et al. 2008 for a review of the potential long-term impacts; see also Gragnolati et al. 2006 for a discussion.

10. The evidence is stronger for the association with childhood morbidity and mortality and contribution to disease burden. For example, in 2004, 19 percent of disability-adjusted life years (DALYs; roughly one lost year of "healthy" life) and 19 percent of deaths among children under five could be attributed to being underweight (Black, Allen, and Zulfigar 2008). The picture is more mixed with respect to the association of childhood undernutrition with adult disease and with adult heights, at least in low- and middle-income countries (Deaton 2007; Victoria et al. 2008).

11. It is notable that considerable debate exists about the correlation between economic growth and health outcomes (see, for example, Deaton 2006 and Das et al. 2006 for a discussion). Starting from a much higher base, improvements in life expectancy in China have, in contrast, been somewhat slower than that in India (based on data from http://www.gapminder.org).

12. India's share of the world's disability-adjusted life years (DALYs) lost was 20 percent in 2004, compared to its 17 percent share of the world's population (WHO statistics on the global burden of disease, 2004 update).

13. Quintiles based on a wealth index, as the NFHS does not canvass information on incomes or consumption.

14. A high degree of inequality is also found in both health utilization and outcomes by social group and gender (see chapter 6 for a discussion).

15. See Peters et al. 2002 for a comparison of child mortality rates in Indian states with those of other countries. The poor states also have poor nutrition outcomes and high mortality.

16. One study in Delhi suggests that poor households visit doctors more than the nonpoor (Das and Sanchez-Paramo 2003).

17. Health insurance coverage in India, particularly among rural households, is extremely low; less than 3 percent of households report any form of health insurance. Coverage is negligible for the poorest, at 0.4 percent, compared to 7 percent of households in the richest quintile (Ajwad 2006).

18. The impoverishing effect of hospitalization can be even greater. One study estimated that one-fourth of individuals hospitalized became poor as a result in 1995–96 (Peters et al. 2002). These estimates are likely to underestimate the negative impact of illness, as only the direct costs of health care are taken into account, while lost earnings are ignored.

19. By 2004–05, all 6-to-10-year-olds were enrolled in primary school; 70 percent of 11 to 14-year-olds were in middle school; and 40 percent of 14-to-18-year-olds were in secondary school. A further 10 percent of 18-to-24-year-olds were enrolled in higher education (from http://www.Indiastat.

com, based on Ministry of Human Resource Development administrative data). The 2009 Annual Survey of Education Report (ASER) survey found that only 4 percent of 6 to 14-year-olds were not in school (Pratham 2010).

20. School attendance is a more accurate indicator of school participation than enrollment rates at the start of the school year, which can mask nonattendance or dropping out during the year.

21. By 2002, 87 percent of villages had a primary school within 1 kilometer, and 78 percent of villages had an upper primary school within the 3-kilometer norm (Sankar 2008). The number of secondary schools has also increased, though they remain less widespread than elementary schools. Significant improvements have been made in physical school infrastructure between 1996 and 2006, and schooling incentives, such as uniforms, textbooks, and cooked midday meals, have also grown (De et al. 2009).

22. However, tribal children continue to lag behind with respect to enrollment and mean years of schooling (Jalan and Murgai 2008). See chapter 6 for a discussion of inequalities across social groups.

23. These estimates are based on enrollment (mean years of schooling) and do not take into account learning outcomes.

24. This could reflect the fact that the increase in school attendance is recent, so that the impact would be seen in younger cohorts.

25. Because of variations in state secondary school systems, learning outcomes as measured by school board examinations are not readily comparable across states and over time (World Bank 2009b).

References

Ajwad, I. 2006. "Coverage, Incidence and Adequacy of Safety Net Programs in India." Background paper for "Social Protection for a Changing India," World Bank, Washington, DC.

Azam, M., and A. Blom. 2008. "Progress in Participation in Tertiary Education in India from 1983 to 2004." Policy Research Working Paper 4793, World Bank, Washington, DC.

Banerjee, A., R. Banerji, E. Duflo, R. Glennerster, and S. Khemani. 2008. "Pitfalls of Participatory Programs: Evidence from a Randomized Evaluation in Education in India." Policy Research Working Paper 4584, World Bank, Washington, DC.

Banerjee, A., S. Cole, E. Duflo, and L. Linden. 2007. "Remedying Education: Evidence from Two Randomized Experiments in India." *Quarterly Journal of Economics* 122 (3): 1235–64.

Banerjee, A., E. Duflo, and R. Glennerster. 2007. "Putting Band Aid on a Corpse: Incentives for Nurses in the Indian Public Health Care System." *Journal of the European Economic Association* 6 (2–3): 487–500.

Berman, P., R. Ahuja, and L. Bhandari. 2010. "The Impoverishing Effect of Healthcare Payments in India: New Methodology and Findings." *Economic and Political Weekly* 45 (16): 65–71.

Black, R. E., L. H. Allen, and A. Zulfigar. 2008. "Maternal and Child Undernutrition: Global and Regional Exposures and Health Consequences." *Lancet* 371: 243–60.

Das, J., J. Hammer, S. Devarajan, and L. Pritchett. 2006. "Will a Wealthier India Be a Healthier India?" Presentation at National Bureau of Economic Research/National Council of Applied Economic Research Conference on Growth in India, New Delhi, January.

Das, J., P. Pandey, and T. Zojanc. 2006. "Learning Levels and Gaps in Pakistan." Policy Research Working Paper 4067, World Bank, Washington, DC.

Das, J., and C. Sanchez-Paramo. 2003. "Short but Not Sweet—New Evidence on Short Duration Morbidities from India." Policy Research Working Paper 2971, World Bank, Washington, DC.

Das, J., and T. Zajonc. 2009. "India Shining and Bharat Drowning: Comparing Two Indian States to the Worldwide Distribution in Mathematics Achievement." *Journal of Development Economics* 92 (2): 175–87.

De, A., J. Drèze, M. Samson, and A. K. Shiva Kumar. 2009. "Struggling to Learn." *The Hindu,* February 18, 2009. http://www.hindu.com/2009/02/18/stories/2009021855921000.htm.

Deaton, A. 2006. "Global Patterns of Income and Health: Facts, Interpretations and Policies." National Bureau of Economic Research Working Paper 12735, NBER, Cambridge, MA.

———. 2007. "Height, Health, and Development." *PNAS* 104 (33): 13232–37.

Deaton, A., and J. Drèze. 2009. "Food and Nutrition in India: Facts and Interpretations." *Economic and Political Weekly* 44 (7): 42–65.

Deaton, Angus. 2008. "Height, Health, and Inequality: The Distribution of Adult Heights in India." *American Economic Review* 98 (2): 468–74.

Drèze, J., and A. Sen. 2002. *India: Development and Participation.* New Delhi: Oxford University Press.

FOCUS. 2006. "Focus on Children under Six." Abridged report by Citizens Initiative for the Rights of Children under Six. New Delhi: Citizens Initiative for the Rights of Children under Six.

Garg, C. C., and A. K. Karan. 2008. "Reducing Out-of-Pocket Expenditures to Reduce Poverty: A Disaggregated Analysis at Rural-Urban and State Level in India." *Health Policy and Planning* 24: 116–28.

GoI (Government of India). 2005. *Financing and Delivery of Health Care Services in India.* New Delhi: National Commission on Macroeconomics and Health, Ministry of Health and Family Welfare.

Goyal, S. 2007. "Learning Achievements in India: A Study of Primary Education in Rajasthan." Manuscript, World Bank, New Delhi.

Gragnolati, M., C. Bredenkamp, M. Shekhar, M. Das Gupta, and Y.-K. Lee. 2006. *India's Undernourished Children: A Call for Reform and Action.* New Delhi: World Bank.

Gupta, I. 2009. "Out-of-Pocket Expenditures and Poverty: Estimates from NSS 61st Round." Paper presented for consideration of the Expert Group on Poverty, Planning Commission, May 12, 2009. http://planningcommission.gov.in/reports/genrep/indrani.pdf.

Haddad, L. 2009. "Lifting the Curse: Overcoming Persistent Undernutrition in India." IDS Research Summary. *IDS Bulletin* 40 (4): 1–8.

Haddad, L., H. Alderman, S. Appleton, L. Song, and Y. Yohannes. 2003. "Reducing Child Malnutrition: How Far Does Income Growth Take Us?" *World Bank Economic Review* 17 (1): 107–31.

Hariss, J., and N. Kohli. 2009. "Notes on the Differing 'States' of Child Undernutrition in Rural India." *IDS Bulletin* 40 (4): 9–15.

IIPS (International Institute for Population Sciences) and Macro International. 2007. *National Family Health Survey (NFHS-3), 2005–06: India.* Mumbai: IIPS.

Jalan, J., and R. Murgai. 2008. "Intergenerational Mobility in Education in India." Manuscript, World Bank, New Delhi.

Kingdon, G. G. 2007. "The Progress of School Education in India." Economic and Social Research Council, Global Poverty Research Group Working Paper 71.

Krishna, A. 2004. "Escaping Poverty and Becoming Poor: Who Gains, Who Loses, and Why?" *World Development* 32 (1): 121–36.

———. 2006. "Pathways Out of and Into Poverty in 36 Villages of Andhra Pradesh, India." *World Development* 34 (2): 271–88.

Muralidharan, K., and M. Kremer. 2008. "Public and Private Schools in Rural India." In *School Choice International: Exploring Public-Private Partnerships*, ed. R. Chakrabarti and P. Petersen. Cambridge, MA: MIT Press.

Muralidharan, K., and V. Sundararaman. 2009. "Teacher Performance Pay: Experimental Evidence from India." National Bureau of Economic Research Working Paper 15323, NBER, Cambridge, MA.

NCERT (National Council of Educational Research and Training, India). 2009. *Learning Achievement of Children in Elementary Education: A Journey from Baseline to Midterm.* New Delhi: NCERT.

Pandey, P., S. Goyal, and V. Sundararaman. 2008. "Public Participation, Teacher Accountability, and School Outcomes." Policy Research Working Paper 4777, World Bank, Washington, DC.

Peters, D., A. Yazbeck, R. Sharma, G. Ramana, L. Pritchett, and A. Wagstaff. 2002. *Better Health Systems for India's Poor: Findings, Analysis and Options.* Washington, DC: World Bank.

Pratham. 2009. "ASER 2008—Annual Status of Education Report (Rural) 2008 (Provisional)." New Delhi: Pratham Resource Center.

————. 2010. "ASER 2009—Annual Status of Education Report (Rural) 2009." New Delhi: Pratham Resource Center.

PROBE Team. 1999. *Public Report on Basic Education in India*. New Delhi: Oxford University Press.

Radhakrishna, R., K. H. Rao, C. Ravi, and B. S. Reddy. 2004. "Chronic Poverty and Malnutrition in the 1990s." *Economic and Political Weekly* 39 (28): 3121–30.

Ramalingaswami, V., U. Jonsson, and J. Rohde. 1996. "The Asian Enigma." In *The Progress of Nations*, ed. P. Adamson. New York: UNICEF.

Riboud, M., Y. Savchenko, and H. Tan. 2007. "The Knowledge Economy and Education and Training in South Asia: A Mapping Exercise of Available Survey Data." Human Development Unit, South Asia Region, World Bank, Washington, DC.

Sankar, D. 2008. "What Is the Progress in Elementary Education Participation in India during the Last Two Decades? An Analysis Using NSS Education Rounds." South Asia Development Sector Discussion Paper 24, World Bank, Washington, DC.

Sen, S. 2008. "Delivery of Social Sector Services and Social Protection in Urban Areas." Background paper for "India 2025: Inputs for an Urban Strategy," World Bank, Washingon, DC.

Swaminathan, M. S. 2009. "Undernutrition in Infants and Young Children in India: A Leadership Agenda for Action." *IDS Bulletin* 40 (4): 103–10.

Tarozzi, Alessandro. 2008. "Growth Reference Charts and the Nutritional Status of Indian Children." *Economics and Human Biology* 6 (3): 455–68.

Victoria, C. G., L. Adair, C. Fall, P. C. Hallal, R. Martorell, L. Richter, and H. S. Sachdev. 2008. "Maternal and Child Undernutrition: Consequences for Adult Health and Human Capital." *Lancet* 371 (January 26): 340–57.

Walton, M. 2009. "The Political Economy of India's Malnutrition Puzzle." *IDS Bulletin* 40 (4): 16–24.

World Bank. 2006. *Inclusive Growth and Service Delivery: Building on India's Success*. New Delhi: World Bank and Macmillan.

————. 2009a. *Moving Out of Poverty: The Promise of Empowerment and Democracy in India*. Washington, DC: World Bank and Palgrave Macmillan.

————. 2009b. "Secondary Education in India: Universalizing Opportunity." Report 48521, World Bank, Washington, DC.

————. 2011. *Social Protection for a Changing India*. New Delhi: World Bank.

5

Rising Inequality:
A Cause for Concern?

India's impressively growing economy offers grounds for hope that the living conditions of its vast population will be transformed within a tantalizingly short time. For that to happen, however, the reach of India's growing prosperity must extend to all segments of society. Chapter 1 has shown that whereas economic growth has indisputably picked up in recent decades, evidence of a marked acceleration in the rate of poverty reduction is harder to find, with the implication that inequality in India may well be on the rise. The distinction between a rising tide that "lifts all ships" and growth that disproportionately favors some population groups has been recognized by the Government of India. For example, the Planning Commission's *Eleventh Five-Year Plan* acknowledges that achieving growth that is broadly distributed poses its own, additional challenges: "The rapid growth achieved in the past several years demonstrates that we have learnt how to bring about growth, but we have yet to achieve comparable success in inclusiveness" (GoI 2008, iii).

Some types of inequality, but not all, are harmful for growth and economic development. Chaudhuri and Ravallion (2006) make a useful distinction between "good" and "bad" inequalities. They identify good inequalities as those that reflect and reinforce the market-based incentives that are needed to foster innovation, entrepreneurship, and growth. In their study of the development experience of China and India, Chaudhuri and Ravallion note that the introduction of the Household Responsibility System in rural China in the early 1980s strengthened incentives for agricultural production and thereby stimulated rural economic growth. As some farm households did better than others, however, inequality in rural areas rose. Similar processes have been observed in India, as when increasing wage dispersion within educational attainment categories reflects more competitive product and labor markets in urban areas (Dutta 2005). Chaudhuri and Ravallion argue that such a process of growth accompanied by widening inequality should not necessarily be viewed in a negative light. They note, however, that "bad" inequalities can also be observed in both China and India. Examples include geographic poverty traps (occurring, for example, when two otherwise identical individuals are not similarly able to escape poverty simply because they live in dissimilar locations), patterns of social exclusion, unequal capacities to enhance human capital, lack of access to credit and insurance, corruption, and uneven influence. Such inequalities prevent individuals from connecting to markets and limit investment in human and physical capital; they are usually rooted in market failures, coordination failures, and governance failures. Where these types of inequalities are deep and pervasive, economic growth is held back. Inequality then has an instrumental impact on economic development and the pace of poverty reduction.

A specific instrumental role of inequality that has received growing attention in recent years relates to the impact of local inequalities on development outcomes. Community-driven development (CDD) initiatives have expanded tremendously throughout the developing world, including India. The term refers to a broad approach in which local communities are empowered to articulate their demands for development projects, to participate in their implementation, and even to contribute to their financing. A concern is often expressed that CDD initiatives may be prone to capture by local elites, who have better information and more influence at the local level and who can thereby appropriate resources or dictate the choice of projects and their implementation. How such a process of local capture would occur and what the presence of local elites implies for the performance of CDD initiatives and their ultimate impact on poverty are issues that have not been settled empirically.[1] A fundamental question in such studies concerns the degree of inequality at the local level. It seems reasonable to suppose that elite capture will be less of a problem if inequality within communities is low. Systematic empirical evidence on the extent of inequality at the local level remains scarce.

In this chapter we examine the extent to which recent rounds of National Sample Survey (NSS) data on per capita consumption can shed light on the extent and evolution of economic inequality during recent decades. We also attempt to understand better what factors shape Indian consumption inequality and how their role has evolved.

We start in the next section with an examination of long-term trends in inequality at the all-India level, spanning the period from 1951 to 2006, and then focus in greater detail on the period since 1983.[2] We note here, however, that statements about the evolution of consumption inequality must remain qualified because, as was seen in box 1.4, chapter 1, many measurement-related issues remain unresolved. We continue with a discussion of why debates about inequality can founder through application of different concepts of inequality. An important distinction relates to absolute versus relative inequality. The former is often invoked when evidence of dramatic increases in inequality over time is presented, whereas the latter tends to provide a more nuanced picture. We document further that assessments of Indian economic inequality also vary depending on whether a concept of income or a concept of consumption is applied. NSS data provide evidence on the distribution of consumption. Other data, notably the 2004 India Human Development Survey collected by the National Council of Applied Economic Research (NCAER) and the University of Maryland, permit an assessment of income inequality. Summary measures of income inequality are much higher than measures of consumption inequality. We show evidence that Indian inequality based on the income concept is not so different from the level of inequality recorded in countries such as Brazil and South Africa, countries commonly singled out as global outliers.

The chapter then presents evidence of consumption inequality at the local level in three major Indian states: West Bengal, Orissa, and Andhra Pradesh. These estimates draw on the poverty mapping exercise mentioned in chapters 1 and 2.[3] An important insight that derives from scrutiny of these local-level inequality estimates in rural areas is that inequality does not appear to be a feature only of richer communities. Indeed, in the state of Andhra Pradesh the evidence points rather to the opposite: inequality of consumption is often particularly high in the poorest rural communities. This finding is of potential importance because, as noted above, poor communities are often targeted with development interventions that rely heavily on their ability to organize themselves and work collaboratively. If local inequality of consumption is also an indication of concentration of power and influence and is possibly associated with stratification and fractiousness, then community-driven development efforts in the poorest communities could be particularly exposed to risk of capture by local elites.

The next section focuses more closely on the population blocs that make up the overall distribution of consumption. A long-standing tradition exists of asking to what extent overall inequality can be decomposed into one component that is due to differences in economic welfare between certain clearly distinguishable groups in the population, and another that reflects how much inequality remains within those groups. We first consider a geographic and sectoral breakdown: how much of inequality observed at the all-India level can be attributed to differences between rural and urban areas, and how much to differences between states? We ask how this has evolved over time. We next consider the breakdown of the population into groups defined in terms of social identity (scheduled caste, scheduled tribe, and so forth), education level, and occupational characteristics.

We find important evidence that the contribution to inequality of differences in education levels has grown between 1983 and 2004–05. We show that in urban areas the share of inequality explained by a simple division of the population into those with and those without primary education shows very little change. But the share of inequality explained when the population is divided into those with and those without a postsecondary education nearly doubles to almost 20 percent in 2004–05, up from only 11 percent in 1983. In rural areas the share of inequality explained with either decomposition rises over time, more so for the graduates. We suggest that this evidence fits well with the story of the growing nonfarm sector presented in chapter 3, as we know that the less the countryside is dominated by agriculture, the more important education is. Even completing primary education increases one's chances of escaping the farm.

The section also provides evidence, via application of an alternative decomposition method, that in some states and sectors, certain social groups (defined in terms of their scheduled caste or scheduled tribe status) are being left behind as overall economic growth has proceeded, whereas in other states the advantaged population groups are clearly pulling ahead. This evidence prompts further attention to the subject of social exclusion, pointing to a need to understand better how and why some population groups are unable to participate fully in the broader Indian development process. Those questions are taken up in detail in the next chapter.

Inequality Dynamics at the All-India Level

Consumption Inequality Has Fallen over the Longer Term in India,. . .

A recent study by Datt and Ravallion (2009) tracks poverty and inequality in India over a period of more than five decades on the basis of the long series of NSS household surveys. The authors indicate that between 1951 and 2006, inequality in rural India, as measured by the Gini coefficient, has declined slightly, while inequality in urban areas declined until the 1980s and then started rising again (figure 5.1). What this would mean for total inequality depends on how adjustments are made for urban-rural cost-of-living differences, but given that the great bulk of the population still lives in rural areas, a long-term downward trend would be expected. In recent decades, with population growth more rapid in urban areas and growing divergence between rural and urban average consumption levels, the consequence has been some rise in inequality at the all-India level, most noticeable in more recent decades (see Datt and Ravallion 2009, and also further below).

... But Is Now on the Increase

Table 5.1 summarizes inequality calculated from unit record data for 1983, 1993–94, and 2004–05 on the basis of a larger set of inequality measures than was examined in figure 5.1.[1] These measures indicate that in rural areas inequality declined unambiguously between

Figure 5.1 Evolution of Inequality, 1951–2006

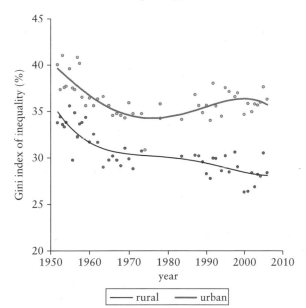

Source: Datt and Ravallion 2009.

Table 5.1 Recent Trends in Inequality

Inequality measures	Rural			Urban			Total		
	1983	1993/94	2004/05	1983	1993/94	2004/05	1983	1993/94	2004/05
Measures of relative inequality									
Gini coefficient	0.3166	0.2854	0.2976	0.3425	0.343	0.3784	0.3237	0.3035	0.3254
Relative mean deviation	0.2232	0.2016	0.2104	0.2457	0.2465	0.2727	0.2291	0.2154	0.2315
Coefficient of variation	1.0245	0.9362	1.0114	0.8364	1.2016	1.2665	0.9801	1.0317	1.1171
Standard deviation of logs	0.5388	0.4833	0.4902	0.5847	0.5871	0.6343	0.5506	0.5129	0.5335
Mehran measure	0.4203	0.3766	0.3857	0.449	0.4484	0.4869	0.4279	0.3979	0.4184
Piesch measure	0.2647	0.2398	0.2535	0.2893	0.2902	0.3241	0.2717	0.2562	0.2789
Kakwani measure	0.0919	0.0762	0.0836	0.1051	0.1053	0.1265	0.0955	0.0851	0.0978
Theil entropy measure	0.1981	0.1708	0.196	0.2196	0.2353	0.2875	0.2046	0.1914	0.2285
Theil mean log deviation measure	0.1539	0.1363	0.1488	0.1844	0.1946	0.2357	0.1619	0.1532	0.1759
Measures of absolute inequality									
P90/10	3.78	3.21	3.20	4.28	4.27	4.84	4.13	3.75	3.92

Source: Authors' calculations based on NSS data.
Note: Inequality estimates based on uniform recall period consumption in 1993/94 all-India rural rupees. Consumption corrected for cost-of-living differences across states and over time using deflators that are implicit in official poverty lines.

1983 and 1993–94 but then increased slightly between 1993–94 and 2004–05. The increase between 1993–94 and 2004–05 would not be reflected in all possible inequality measures. Growth incidence curves (GIC) indicate that between this latter pair of years the growth rate of consumption of the poorest percentiles was above average. This implies that a summary measure of inequality that attached the greatest possible weight to gains among the poorest segments of the distribution could conceivably record a decline in overall inequality.[5]

For urban areas, table 5.1 again suggests that an assessment of inequality change between 1983 and 1993–94 hinges on the specific measure of inequality that is employed. Between these two years, the Gini coefficient records a slight increase in inequality. The coefficient of variation implies a more significant increase in inequality, while the Mehran measure of inequality suggests that inequality fell. It is thus clear that judgments as to what happened to urban inequality between 1983 and 1993–94 will not command universal agreement. Unanimity is more likely to be achieved for the comparison of urban inequality between 1993–94 and 2004–05. Here, all summary measures of inequality reported in table 5.1 document a sizable increase in inequality.

These Results Understate the Increase in Inequality Because, as Noted Earlier, It Is Likely That the Household Consumption Surveys Are Missing Increases in Top-End Incomes and Rural-Urban Income Gaps Are Being Understated

Whereas the survey data we examine do show an increase in inequality, it is not a dramatic increase. We have already noted (box 1.3, chapter 1) that the survey data likely underreport consumption at the top end.

The all-India inequality trends have been estimated by correcting for cost-of-living differences between rural and urban areas, using the deflators implicit in the official poverty lines. However, it is generally agreed that the implicit cost-of-living adjustments contained in these poverty lines are particularly unconvincing for comparisons of rural versus urban consumption levels, especially so in certain states (Deaton and Tarozzi 2005). They imply, for example, that the urban cost of living in some states is as much as 50 percent higher than in rural areas. As the deflators in the official poverty lines probably overcorrect for cost-of-living differences, at least in some places, inequality measured at the all-India level is likely to be understated.[6]

Increases in Wealth Holdings Are Also Driving Perceptions of Increased Inequality

Certainly a popular perception exists that inequality has increased sharply. One rea0son for the dissonance between perceptions and the relatively modest rise in inequality suggested by the estimates reported in table 5.1 relates to the distinction between relative and absolute concepts of inequality. The former approach separates out average income levels from assessments of inequality, whereas the latter looks simultaneously at both changes in the shape of the income distribution and changes in overall income levels.[7] Ravallion (2004) notes that in debates about the impact of globalization on income inequality, perceptions that inequality is rising appear often to relate to absolute inequality rather than relative inequality. However, when we probe this conjecture for the case of India, we find relatively muted support: A commonly used "P90/10" measure of absolute inequality (estimated as the ratio of the average per capita consumption level of the top decile and that of the poorest decile; see table 5.1) shows that patterns of change in absolute inequality are broadly aligned with those observed in relative inequality.

A further possible explanation for the perception of rising inequality could be that rich Indians—who are unlikely to be captured in NSS data—did extraordinarily well during the boom of the 1990s. Banerjee and Piketty (2003) examined individual tax return data to show that in 1999–2000, the gap in per capita income between the 99th and 99.5th percentile was almost four times as large as the gap between the median person and the 95th percentile. Incomes of the super-rich, at the 99.99th percentile, grew by over 285 percent between 1987–88 and 1999–2000. Wealth inequalities are also on the rise. A recent study shows that between 1996 and 2008, wealth holdings of Indian billionaires rose from 0.8 percent of GDP to 23 percent (Walton 2010). The study not only indicates that the present concentration of wealth in India is much higher than was seen only a few years earlier, but also suggests that India stands out relative to other countries with similar per capita incomes.[8] Ahya and Sheth (cited in Topalova 2008) found an increase in wealth in India between 2003 and 2007 equal to the country's total GDP in 2007. Three key sources of wealth are identified: the equity market, the residential property market, and gold. With only 4 percent to 7 percent of the population participating in the stock market, less than half (47 percent) of the population owning a *pucca* home, and the top 34 percent of Indian households owning 71 percent of the value of consumer durables (including gold and jewelry), Ahya and

Sheth conclude that wealth accretion in India has been concentrated in a very small segment of the population. Bardhan (2007) focused on comparing India with China and found that inequalities, particularly in land and education, are much greater in India. He warns that relative backwardness in education and in the status of women in India implies that the forces that perpetuate inequality are stronger in India than in China.

Finally, Crost, de Janvry, and Sadoulet (2009) point to another possible source of dissonance between conventionally measured inequality and inequality as it is popularly perceived. They argue that popular perceptions of inequality are quite possibly based on nominal differences in income or consumption levels, rather than on income differences that have been corrected for spatial price variation. They cite Roos (2006), who argues that nominal differences in income tend to dominate in public discussion and popular perceptions of disparity between eastern and western Germany but that real differences after correcting for price variation in the two areas are much less marked. As mentioned above, our estimates of inequality are based on rural and urban sectors' consumption levels after correction for price variation within each sector (table 5.1). These corrections lessen the gap between the consumption levels of the richest and poorest and thereby lessen measured inequality. To the extent that popular perceptions about inequality trends do not match the inequality statistics that we report, it is possible that the dissonance is partly attributable to the fact that popular views may not fully take account of price differences in different places.

Inequality May Be Higher in India Than Is Often Thought

How unequal is India in the global context? International comparisons of inequality are the focus of a large body of research and also of a great deal of discussion.[9] In this literature, inequality in India is generally judged to be relatively modest by international standards. Well-known outliers in such international comparisons are countries such as Brazil and South Africa. In 2005, for example, the Gini coefficient for income inequality in Brazil was calculated to be 0.57 (World Bank 2007), starkly higher than the Gini of 0.325 in 2004–05 reported for India. It is important to realize, however, that a simple comparison between Brazil and India is not legitimate, not least because the welfare concept applied in the Brazilian case is per capita income, whereas in India it is per capita consumption.[10] The fact that certain countries have tended to measure inequality on the basis of consumption, while others have estimated it from income data, renders international comparisons difficult. This point has been recognized in the literature, but efforts to correct for it and to achieve strict comparability have not met with universal approval.

The 2004–05 NCAER–University of Maryland survey permits for the first time a calculation of income inequality in India, based on a fairly comprehensive definition of household income. Estimates based on this measure (including correction for spatial price variation within rural and urban areas separately, using the same poverty-line-based price indexes as applied to NSS consumption data) indicate that income inequality in India in 2004–05, as measured by the Gini coefficient, was 0.54. That level still places India below Brazil in overall income inequality (0.54 relative to 0.57), but the gap between the two countries is much smaller than usually assumed. Indeed, as figure 5.2 illustrates, when inequality in India is measured on the basis of per capita income, it stands among those countries with the highest recorded inequality rates. It is noteworthy, as well, that the shift from consumption to income implies that India dramatically leapfrogs China in international rankings of inequality (figure 5.2).

The gap between the income and consumption Gini is large in India. For example, the consumption Gini for Brazil in 2004 is 0.479—still a good deal higher than what is reported for India based on NSS consumption data for the same year.[11] Why the difference between India's consumption and income Gini measures of inequality is so large remains to be explained, but the finding at a minimum casts doubt on the often-propounded notion that inequality is low in India.

Inequality at the Local Level in Three States

Community-based development (CBD) initiatives, in which poor communities are required to identify, apply for funding for, design, implement, and manage their projects, are a growing feature of the Indian and the international development landscape (Mansuri and Rao 2003).[12] These initiatives aim to improve poverty targeting and the implementation of projects by making use of information at the local level and drawing on local participation. However, in practice those potential benefits may be outweighed by the possibility of resources being "captured" by local elites.[13] In their review of the CBD approach, Mansuri and Rao (2003) argue that although gains from CBD efforts are potentially large, important risks are also inherent in the approach.

A common approach within the CBD framework is to categorize communities by easily observable characteristics and then adapt

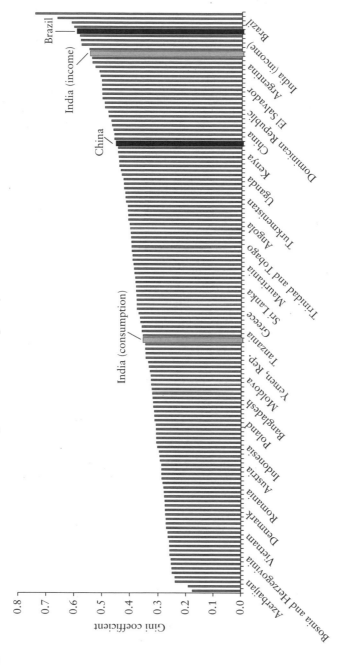

Figure 5.2 India in International Comparisons of Inequality

Sources: Consumption Gini from NSS 61st round; income Gini from 2004–05 NCAER–University of Maryland India Human Development Survey (Dubey 2008).

Note: Consumption Gini = 0.325; income Gini = 0.535.

plans for different groups. For example, because local-level data on poverty are generally unavailable, government programs often draw on proxy indicators that are believed to be correlated with local poverty conditions to determine communities' eligibility for various projects. But information on *inequality* outcomes at the local level has not similarly made its way into program design. There seem to be two main reasons why local inequality is not explicitly considered in program design. First, local inequality estimates are relatively scarce. Although proxy indexes have been developed for the missing income- or consumption-based poverty measure, such proxies have not been available for income inequality. Second, when the target of an intervention is a small, poor community, inequality may not be considered of primary importance: it seems natural to assume that in the poorest communities livelihoods are at the subsistence level with little scope for pronounced variation in well-being across households and individuals.

We draw on the small-area estimation pilot exercise in the states of West Bengal, Orissa, and Andhra Pradesh to show that considerable heterogeneity in inequality is present across blocks (*tehsils*) in the three states.[14] We find that this heterogeneity in local inequality levels is present even when we focus our attention on the poorest communities in rural areas. The combined implication of these findings is that information on local inequality is, in principle, available for use by program implementers and could help to categorize communities even after conditioning on local poverty and type of area.

Inequality Affects Poor and Rich Communities Alike

Map 5.1 depicts the distribution of rural poverty and inequality (as captured by the Gini coefficient) across *tehsils* in the states of West Bengal, Orissa, and Andhra Pradesh, respectively (each *tehsil* comprises roughly 10,000 to 30,000 households). As map 5.1 shows clearly, the spatial distributions of poverty and inequality are not identical. In some places pockets of high poverty coincide with low inequality; other places show both poverty and significant inequality. In general, inequality seems greater in the western *tehsils* of Andhra Pradesh, in the north and northwestern regions of Orissa (as well as in the areas to the immediate west and south of the capital, Bhubaneswar), and around the delta region of southern West Bengal.

Figures 5.3 through 5.5 focus more closely on the association between poverty and inequality in the three states. The top panel in figure 5.3 presents a nonparametric regression line of local, *tehsil*-level

Map 5.1 Spatial Distributions of Poverty and Inequality at the Local Level Are Not Identical

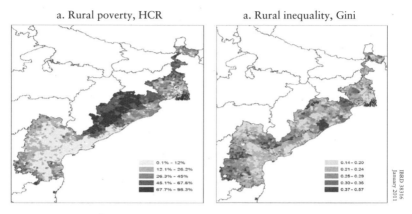

Source: Gangopadhyay et al. 2010.
Note: Estimates reported at the *tehsil* level, HCR = head-count rate.

inequality on the incidence of poverty in each tehsil and shows that in rural West Bengal, on average, poorer communities are indeed more equal. Even so, even among the poorest 20 percent of tehsils, a considerable degree of heterogeneity appears in measured inequality (panel b). The median level of inequality among the poorer tehsils is roughly the same as in other tehsils, and a fair amount of variation is seen around that median.

The picture in rural Orissa (not shown) is rather similar. In that state inequality is, on average, highest in the middle ranks of tehsils in poverty terms. Median inequality is least among the poorest tehsils. However, in Orissa, as was seen in Andhra Pradesh, local-level inequality estimates suggest, even among poor tehsils, nonnegligible variation across tehsils in measured inequality, cautioning against a blanket assertion that living standards are equally distributed in all poor tehsils.

The evidence from Andhra Pradesh further reinforces the argument against the presumption that inequality is low in poorer communities. On average, inequality displays a strongly positive relationship with poverty among tehsils in rural Andhra Pradesh (figure 5.4). Not only is median inequality highest among the poorest tehsils, but measured inequality spans the largest range of values.

The combined picture across all three states appears to follow a Kuznet's relationship between rural poverty and inequality (figure 5.5). On average, inequality is lowest among the least poor and the most poor tehsils; it is highest among the medium poor. As was argued

Figure 5.3 Local Poverty and Inequality in Rural West Bengal

a. Inequality and poverty

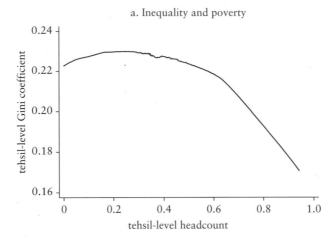

b. Tehsil-level inequality estimates within poverty quintiles

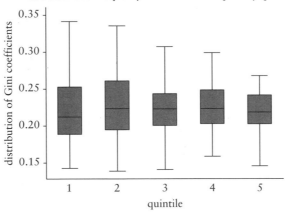

Source: Gangopadhyay et al. 2010.

Note: Panel a is the nonparametric relationship between inequality and poverty at the tehsil level. Panel b is the box-plot distribution of tehsil inequality estimates for quintiles of tehsils drawn on poverty rates. Box-plot 1 represents tehsils in the quintile with lowest poverty, and 5 the quintile of poorest tehsils.

above, a great deal of variation is seen in inequality among tehsils classified in terms of poverty status. The most variation is observed among the 4th quintile of tehsils in poverty terms, confirming again that in general it should not be presumed that poor communities are homogeneous.

In sum, the findings reported here suggest that local inequality can be an important source of additional information to policy

Figure 5.4 Local Poverty and Inequality in Rural Andhra Pradesh

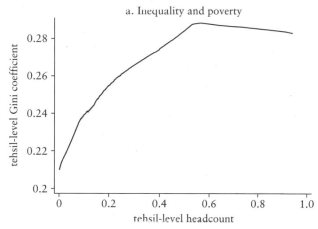

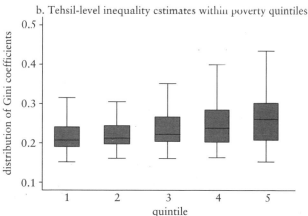

Source: Gangopadhyay et al 2010.
Note: Panel a is the nonparametric relationship between inequality and poverty at the tehsil level. Panel b is the box-plot distribution of tehsil inequality estimates for quintiles of tehsils drawn on poverty rates. Box-plot 1 represents tehsils in the quintile with lowest poverty, and 5 the quintile of poorest tehsils.

makers, even after controlling for the type of area and the poverty levels of localities. It is possible that use of such information can enhance desired outcomes. For example, for public programs where it is intended that local communities themselves identify poor beneficiaries, eligible communities could be categorized broadly as localities of low, middle, and high inequality. Random audits and means-tested targeting by the central government (as are conducted, for example, in Mexico's PROGRESA program) could then

Figure 5.5 Across States, Rural Inequality and Poverty
Appear to Follow a Kuznet's Relationship

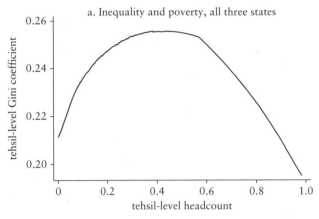

a. Inequality and poverty, all three states

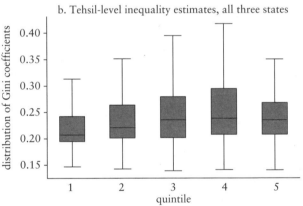

b. Tehsil-level inequality estimates, all three states

Source: Gangopadhyay et al 2010.
Note: Panel a is the nonparametric relationship between inequality and poverty at the
tehsil level. Panel b is the box-plot distribution of tehsil inequality estimates for quintiles
of tehsils drawn on poverty rates. Box-plot 1 represents tehsils in the quintile with lowest
poverty, and 5 the quintile of poorest tehsils. Data exclude outside values.

be considered to improve pro-poor targeting in the middle and
high-inequality communities.

Clearly, a first priority is to undertake further and more systematic research into the relationship between local inequality and
various development outcomes. A critical question concerns the
manner and extent to which current development practices interact
with local inequality. Better estimates of local-level consumption
inequality, made possible through the application of techniques
such as the small-area estimation method, offer new opportunities

for analysis. At present, micro-level estimation of welfare based on the methodology described here has been completed in the three states discussed above and is under way in the remaining states of India.

The Structure of Indian Inequality

In a country as vast as India it is natural to ask how much of overall inequality, or even of inequality in rural and urban areas separately, can be attributed to differences between particular subgroups in the population: Is Indian inequality as high as it is because people belonging to group A are so much richer than those in groups B and C, or because those in group C are so much poorer than members of A and B?

One obvious point of departure is to ask how much overall inequality is attributable to differences between Indian states. Many of the states are enormous, in both population size and geographic area. States often represent distinct populations with their own social, cultural, and historical features. The geography of states varies tremendously, implying different patterns of human settlement and economic organization. Indian states also enjoy a considerable degree of economic and political autonomy. To what extent do differences across states account for overall Indian inequality? Do the different trajectories of states in recent decades account for the recent evolution of Indian inequality?

The contribution of state differences to overall inequality has traditionally been assessed on the basis of inequality decompositions. This procedure breaks down overall inequality to determine a component that represents how much overall inequality would remain if no differences existed in average consumption levels across states. What is left is denoted "within-state" inequality. A second component then captures how much inequality would remain if consumption levels within states were equalized, and only differences across groups in average per capita consumption remained ("between-state" inequality). The ratio of between-state inequality to total inequality is labeled "the between-state contribution" and takes a value between 0 and 1.[15] Not all inequality measures lend themselves to a neat decomposition in this manner, but the widely used General Entropy (GE) class of inequality measures is readily decomposable and is able to accommodate a very wide range of normative judgments about the relative importance of different parts of the income distribution via selection of a specific parameter value (Bourguignon 1979; Shorrocks 1980, 1984; Cowell 1980). Below we examine the between-group contribution to total inequality based on a variety of group definitions.

Standard decomposition analysis offers only a partial perspective on group differences. A recent study proposes an additional, complementary perspective (Elbers et al. 2008). This approach considers a given group definition and asks to what extent the groups making up the definition neatly divide the income distribution into non-overlapping "partitions." For example, if a population is divided into two groups, the approach asks whether the richest person in the poorer group is still poorer than the poorest person in the richer group. Because this approach is not so much concerned with the degree of within-group inequality, it does not cleanly decompose overall inequality. But it retains some appeal in examining group differences in a way that standard decomposition analysis does not explicitly consider. For example, when the South African population is divided into two groups—whites versus all nonwhites—the resulting consumption distribution is roughly 80 percent of the way to being fully partitioned (Elbers et al. 2008). This finding is consistent with the widely held perception of markedly greater economic opportunities for whites than nonwhites in South Africa. It can be contrasted with results from the standard inequality decomposition procedure, which finds that only 27 percent of overall inequality can be attributed to between-group differences with this white-nonwhite population breakdown. The two decomposition techniques focus on different aspects of group differences—with the standard approach placing a great deal of emphasis both on differences in means and on within-group inequality, while the approach of Elbers et al. (2008) focuses specifically on the question of whether the groups partition the income distribution, irrespective of the degree of inequality within each of the groups.

Growing Divergence across States in Mean Incomes Does Not Explain the Increase in Inequality Observed in the Survey Data

Differences across states are often pointed to as the main source of rising inequality. Indeed, inequality in mean incomes across states is increasing according to the national accounts (figure 5.6). In the 1970s rich states used to have average incomes twice those of poor states; now the ratio is closer to four. This dispersion has been most noticeable between states such as Bihar and the more dynamic states such as Tamil Nadu or Gujarat. Within the set of high-income states, however, dispersion has actually gone down; rather than the states'

Figure 5.6 Spatial Differences in Income between States Have Grown

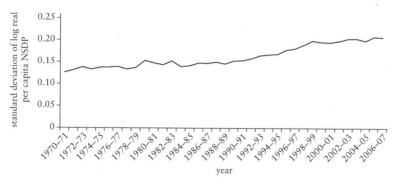

Source: Walton 2010.
Note: Based on data for 23 Indian states.

growing apart, real per capita net state domestic product (NSDP) figures have converged for the states of Gujarat, Haryana, Karnataka, Kerala, Maharashtra, Punjab, Tamil Nadu, and West Bengal (Walton 2008).

Table 5.2 reports the contribution to overall per capita consumption inequality (as reflected in NSS survey data) from differences between states, separately for rural and urban areas.[16] In 1983, 10.5 percent of overall rural inequality (summarized by the Theil L measure—GE(0)) could be accounted for by differences in average per capita consumption between Indian states. State differences accounted for a lower percentage of overall inequality (which itself was also less pronounced) in 1993–94—8.9 percent, according to this measure. By 2004–05 the between-state contribution had risen again to 10.7 percent. In urban areas as well, the overwhelming contribution to total urban inequality comes from differences across individuals, irrespective of state of residence.

These decompositions point to two important findings. First, between-state differences do not appear to be terribly significant in helping to understand patterns of inequality in rural and urban India.[17] In all three survey periods, and irrespective of which particular inequality measure is being decomposed, the overwhelming share of total inequality can be attributed to differences across individuals irrespective of the state they reside in. Second, although the between-state contribution is generally small, the assessed importance of between-state differences is even less when inequality measures GE(1) and GE(2) that put more weight to inequality among the rich are considered.

Table 5.2 Inequality Decomposition across States
percent

	1983			1993–94			2004–05		
	GE(0)	GE(1)	GE(2)	GE(0)	GE(1)	GE(2)	GE(0)	GE(1)	GE(2)
Rural									
Overall inequality	16.2	19.1	51.8	13.6	17.1	43.8	14.9	19.6	51.1
Between-group inequality as a percentage of overall inequality	10.5	8.9	3.3	8.9	7.1	2.8	10.7	8.4	3.3
Urban									
Overall inequality	19.0	21.5	34.6	19.5	23.5	72.2	23.6	28.8	80.2
Between-group inequality as a percentage of overall inequality	4.9	4.3	2.8	7.1	6.2	2.2	5.5	4.7	1.8

Source: Authors' calculations based on NSS data.
Note: General Entropy inequality estimates based on uniform recall period consumption in 1993/94 all-India rural rupees. Consumption corrected for cost-of-living differences across states and over time using deflators that are implicit in official poverty lines.

Table 5.3 checks to see whether the complementary Elbers et al. (2008) approach to thinking about the structure of the consumption distribution yields a more important role for geography than was observed with the between-state analysis. Table 5.3 breaks rural India into different regional groupings (aggregating up from the state level) based on geographic contiguity. In row 1, inequality as summarized by the Theil T measure is decomposed, in the standard way, based on four regional groups representing the North (and Northwest), South, East (and Northeast), and West of the country. Column 1 indicates that in 1983, the contribution to total inequality of this between-region component was 5.2 percent.[18] In 2005, the standard decomposition by these regions accounted for 4.2 percent of total inequality. Thus, little evidence appears that between-region differences are very important for understanding overall inequality. In addition, no evidence is seen of regional differences becoming more important over time.

When one applies the "partitioning" approach introduced by Elbers et al. (2008) the picture of regional differences is not very different (columns 2 and 4 of table 5.3). In 1983, the overall distribution of per capita consumption was only 7.6 percent of the way toward a full partitioning between the four regions under consideration (in the sense that the regions divide the overall

Table 5.3 Decomposition of Rural Inequality by Region

	1983		2004–05	
Region	Standard between-group contribution	Elbers et al. partitioning index	Standard between-group contribution	Elbers et al. partitioning index
Overall inequality (Theil T measure)	0.192	0.192	0.196	0.196
North, South, East, and West	0.052	0.076	0.042	0.068
North versus rest	0.004	0.008	0.000	0.000
East versus rest	0.051	0.092	0.030	0.050
South versus rest	0.012	0.022	0.030	0.060
West versus rest	0.002	0.004	0.000	0.000
High-growth states versus rest[a]	0.003	0.005	0.014	0.031

Source: Authors' calculations based on NSS data.

Note: a. High-growth states refer to Gujarat, Haryana, Karnataka, Kerala, Maharashtra, Punjab, Tamil Nadu, and West Bengal. See text and notes to table 5.1 for further definitions.

consumption distribution into neat, nonoverlapping segments represented by the respective regional groups). Comparing this figure with the 80 percent that obtains when the South African consumption distribution is divided into white and nonwhite subgroups, the impression is of a low degree of partitioning of the consumption distribution and hence a rather low importance for regional differences in an understanding of consumption inequality in rural India.

Exploring alternative regional group definitions provides few additional insights (rows 2 through 6). Some suggestion appears that a comparison of the East versus the rest of India is qualitatively more important, as the between-group contribution here is 5.1 percent, only marginally lower than the 5.2 percent in 1983 obtained with a four-way breakdown of India into regions.

The Elbers et al. (2008) partitioning index indicates some subtle qualifications to that assessment, but the overall picture remains. In 1983, the rural Indian consumption distribution was approximately 9 percent of the way toward fully partitioned between the East and the rest of India. That had declined to 5 percent by 2005. However, whereas in 1983 the distribution was only 2.2 percent of the way toward full partitioning between the South and the rest of rural India, by 2005 that had increased to 6 percent. Although regional differences do not appear particularly important even using the Elbers et al. (2008) perspective, some suggestion appears that the South is becoming more separate from the rest of India over time—a faint indication of regional change that is not being picked up in the standard decomposition analysis.

Finally, despite some evidence of the rich states' converging in terms of per capita net state domestic product—and pulling away from the poorer states—no evidence indicates that this particular regional breakdown provides a deeper understanding of consumption inequality than the regional breakdowns based on geographic location and state contiguity discussed above. The NSS data do not suggest that rich states are standing apart from the rest of the country or give evidence of any major change in that respect over time.

Table 5.4 provides analogous evidence on the importance of geographic differences for inequality in urban India. The picture is, if anything, even more suggestive that a geographic breakdown of the country provides little insight for an understanding of the structure of urban consumption inequality.

Thus, despite the clear evidence of divergence across states in incomes as measured by the national accounts, a decomposition analysis of inequality using survey data between states, or between

Table 5.4 Decomposition of Urban Inequality by Region

Region	1983		2004–05	
	Standard between-group contribution	Elbers et al. partitioning index	Standard between-group contribution	Elbers et al. partitioning index
Overall inequality (Theil T measure)	0.215	0.215	0.288	0.288
North, South, East, and West	0.003	0.004	0.010	0.013
North versus rest	0.002	0.004	0.002	0.003
East versus rest	0.000	0.000	0.004	0.008
South versus rest	0.001	0.001	0.000	0.000
West versus rest	0.001	0.001	0.007	0.013
High-growth states versus rest[a]	0.005	0.010	0.007	0.014

Source: Authors' calculations based on NSS data.

a. High-growth states refer to Gujarat, Haryana, Karnataka, Kerala, Maharashtra, Punjab, Tamil Nadu, and West Bengal. See text and notes to table 5.1 for further definitions.

high-growth and low-growth regions, reveals that only a very small, albeit growing, share of overall consumption inequality can be attributed to differences in mean consumption levels. In other words, within-state and within-region inequality dominates. If the growing spatial disparities are driving increased inequality, it is not being captured by the survey data, perhaps because the spatial disparities are growing fastest at the top, non-sampled, end of the distribution.

At the All-India Level, Differences between Social Groups Explain Only a Small Share of Total Inequality, but in Some States, Group Differences Are Important and Growing

One can use criteria other than state and regional differences to define population subgroups. In India a natural definition to consider is differences across social groups—distinguishing among, for example, scheduled tribes (ST), scheduled castes (SC), Muslims, and all Others. This breakdown is far from ideal, as it does not permit any kind of detailed assessment of differences across subgroups within these broad categories. However, no more detailed breakdown of the population is available from the NSS data.[19] Tables 5.5 and 5.6 examine the contribution of this group breakdown to consumption inequality at the all-India level in 1983 and 2004–05.

Table 5.5 Decomposition of Rural Inequality by Social Group

	1983		2004–05	
Group	Standard between-group contribution	Elbers et al. partitioning index	Standard between-group contribution	Elbers et al. partitioning index
Overall inequality (Theil T measure)	0.192	0.192	0.196	0.196
All India				
ST, SC, MUS, and OTH	0.041	0.062	0.032	0.067
ST versus rest	0.015	0.033	0.011	0.030
SC versus rest	0.014	0.028	0.013	0.036
MUS versus rest	0.002	0.005	0.001	0.003
OTH versus rest	0.039	0.083	0.029	0.099
ST and SC versus rest	0.033	0.068	0.026	0.080
ST and MUS versus rest	0.016	0.033	0.010	0.027
ST and OTH versus rest	0.018	0.036	0.014	0.044
Selected states				
Bihar: SC versus rest	0.024	0.069	0.023	0.127
Haryana: OTH versus rest	0.039	0.127	0.104	0.357
Orissa: ST versus rest	0.073	0.229	0.068	0.226
Punjab: OTH versus rest	0.059	0.236	0.034	0.304

Source: Authors. Estimates based on respective NSS survey rounds.

Note: ST = scheduled tribes; SC = scheduled castes; MUS = Muslims; OTH = all others.

(Chapter 6 of the book pursues the nature of caste and other social-group differences in a more holistic manner that looks beyond the consumption dimension and explicitly considers overall social exclusion of these population groups.)

At the all-India level, the contribution of group differences (defined as social group membership) to overall rural inequality is small and has been declining—from 4 percent in 1983, based on the standard decomposition procedure, to 3 percent in 2004–05 (table 5.5). The partitioning index of Elbers and colleagues indicates as

Table 5.6 Decomposition of Urban Inequality by Social Group

Group	1983		2004–05	
	Standard between- group contribution	*Elbers et al. partitioning index*	*Standard between- group contribution*	*Elbers et al. partitioning index*
Overall inequality				
(Theil T measure)	0.215	0.215	0.288	0.288
All India				
ST, SC, MUS,				
and OTH	0.052	0.064	0.071	0.088
ST versus rest	0.003	0.008	0.003	0.007
SC versus rest	0.015	0.026	0.028	0.048
MUS versus rest	0.025	0.042	0.026	0.046
OTH versus rest	0.052	0.088	0.071	0.134
ST and SC versus				
rest	0.019	0.031	0.031	0.055
ST and MUS				
versus rest	0.029	0.048	0.030	0.053
ST and OTH				
versus rest	0.047	0.078	0.065	0.120
Selected states				
Himachal Pradesh:				
OTH versus rest	0.043	0.102	0.093	0.239
Karnataka: OTH				
versus rest	0.036	0.057	0.102	0.163
Punjab: OTH				
versus rest	0.036	0.071	0.063	0.279
West Bengal: OTH				
versus rest	0.054	0.097	0.114	0.219
Delhi: OTH				
versus rest	0.118	0.220	0.181	0.297
Orissa: ST and				
SC versus rest	0.070	0.129	0.069	0.152

Source: Authors' estimates based on respective NSS survey rounds.

Note: ST = scheduled tribes; SC = scheduled castes; MUS = Muslims; OTH = all others.

well that social group differences do not account for much of the overall inequality of consumption in rural areas. Treating the four groups separately, the consumption distribution is about 7 percent of the way toward being neatly partitioned into four nonoverlapping segments that respectively constitute these population groups. A slightly greater importance is given to group differences when the population is divided into two groups representing the "Others" versus all SCs, STs, and Muslims together (row 5, in table 5.5). Yet again, it is important to recognize that at the all-India level one certainly cannot speak of a partitioning of the consumption distribution among these four groups (taken separately, or combined in various ways).

When states are singled out for separate scrutiny, a different picture can emerge. In the case of Bihar, for example, the Elbers et al. partitioning index nearly doubles (from 7 percent to 13 percent) between 1983 and 2005 when the population is divided into SCs versus the rest. In rural Haryana and Punjab, the Elbers et al. approach suggests that a relatively advantaged segment of the rural population (the "Others") is pulling away from other groups, and that little insight is gained from treating the SCs, STs, and Muslims separately. At the state level overall, therefore, the qualitative conclusion is that in certain states, the construct of social groups helps to understand the nature of inequality and the way inequality has changed over time in at least one potentially important respect.

In urban areas, at the all-India level, the picture is, again, somewhat muted (table 5.6); it appears to be rather unhelpful to assess the role and importance of social groups at the national level. However, in states such as Himachal Pradesh, Karnataka, Punjab, West Bengal, and Delhi, significant and growing differences appear between the advantaged segments of society (the "Others") and an aggregation of all disadvantaged population groups (the "Rest"). The picture is one of the more advantaged social groups possibly taking better advantage of the new opportunities offered by the galvanizing urban economic environment over the past 25 years, resulting in a tendency for income distribution to partition between these two groups. This process, as documented most clearly with the Elbers et al. partitioning index, suggests that a certain form of polarization is taking place, one that is not captured with conventional inequality decomposition analysis (nor on the basis of the nascent but growing polarization measurement approach).[20]

To summarize the discussion so far, we have found in the analysis above that scrutinizing group differences solely in terms of geographic location contributes only modestly to an understanding of the structure of consumption inequality. This conclusion is somewhat surprising and stands in possible contrast to popular perceptions. When we pursue the alternative route of defining population groups by social group membership, however, in some states, though not all, group differences defined in this way are indeed quite salient to an understanding of consumption inequality and its evolution over time. To better gauge the significance of this finding, a more systematic and comprehensive assessment of social exclusion between social groups is attempted in the next chapter. The chapter takes a less-formal approach to consider group differences, on average, and to look beyond consumption to examine also differences in health, education, earnings, and occupation. The analysis points both to the persistence of long-standing patterns of disadvantage and to evidence of progress toward greater integration in certain settings.

Increased Returns to Education Appear to Be an Important Factor Driving Increasing Inequality

In rural areas, differences among four groups, defined in terms of broad schooling achievement of the household head, accounted for just over 5 percent of total inequality in 1983, rising to just under 10 percent in 2005 (table 5.7, row 1, columns 1 and 3). Although the percentage contribution is low even in 2004–05, the evidence points to a significant increase in importance over time, particularly when groups are defined in other ways. For example, if the population is divided into two groups, those with postsecondary education and the rest, the standard between-group inequality contribution rises sixfold, from 0.008 to 0.05 (the partitioning index rises from 0.028 to 0.105). If the population is divided into those with only up-to-primary education versus everyone else, both the standard between-group contribution and the partitioning index roughly double in size. The picture is one in which in rural areas, education differences, while they do not fully explain consumption inequality, seem to be growing in importance.

These conclusions are more clearly visible at the level of certain states. In rural Bihar, for example, the Elbers et al. index suggests that it is particularly the distinction between those with beyond-secondary schooling and those with secondary schooling and less that is salient to an understanding of inequality. Between 1983 and 2005, the index increased in Bihar such that in the latter year the rural consumption distribution was nearly a third of the way toward full partitioning of the population in terms of these two groups. The picture is even more striking in rural Haryana, where by 2005 the distribution of consumption was more than two-fifths of the way toward full partitioning between those with beyond-secondary schooling and the rest of the population. This is all the more striking because we have virtually no evidence of any distinction between those with schooling beyond secondary school and the rest of the population in 1983, most likely because of the very small population with such credentials in the earlier period.

In rural Karnataka and Punjab, the key distinction appears to be between those with less-than-primary education and the rest of the

Table 5.7 Decomposition of Rural Inequality by Education Class

Group	1983		2004–05	
	Standard between-group contribution	*Elbers et al. partitioning index*	*Standard between-group contribution*	*Elbers et al. partitioning index*
Overall inequality (Theil T measure)	0.192	0.192	0.196	0.196
All India				
BP, PM, Sec, and Grad	0.052	0.067	0.096	0.122
BP versus rest	0.041	0.075	0.058	0.135
Grad versus rest	0.008	0.028	0.050	0.105
BP and PM versus rest	0.031	0.066	0.063	0.119
Selected states				
Bihar: Grad versus rest	0.015	0.088	0.053	0.322
Haryana: Grad versus rest	0.001	0.004	0.276	0.424
Karnataka: BP versus rest	0.044	0.083	0.094	0.287
Kerala: BP and PM versus rest	0.104	0.190	0.100	0.223
Punjab: BP versus rest	0.014	0.032	0.075	0.207
Uttar Pradesh: BP and PM versus rest	0.017	0.037	0.039	0.073

Source: Authors' calculations based on NSS data.

Note: BP = below primary; PM = primary and middle school; Sec = secondary; Grad = any postsecondary.

population (table 5.7). In those two states the salience of schooling achievement to an understanding of inequality has increased dramatically. In Kerala those who have completed middle school or more have come to stand apart from the rest of the population, but the process has been more gradual than in the previously considered states. In Uttar Pradesh, on the other hand, group differences on the basis of education seem still to be of negligible importance, even in 2005. The experiences of different states vary dramatically, underscoring the need to look beyond the all-India level.

The rising importance of education to understanding the evolution of inequality is also evident in urban areas (table 5.8). The

Table 5.8 Decomposition of Urban Inequality by Education Class

| Group | 1983 | | 2004–05 | |
	Standard between-group contribution	Elbers et al. partitioning index	Standard between-group contribution	Elbers et al. partitioning index
Overall inequality (Theil T measure)	0.215	0.215	0.288	0.288
All India				
BP, PM, Sec, and Grad	0.197	0.237	0.255	0.353
BP versus rest	0.093	0.171	0.102	0.184
Grad versus rest	0.111	0.205	0.193	0.336
BP and PM versus rest	0.163	0.271	0.189	0.375
Selected states				
Andhra Pradesh: BP and PM versus rest	0.134	0.236	0.233	0.462
Bihar: BP and PM versus rest	0.132	0.216	0.276	0.445
Himachal Pradesh: Grad versus rest	0.157	0.229	0.292	0.551
Karnataka: BP and PM versus rest	0.196	0.312	0.267	0.440
Orissa: BP and PM versus rest	0.139	0.218	0.332	0.538
Punjab: BP and PM versus rest	0.065	0.122	0.117	0.608
West Bengal: BP and PM versus rest	0.169	0.292	0.271	0.565

Source: Authors' calculations based on NSS data.

Note: BP = below primary; PM = primary and middle school; Sec = secondary; Grad = any postsecondary.

standard decomposition procedure reveals that for urban areas the between-group contribution rose from 0.197 to 0.255 between 1983 and 2005, indicating that as much as a quarter of overall urban inequality in 2005 could be attributable to differences in average per capita consumption across our four schooling groups. The Elbers et al. partitioning index shows that the most important distinction at the all-India level is between the population with up-to-middle schooling versus the rest of the population. In this particular breakdown the partitioning index suggests that the urban consumption distribution has grown sharply, to nearly two-fifths of the way toward a full partitioning.

The picture for urban areas is fairly striking, even at the all-India level, but the salience of education becomes even more apparent within certain states. In urban Andhra Pradesh and Bihar, for example, two groups comprising those with up-to-middle schooling versus the rest result in a consumption distribution that is nearly halfway to becoming fully partitioned. In Himachal Pradesh, on the other hand, the most salient group breakdown is between those with beyond-secondary schooling and the rest of the population. Other states that stand out in terms of the importance of schooling as a basis for subdividing the urban population include Karnataka, Orissa, Punjab, and West Bengal.

In sum, the experience documented in these states reveals that although overall inequality does not always change dramatically (although a dramatic increase is notable in urban Punjab), a great deal of reshuffling may nonetheless be occurring within the distribution of consumption. The evidence discussed above suggests that schooling is increasingly salient to our understanding of the underlying structure of consumption inequality in India. In the urban sectors of most states, and not a few rural areas, those population groups with little education are increasingly standing apart from the rest, whereas those with the most education also stand apart but at the other end of the consumption distribution. This picture accords well with the discussion in earlier chapters documenting the growing importance of the nonfarm sector in rural areas and the growing importance of urban growth for both urban and rural poverty reduction. These newly important sectors are known to be considerably more education intensive than traditional sectors such as agriculture.

That education is a source of rising inequality appears paradoxical because, as demonstrated in the previous chapter, access to education is becoming much more equal over time. However, returns to education have been increasing, and rewards to skills are becoming more unequal (Dutta 2005). Moreover, as also discussed in chapter 4, inequalities in learning outcomes are high in India.

In Some States, Rural Households Dependent on Agricultural Wage Labor and Urban Households That Depend on Casual Wage Employment Are Falling Behind

A final group breakdown that we consider relates to occupational groups based on a household's primary means of livelihood. It is of inherent interest to understand to what extent the structure of inequality is associated with occupational status. In particular we desire to know how occupational status might have become more or less pertinent to an understanding of inequality over time, against a background of rapid economic growth and structural change. It is also the case that certain occupations are associated with a degree of persistence over time. For example, village studies have documented that mobility out of agricultural wage labor is often rather limited (Lanjouw and Stern 1998), although as chapter 3 shows, a shift appears to be under way since the mid-1990s (and see also chapter 6).

The statistics in table 5.9 indicate that in rural areas, differences between occupational groups at the all-India level appear to be of very limited importance to an understanding of inequality. We consider four broad occupation groups: the self-employed in agriculture, agricultural wage labor, self-employed in the nonagricultural sector, and nonagricultural wage labor and other activities. The standard between-group contribution to overall inequality shows not only that

Table 5.9 Decomposition of Rural Inequality by Occupational Group

	1983		2004–05	
Group	Standard between-group contribution	Elbers et al. partitioning index	Standard between-group contribution	Elbers et al. partitioning index
Overall inequality (Theil T measure)	0.192	0.192	0.196	0.196
All India				
SN,AL,OT and SA	0.063	0.084	0.054	0.082
SA versus rest	0.022	0.046	0.004	0.008
AL versus rest	0.059	0.109	0.051	0.101
SN versus rest	0.000	0.000	0.003	0.005
OT versus rest	0.009	0.016	0.014	0.026
OT and SN versus rest	0.005	0.010	0.019	0.040
Selected states				
Bihar: AL versus rest	0.110	0.210	0.123	0.241
Maharashtra: AL versus rest	0.115	0.192	0.113	0.204
Punjab: AL versus rest	0.073	0.171	0.111	0.222
Tamil Nadu: AL versus rest	0.058	0.153	0.082	0.207

Source: Authors' calculations based on NSS data.

Note: SA = self-employed in agriculture; AL = agricultural wage labor; SN = self-employed in nonagriculture; OT = nonagricultural labor and other.

between-group differences are modest, but that they appear to be declining over time. The all-India picture masks important variation across states, and as the Elbers et al. index shows, the salient occupational group breakdown in rural areas is agricultural laborers versus all other occupation groups. In rural Bihar, Maharashtra, Punjab, and Tamil Nadu, agricultural laborers tend to stand apart from the rest of the population, and increasingly so over time. Chapter 6 discusses further how occupational group definitions and social group definitions overlap in important ways. For example, scheduled caste households are generally highly represented among agricultural labor households.

In urban areas the occupational group breakdown comprises self-employment, salaried employment, casual wage employment, and all other occupations. Again, the all-India picture points to a relatively muted importance of occupational status, although with some increase in significance over time (table 5.10), most evidently in the

Table 5.10 Decomposition of Urban Inequality by Occupational Group

	1983		2004–05	
Group	Standard between-group contribution	Elbers et al. partitioning index	Standard between-group contribution	Elbers et al. partitioning index
Overall inequality (Theil T measure)	0.215	0.215	0.288	0.288
All India				
SF, REG, CAS, and OT	0.064	0.078	0.083	0.100
SF versus rest	0.009	0.017	0.006	0.010
REG versus rest	0.043	0.078	0.022	0.037
CAS versus rest	0.036	0.063	0.063	0.109
OT versus rest	0.000	0.000	0.010	0.017
Selected states				
Gujurat: CAS versus rest	0.029	0.061	0.099	0.221
Haryana: CAS versus rest	0.015	0.023	0.256	0.410
Karnataka: CAS versus rest	0.042	0.074	0.169	0.432
UP: SF, REG, CAS, and OT (4!)	0.077	0.089	0.230	0.346

Source: Authors' calculations based on NSS data.

Note: SF = self-employment; REG = regular salaried employment; CAS = casual wage employment; OT = all other activities and occupations; UP = Uttar Pradesh.

case of a two-group breakdown between casual wage laborers and the rest of the urban population.

For some states occupational group differences are more pronounced. In Gujarat the Elbers et al. index shows more than a fifth of the way toward complete partitioning of the consumption distribution between casual laborers and the rest in 2005, up from only 6 percent in 1983 (table 5.10). In Haryana and Karnataka the picture is more striking still, with sharp differences emerging between households that rely on casual wage employment for earnings, and the rest. In Uttar Pradesh, by contrast, the Elbers et al. index points to the salience of the original four-way breakdown of the population. Here both the partitioning index and the standard decomposition analysis point to a sharp increase in group differences in terms of these occupational characteristics over time.

Notes

1. Galasso and Ravallion (2005) found that the targeting performance of the Food for Education program in Bangladesh is worse in communities where land inequality is greater. Foster and Rosenzweig (2003) found that increases in the population weight of the poor increase the likelihood of receiving pro-poor projects (such as rural roads) in Indian villages that have democratically elected *panchayats,* but not in villages with more traditional leadership structures. Araujo et al. (2008) found that, controlling for poverty, unequal communities in Ecuador are less likely to select projects that provide private goods to the poor and favor projects that impart public goods to the community as a whole.

2. Our attention is confined to consumption and, to some extent, per capita income as measures of economic well-being. We do not focus here on the distribution of important additional dimensions of welfare, such as education and health, which also merit close attention. To the extent that we touch on these dimensions at all, it is insofar as they are helpful in understanding patterns and trends in the distributions of income and consumption.

3. The resulting inequality estimates are found to correlate rather well with population characteristics such as population size, educational outcomes, occupational diversification, and so on. This provides some indirect evidence that these inequality estimates—although based on a rather complex statistical forecasting procedure—do contain information and are not just statistical "noise."

4. We have no single, ideal summary measure of inequality. Each summary measure carries within it its own implicit, or sometimes explicit, normative judgment as to the weight and importance that should be given to certain segments of the income distribution (Atkinson 1970). Because of

this feature of inequality measures, it is common practice to calculate a wide range of measures and to confine strong categorical statements about inequality comparisons to situations when those statements are robust across a range of measures. An alternative approach, drawing on results from the stochastic dominance literature, has developed as a complementary way in which to make inequality comparisons. In that approach the goal is to delineate the range of normative judgments over which a specific inequality comparison is robust (see Atkinson 1970; Davidson and Duclos 2000).

5. A "Rawlsian" measure of inequality that focused exclusively on the incomes of the poorest, such as an Atkinson measure with a particularly high inequality aversion parameter value, would presumably conclude that rural inequality fell between these two years (see Atkinson 1970).

6. The *Report of the Expert Group to Review the Methodology for Estimation of Poverty* (GoI 2009) indicates, indeed, that poverty lines other than those that are currently endorsed officially can imply very different patterns of sectoral and interstate price variation. For a summary of the new poverty lines proposed by the expert group, see chapter 1.

7. A study by Beck (1994) documents that in the late 1980s villagers in three West Bengal villages believed that living standards in their villages had worsened, even though they acknowledged that average incomes had grown and that even the poorest had seen their incomes rise during the period. The villagers attached considerable weight to the fact that the absolute gap between the incomes of the poorest and the richest segments had widened. A doubling of all incomes in these villages would have clearly resulted in a widening of this absolute gap and could have prompted such a reaction. But such a doubling would have left relative inequality unaffected. Unless the rich had benefited *proportionately* more than the poor, relative inequality as it is conventionally measured would not have risen and could even have declined.

8. The study also indicates that with the unfolding financial crisis, the value of wealth holdings of Indian billionaires had fallen significantly by the end of 2008.

9. Deininger and Squire 1996, Milanovic 2005, the WIDER World Income Inequality Database (UN 2008), and the *World Development Report 2005* (World Bank 2004) provide cross-country databases of summary inequality measures that underpin a large literature undertaking international comparisons of inequality. Deaton 2010 summarizes the myriad difficulties in making such international comparisons.

10. The calculation for Brazil, moreover, applies a rather problematic definition of per capita income that is based largely on earnings and not terribly well placed to capture certain incomes, such as informal sector self-employment income or subsistence agriculture; see Elbers et al. 2002.

11. In 2004, the Brazilian Statistical Bureau (Institute Brasileiro de Geografia e Estadistica, or IBGE) fielded the *Pesquisa de Orcamentos*

Familiales (POF), the first nationally representative consumption survey in Brazil since the 1970s. The *World Development Report 2008* (World Bank 2007) presents estimates of consumption-based inequality in Brazil for 2004, based on a comprehensive concept of consumption and following also adjustment for spatial price variation based on poverty lines derived from POF survey data.

12. Mansuri and Rao (2003) distinguish CBD from community-driven development (CDD), popularized by the World Bank, in that the latter refers to projects in which communities have direct control over key project decisions, as well as the management of investment funds. "CBD" can be thought of as a broader umbrella term that accommodates, but is not restricted to, the World Bank's CDD concept.

13. A growing theoretical and empirical literature explores the relationship between inequality and local development outcomes. For recent contributions see, for example, Alesina and La Ferrara 2000; Araujo et al. 2008; Baland and Platteau 1999, 2003, 2007; Bardhan and Mookherjee 1999; Dayton-Johnson 2000; Dayton-Johnson and Bardhan 2002; Galasso and Ravallion 2005; Khwaja 2002; La Ferrara 2002.

14. Box 1.4 in chapter 1 describes the poverty mapping project based on small-area estimation methods. More detail is available in Gangopadhyay et al. (2010). Estimates of *tehsil*-level inequality obtained for the states considered here correlate well with a number of *tehsil* characteristics, adding to the notion that the estimates represent more than just statistical "noise" (Gangopadhyay et al. 2010).

15. Decomposition analysis can also be straightforwardly applied to groups defined in terms of nongeographic characteristics. Ferreira and Gignoux (2008) argue that between-group inequality can provide a useful statistic on the importance of inequality of opportunity. If groups are defined in terms of characteristics over which individuals have no control and that can be viewed as "morally irrelevant," one can interpret the between-group inequality contribution as a lower boundary on the possible extent of inequality of opportunity in a given setting. Why should any systematic differences exist between groups of people who are distinguished from each other only on the basis of characteristics that society agrees are not pertinent? If such differences exist, Ferreira and Gignoux (2008) argue, it provides *prime facie* evidence of inequality of opportunity across such groups. The between-group contribution to inequality provides a statistic that summarizes the extent to which group means differ across groups. Ferreira and Gignoux (2008) suggest that it provides a lower boundary estimate, however, because additional exogenous circumstance indicators may always exist that would add to the overall number of groups (and thereby raise the between-group contribution to inequality) but that are not available in the data to be incorporated into the analysis.

16. Three measures from the General Entropy (GE) class are reported, with parameter c taking the value of 0, 1, or 2. Lower values of c are

associated with greater sensitivity to inequality among the poor, and higher values of *c* place more weight on inequality among the rich. A *c* value of 1 yields the well-known Theil entropy measure, a value of 0 provides the Theil L or mean log deviation, and a value of 2 is ordinally equivalent to the squared coefficient of variation.

17. This finding is consistent with other studies. For example, Gajwani, Kanbur, and Zhang (2006) found a similarly low between-group contribution when groups are defined in terms of inland or coastal or north-south location of residence.

18. This is less than the between-region component of 8.9 percent (for the Theil T measure) in table 2 because in standard decomposition analysis the between-group contribution to inequality tends to fall as the number of groups under consideration decreases.

19. Lanjouw and Rao (2009) explored inequality across fine caste groupings in two Indian villages, underscoring that the "scheduled caste" category is in many respects an unsatisfactory classification, as it masks a great deal of important heterogeneity within the category.

20. The Elbers et al. (2008) partitioning approach shares some notional similarities with the analysis of "polarization" that has received growing attention in the literature in recent years (see Duclos, Esteban, and Ray 2004, for a recent review). However, polarization measures and the Elbers et al. statistic do not always yield identical orderings; the former respond to changes in within-group inequality, whereas the latter focuses solely on the degree to which distributions can be characterized as "partitioned," independent of the degree of within-group inequality.

References

Alesina, A., and E. La Ferrara. 2000. "Participation in Heterogeneous Communities." *Quarterly Journal of Economics* 115 (3): 847–904.

Araujo, M. C., F. H. G. Ferreira, P. Lanjouw, and B. Özler. 2008. "Local Inequality and Project Choice: Theory and Evidence from Ecuador." *Journal of Public Economics* 92 (5–6): 1022–46.

Atkinson, A. B. 1970. "On the Measurement of Inequality." *Journal of Economic Theory* 2: 244–63.

Baland, J. M., and J. P. Platteau. 1999. "The Ambiguous Impact of Inequality on Local Resource Management." *World Development* 27: 773–88.

———. 2003. "Economics of Common Property Management." In *The Handbook of Environmental Economics*, vol. 1, ed. K. G Mäler and J. R. Vincent. North Holland, Netherlands: Elsevier Science Publishers.

———. 2007. "Collective Action on the Commons: The Role of Inequality." In *Inequality, Cooperation and Environmental Sustainability*, ed.

J. M. Baland, P. Bardhan, and S. Bowles. Princeton, NJ: Princeton University Press.

Banerjee, A. V., and T. Piketty. 2003. "Top Indian Incomes: 1956–2000." *World Bank Economic Review* 19 (1): 1–20.

Bardhan, P. 2007. "Poverty and Inequality in China and India: Elusive Link with Globalisation." *Economic and Political Weekly* 42 (38): 3849–52.

Bardhan, P., and D. Mookherjee. 1999. "Relative Capture of Local and National Governments: An Essay in the Political Economy of Decentralization." Working Paper, Institute for Economic Development, Boston University.

Beck, T. 1994. *The Experience of Poverty: Fighting for Respect and Resources in Village India.* London: Intermediate Technology Publications.

Bourguignon, F. 1979. "Decomposable Income Inequality Measures." *Econometrica* 47: 901–20.

Chaudhuri, S., and M. Ravallion. 2006. "Partially Awakened Giants: Uneven Growth in China and India." In *Dancing with Giants: China, India and the Global Economy*, ed. L. A. Winters and S. Yusuf. Washington, DC: World Bank.

Cowell, F. A. 1980. "On the Structure of Additive Inequality Measures." *Review of Economic Studies* 47: 521–31.

Crost, B., A. de Janvry, and E. Sadoulet. 2009. "Analyzing Income Disparities in India Using Relative Distribution Methods." Unpublished manuscript, Department of Agriculture and Resource Economics, University of California, Berkeley.

Datt, G., and M. Ravallion. 2009. "Has Poverty in India Become Less Responsive to Economic Growth?" Background paper prepared for India Poverty Assessment Report, World Bank, Washington, DC.

Davidson, R., and J.-Y. Duclos. 2000. "Statistical Inference for Stochastic Dominance and for the Measurement of Poverty and Inequality." *Econometrica* 68 (6): 1435–64.

Dayton-Johnson, J. 2000. "Determinants of Collective Action on the Local Commons: A Model with Evidence from Mexico." *Journal of Development Economics* 62 (1): 181–208.

Dayton-Johnson, J., and P. Bardhan. 2002. "Inequality and Conservation on the Local Commons: A Theoretical Exercise." *Economic Journal* 112 (481): 577–602.

Deaton, A. 2010. "Price Indexes, Inequality and the Measurement of World Poverty." *American Economic Review* 100 (1): 1–34.

Deaton, A., and A. Tarozzi. 2005. "Prices and Poverty in India." In *The Great Indian Poverty Debate*, ed. A. Deaton and V. Kozel, chapter 16. New Delhi: Macmillan India.

Deininger, K., and L. Squire. 1996. "A New Data Set Measuring Income Inequality." *World Bank Economic Review* 10 (3): 565–91.

Dubey, A. 2008. "Consumption, Income, and Inequality in India." Background paper for the India Poverty Assessment Report, World Bank, Washington, DC.

Duclos, J.-Y., J. Esteban, and D. Ray. 2004. "Polarization: Concepts, Measurement, Estimation." *Econometrica* 72: 1737–72.

Dutta, P. Vasudeva. 2005. "Accounting for Wage Inequality in India." *Indian Journal of Labour Economics* 48 (2): 273–95.

Elbers, C., J. O. Lanjouw, P. Lanjouw, and P. G. Leite. 2002. "Poverty and Inequality in Brazil: New Estimates from Combined PPV-PNAD Data." Unpublished manuscript, Development Economics Research Group, World Bank, Washington, DC.

Elbers, C., P. Lanjouw, J. A. Mistiaen, and B. Özler. 2008. "Re-interpreting Between-Group Inequality." *Journal of Economic Inequality* 6 (3): 231–45.

Ferreira, F. H. G., and J. Gignoux. 2008. "The Measurement of Inequality of Opportunity: Theory and an Application to Latin America." Policy Research Working Paper 4659, World Bank, Washington, DC.

Foster, A., and M. Rosenzweig. 2003. "Agricultural Development, Industrialization and Rural Inequality." Unpublished manuscript, Brown University and Harvard University.

Gajwani K., R. Kanbur, and X. Zhang. 2006. "Patterns of Spatial Convergence and Divergence in India and China." Paper prepared for the Annual Bank Conference on Development Economics, St. Petersburg, January 18–19.

Galasso, E., and M. Ravallion. 2005. "Decentralized Targeting of an Anti-Poverty Program." *Journal of Public Economics* 89 (4): 705–27.

Gangopadhyay, S., P. Lanjouw, T. Vishwanath, and N. Yoshida. 2010. "Identifying Pockets of Poverty: Insights from Poverty Mapping Experiments in Andhra Pradesh, Orissa and West Bengal." *Indian Journal of Human Development* 4 (1).

GoI (Government of India) Planning Commission. 2008. *Eleventh Five-Year Plan 2007–12*. New Delhi: Oxford University Press.

———. 2009. *Report of the Expert Group to Review the Methodology for Estimation of Poverty*. New Delhi: Government of India.

Khwaja, A. 2002. "Can Good Projects Succeed in Bad Communities? Collective Action in the Himalayas." Working paper, Department of Economics, Harvard University, Cambridge, MA.

La Ferrara, E. 2002. "Inequality and Group Participation: Theory and Evidence from Rural Tanzania." *Journal of Public Economics* 85 (2): 235–73.

Lanjouw, P., and V. Rao. 2009. "Revisiting Between-Group Inequality Measurement: An Application to the Dynamics of Caste Inequality in Two Indian Villages." Draft, Development Economics Research Group, World Bank, Washington, DC.

Lanjouw, P., and N. Stern, eds. 1998. *Economic Development in Palanpur over Five Decades*. Oxford: Oxford University Press.

Mansuri, G., and V. Rao. 2003. "Evaluating Community Driven Development: A Review of the Evidence." Unpublished manuscript, Development Economics Research Group, World Bank, Washington, DC.

Milanovic, B. 2005. *Worlds Apart. Measuring International and Global Inequality*. Princeton, NJ: Princeton University Press.

Ravallion, M. 2004. "Competing Concepts of Inequality in the Globalization Debate." Policy Research Working Paper 3243, World Bank, Washington, DC.

Roos, M. W. M. 2006. "Earnings Disparities in Unified Germany: Nominal versus Real." *Jahrbuch für Regionalwissenschaft* 26: 171–89.

Shorrocks, A. F. 1980. "The Class of Additively Decomposable Inequality Measures." *Econometrica* 48 (3): 613–25.

———. 1984. "Inequality Decomposition by Population Subgroups." *Econometrica* 52: 1369–85.

Topalova, P. 2008. "India: Is the Rising Tide Lifting All Boats?" IMF Working Papers 08/54, International Monetary Fund, Washington, DC.

UN (United Nations). 2008. "World Income Inequality Database." UNU-WIDER, World Institute for Development Economics Research, Helsinki.

Walton, M. 2010. "Inequality, Rents and the Long-Run Transformation of India." Unpublished manuscript, Kennedy School of Government, Harvard University, Cambridge, MA.

World Bank. 2004. *World Development Report 2005: A Better Investment Climate for Everyone*. Washington, DC: World Bank.

———. 2007. *World Development Report 2008: Agriculture for Development*. Washington, DC: World Bank.

6

Social Exclusion: Who Is Being Left Behind?

It is well recognized that poverty alone is not a comprehensive marker of deprivation. In India in particular, historical and cultural factors have created a unique system of stratification along lines of caste, tribe, and gender. The evidence presented in chapter 5 shows that in some regions, scheduled castes and scheduled tribes are being left behind, even as overall economic growth has proceeded. This chapter goes beneath the numbers laid out in chapter 5 to explore the hows and whys of poor outcomes for certain groups. We ask in this chapter:

> During the period of rapid economic growth, what happened to entrenched group inequalities? Were there ways in which excluded groups broke out of the "traps" or did "traps" trump opportunities?

We use the term "social exclusion" to distinguish it from poverty and to draw attention to the peculiar normative structures that have rendered some groups outsiders. The term was first used in the 1970s in France to distinguish "the excluded," who then comprised a wide variety of people: the disabled, suicidal and elderly persons, and abused children, among others (Silver 1994). Since then, it has been used in the social science literature to distinguish from, and add to, the concept of poverty and to denote social practices that "keep groups out." Usually, excluded groups are ethnic and/or religious minorities who, by virtue of their distinct cultural practices, are considered "the other."

The concept of social exclusion has been applied more widely to groups left out of development processes and in specific regional contexts. A report on Latin America points out that social exclusion is "multidimensional, and deprivation in one sphere interacts with deprivation in other areas to deepen the limits on the functionings of the excluded" (IADB 2007, 11). Sen (2000, 45) calls processes and relations that constrain individuals "relational roots of deprivation," whereby membership in a particular group (women, lower castes, indigenous people, or the disabled) limits the ability of individuals to acquire or use their capabilities to achieve a desired outcome. Culturally rooted systems perpetuate inequality, and rather than a "culture of poverty" that afflicts disadvantaged groups, in fact it is these "inequality traps" that prevent them from breaking out. Therefore,

> cultural factors can play a role in sustaining inter-group differences in wealth, status and power. Where the mechanisms involved are self-enforcing this can be considered to be an "inequality trap." Where such an inequality trap exists, it implies that subordinate groups are maintained at least in relative poverty, and that these are associated, in part, with culturally shaped behaviors, including endogenous preferences that can limit the prospects of poorer, or subordinate, groups. (Walton 2007, 2)

This chapter is organized along three axes—caste, tribe, and gender. It is by these that exclusion usually operates in India.[1] Our evidence builds on the vast academic and activist literature and debate on exclusion, but this chapter is by no means an attempt to provide a comprehensive survey of the literature or even a review of all the issues involved. The facts that each of these groups is highly heterogeneous and that outcomes and processes differ by state, by district, and by type of caste or tribe make the task even more challenging and make generalizations that much more difficult. Therefore, we focus on a select set of issues, drawing on both large datasets and qualitative work.

The preceding chapter has already touched on social groups' "contribution" to consumption inequality, based on several decomposition techniques. At the national level, it was found that in the National Sample Survey (NSS) consumption data, within-group heterogeneity is so considerable that a focus on between-group differences appears to contribute only modestly to an understanding of consumption inequality. The analysis further showed, however, that exploring group differences at the state level leads, in some places, to a much stronger perceived role for differences between groups. The analysis in the preceding chapter has limits. The techniques that were applied produce summary statistics that are sensitive either to the presence of within-group differences or to the presence of extreme values in the data that can cloud an assessment of group partitioning.

We revisit the issues here, employing less formal decomposition techniques and looking beyond only consumption as the welfare indicator of interest. Our analysis is based largely on group averages and other broad measures of central tendency. We find that although poverty has declined for all social groups over the last two decades, scheduled castes (SCs) today (2004–05) experience levels of poverty seen in the general population 10 years earlier (1983). Scheduled tribes (STs) are falling behind because their pace of improvement is slower (and indeed, their poverty is increasing in rural areas of some states). Today scheduled tribes lag 20 years behind the general population (see also Kijima 2006; Deshpande 2001). We explore some of the nuances of this exclusion. We also find that caste seems to be reinventing itself in response to economic opportunities, and far from its static stereotype, is an evolving, dynamic institution with mixed results. Finally, our evidence shows that although considerable progress has been achieved, female disadvantage in India continues, and women die unnecessarily both in infancy and in motherhood, with the poorest outcomes among scheduled castes and scheduled tribes.

Caste. Caste has been the predominant marker of deprivation and privilege in India. It is rooted in a ritually backed ordering of occupations drawn from ancient Hindu texts.[2] Stratification along caste lines is solidified through a system of occupational segregation and rules of purity and pollution, which play out in strict adherence to norms of intermarriage and who may eat with whom. In practice, the caste system developed into a broad social framework, and each caste has hundreds of endogamous subcastes, or *jatis,* which are the operative social units. Over time, several subcastes or *jatis* within the scheduled caste category chose to identify themselves under a broad umbrella term as the "Dalits," or the oppressed people. The term united them politically in a process more empowering than being identified by their individual names, which were (and continue to be) associated with ritually impure occupations.[3] However, caste today is not, nor has it ever been, an immutable institution. It adapts over time to changing opportunities and circumstances (Srinivas 1966). In the last 20 years of rapid economic growth, too, we find that the nature of outcomes based on caste has changed, but this comes out more through micro-level evidence than in the aggregate.

Regardless of its historically dynamic nature, caste has had dire implications for poverty and other welfare outcomes, especially because occupations are passed down over generations, making it difficult for lower castes to move up (Thorat 2007). Recognizing the unfair disadvantage that certain castes and tribes had borne through history, the Constitution of independent India put in place a set of laws that mandated punitive action against discrimination, on the one hand, and affirmative action in public employment and publicly funded education, on the other. It is generally accepted that job quotas in public employment have been successful in helping historically marginalized groups find a space in the public arena. However, concern also exists that elites within those groups have monopolized the gains in employment. We focused on access to, or exclusion from, two arenas, education and the labor market, to see the nature of change over the last two decades, and we found that Dalit men in particular have had the greatest convergence in educational outcomes with their so-called upper-caste counterparts. In employment, too, there are signs of change, and Dalits who had always been casual laborers are now looking toward, and succeeding in, self-employment. But that is far from the norm, and historical inequalities continue to play out.

Tribe. Tribal groups in India are considered to be the earliest inhabitants of a country that experienced waves of invaders and other settlers so diverse that it becomes impossible to identify ethnic groups from a "purist" perspective. The self-preferred term "Adivasi" is commonly translated as "original inhabitants" and literally means "[adi] earliest time" and "[vasi] resident of." According to the 2001 Population Census, India has 84.3 million Adivasis, making up 8.1 percent of the total population of the country. The Constitution Order 1950 declared 212 tribes, located in 14 states, "scheduled tribes." The Government of India today identifies 533 tribes, 62 of them located in the state of Orissa (see http://www.tribal.nic.in/index1.html).

Although scheduled tribes do not face ritually endorsed exclusion in the form of untouchability, as do Dalits, when exclusion is defined more broadly, in terms of being "prevent[ed] ... from entering or participating" or "being considered or accepted" (*Encarta Online Edition*), scheduled tribes fit squarely within the concept of excluded people. The major difference in the development status of the scheduled castes (SCs) and scheduled tribes (STs) is that whereas the former lived among, but were segregated socially from, the mainstream and from upper caste groups, the latter were isolated physically and hence socially (Béteille 1991), although the degree of isolation remains in question. Anthropological literature suggests that tribals are in more ways integrated into the mainstream than is recognized, and, in turn, local dominant cultures changed through their contact with Adivasis. Evidence is also seen of tribes emulating norms and traditions of the caste system, especially as they become more socially mobile (Sinha 1958; Dreze and Gazdar 1997).

Adivasis mostly report themselves in national surveys as self-employed farmers. They have historically had close cultural and economic relations with land, forests, and natural resources. With increasing state ownership of land and forests, the relationship of Adivasis with their traditional resources diminished, but they could not find space in the new development paradigm. Over time, the geographic dispersion and attendant isolation of STs have manifested in relative and often absolute deprivation for them. The remotest tribal communities show the poorest outcomes.

The response of the state to the vulnerability of scheduled tribes has been proactive, with strong constitutional backing. Schedule V of the Indian Constitution identifies special privileges for those areas where the majority of the population belong to scheduled tribes. Schedule VI is different in that it applies special privileges to tribals who reside in the northeastern states of India.[4] In areas where scheduled tribes are a minority or the Scheduled V areas located within other states, Adivasis are among the most impoverished and marginalized.

In this chapter we focus on analysis of national data to ask how tribals fare vis-à-vis the rest of the population. We focus on two major markers of tribal deprivation—poverty levels, which are higher than the national average and in comparison with other groups (including the scheduled castes), and child mortality.[5] We also discuss the difficulties that tribal groups face in obtaining access to services such as health care, and in particular the institutional and governance-related challenges that may explain poor access and some of the outcomes. Unfortunately, national-level data do not let us analyze tribal outcomes below the state level. It is well known through micro-level studies, for instance, that substantial internal diversity exists among scheduled tribes even within states. The chapter draws on such state-level analyses wherever possible. Northeastern states are excluded from the analysis because of their very different context and a range of institutional and fiscal issues that go beyond the scope of this diagnostic.

Gender. Gender inequalities in India are well documented. Female deprivation finds its starkest manifestation in high female mortality rates. Both very young girls and women in their reproductive years are at unnatural risk of death due to neglect, or in the case of female fetuses, at risk of being aborted. A system of village exogamy that distances married women socially and geographically from their natal families, combined with very young ages of marriage and motherhood, has made women collectively at greater risk of poor health and mortality (Dyson and Moore 1983).

Focusing on selected indicators, we show that in terms of both level and pace of improvement, India lags behind many countries of its income level where gender equality is concerned. We also focus in this chapter on threats to women's physical security, both within the home and outside, and the fact that those threats also account for poor access to services such as health care and consequent poor outcomes for them.

Considerable heterogeneity is evident in outcomes among women. Absolute levels of most human development outcomes are particularly low for Dalit and Adivasi women, who suffer from multiple disadvantages of social identity, residence, and gender. Though their labor market outcomes are slightly better than those of other Indian women, that must be tempered by the fact that Dalit and Adivasi women end up in the labor force mostly as casual workers out of necessity.

We draw our evidence from multiple sources of data, both quantitative and qualitative. Our quantitative analysis is based on multiple rounds of the Indian National Sample Survey (NSS); the Indian Population Census; two rounds of the Indian National Family Health Survey (NFHS; 1998 and 2005); several rounds of multicountry Demographic and Health Surveys; and the Reproductive Child Health Survey II (2005). The chapter also builds on independent background papers commissioned for this book (Desai, Noon, and Vanneman 2008; Jodhka 2008; Dubey et al. 2008; Burra 2008; Witsoe 2008) and qualitative evidence from the World Bank's study *Moving Out of Poverty* (Narayan, Pritchett, and Kapoor 2009).

Exclusion by Caste

This part of the chapter focuses on labor market and education outcomes for Dalits, primarily using data from the NSS, supplemented by evidence from recent microstudies. We highlight that although evidence appears of both occupation segregation and wage differentials between Dalits and other groups, some upward mobility is evident, both vertically to better-paying jobs within occupations and horizontally to new occupations. Caste thus appears to be not the immutable frame that conventional stereotypes suggest, but an institution that is malleable to policy and changing opportunities. Education indicators tell a similar story, with improvements but large and persistent differences.

Dalits Are Concentrated in Casual Work and, If in the Regular Salaried Sector, in Lower-Paying Jobs

Nearly 30 percent of Dalits are engaged in low-skilled casual jobs, compared to 8 percent general category (non-SC/ST/OBC) individuals (table 6.1). This condition is related to the fact that the Dalits are largely landless. Only 19 percent of Dalit men—as against 44 percent of Adivasi men, 32 percent of other backward caste (OBC) men, and 35 percent of men from the "general" category—are self-employed farmers in rural areas. Dalits are also less likely than other groups to have their own business enterprises, particularly in urban areas.

A similar pattern is evident from the distribution of occupational and industrial affiliations by social group (figure 6.1). Dalits (both wage workers and the self-employed) are much more likely to be working in agricultural and allied industries, in construction, and in blue-collar jobs, relative to general caste households. Only 2 percent of scheduled caste prime-age working individuals are in higher-paying professional or technical occupations, compared to 8 percent of general caste households. Even in the public sector traditional caste patterns are replicated: that more than 65 percent of sweepers in central government ministries are Dalits indicates that they are more likely to undertake ritually unclean and manual work (Das and Dutta 2007).

Concentration of Dalits in casual work or in lower-paid occupations, relative to other groups, is related to differences in education level, but that is only a part of the story. Differences in occupation persist even when "observationally equivalent" persons (that is, persons with the same level of education, in the same region, and so forth) are compared.[6]

Table 6.1 Nearly One-Third of Scheduled Castes Are Employed as Casual Laborers

percent

Employment type	SC	OBC	General	All
Self-employment	28	41	37	38
Regular employment	9	9	14	10
Casual labor	29	16	8	17
Unemployment	3	3	3	3
Not in labor force	30	32	38	33

Source: Das and Dutta 2007.

Note: Based on 2004–05 employment and unemployment schedule NSS data. Statistics pertain to men and women between 20 and 65 years of age. SC = scheduled caste; OBC = other backward caste.

Figure 6.1 An Overwhelming Majority of Scheduled Castes
Work in Lower-Paying Occupations and Jobs

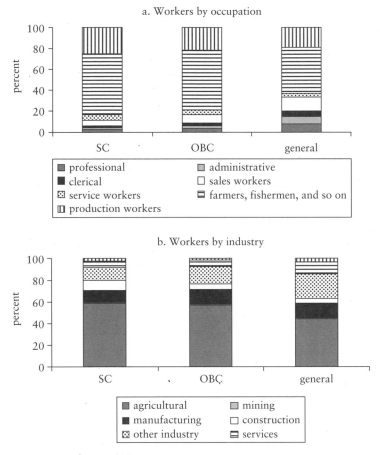

a. Workers by occupation

b. Workers by industry

Source: Das and Dutta 2007.
Note: Based on 2004–05 employment and unemployment schedule NSS data.
Statistics pertain to men and women between 20 and 65 years of age. SC = scheduled
caste; OBC = other backward caste.

In urban areas an SC status confers an advantage. SCs are more
likely to find regular salaried work, which is still predominantly in
the public sector and where reservation policy applies. However,
the combined effects of caste and education indicate that SC men
suffer a disadvantage in regular salaried jobs if they have postprimary education. This may be a corollary of an increasing supply
of educated scheduled caste men over time and an otherwise effi-
cient reservation policy, creating a system of rationing of jobs for

SCs, who cannot compete in the nonreserved salaried job market (Das 2006).[7]

Unlike the urban public sector, Dalits face a disadvantage in the urban *private* sector where, recent research establishes, they are less likely to secure a job despite being as qualified as other caste students (Deshpande and Newman 2007). For example, they find it harder to pass through hiring screens set up by employers (Thorat and Atwell 2007). Jodhka and Newman (2007) found by interviewing human resource managers on the hiring practices of their firms that caste-based stereotypes do color the hiring process, so that very low caste (and very high caste) candidates are disadvantaged. It is possible that such caste-based stereotyping with respect to productive characteristics is unconscious, in which case discrimination in hiring practices may not be overt. Instead, it may be manifest in the interaction between employer and job applicant, which may result in a scheduled caste worker withdrawing from the job queue.

It is worth noting that only screening based on subjective criteria, such as stereotypes of caste identities, would be discriminatory. Screening based on correctly perceived differences in productivity would not. However, employer perceptions of caste-based differences could be proved correct only because they are self-fulfilling. Hoff and Pandey (2004) provide experimental evidence of a significant negative impact of announcing caste identities with the test scores of scheduled caste children who otherwise performed on par with their peers. Segregation of children into high and low caste groups only deepened the decline in performance of the latter.

Wage Differentials between Dalits and Others Are a Testimony to Their Continued Disadvantage in the Labor Market. Difference in Access to Occupations—or "Glass Walls"—Is an Important Determinant of the Wage Gap

The influence of caste affiliation on wages is a much-noted feature of the Indian labor market (see, for example, Banerjee and Knight 1985; Das 2006; Unni 2001). That Dalits are less likely to be employed in high-paying jobs (both vertically, within the same employment type, and horizontally across occupations) means that, on average, they have lower wages and earnings. NSS wage data from 2004–05 show that SC and OBC individuals earn less, on average, than general caste workers in all occupational categories, with the gap bigger in predominantly white-collar occupations (Das and Dutta 2007). Using data from the 2004–05 India Human Development Survey, Desai, Noon, and Vanneman (2008) show that as with wages, an earnings gap between Dalits and other social groups is also present when nonwage sources of income (such as income from farming and business) are taken into account.

Kernel density plots of wages by social group in 2004–05 largely bear out the expectation that SC workers in regular jobs are less likely to hold the better-paying positions: the distribution of regular wages for general caste workers lies to the right of the distribution for SC and OBC workers (figure 6.2). Given that casual workers are in large part a homogeneous pool of low-skilled workers, the casual wage distributions of different social groups are nearly identical.

In addition to differences in types of jobs, these wage gaps could be related to structural characteristics such as age and education. The Desai, Noon, and Vanneman (2008) study mentioned earlier shows, for example, that personal resources, particularly social connections, and other forms of capital (as measured by indicators of education, newspaper readership, and the like) are important determinants of earnings. Dalits lack both social and cultural capital, which puts them at a disadvantage. Unequal treatment of similar workers, or wage discrimination, may also occur.

To understand the sources of the wage gap between Dalits and wage workers from other groups, Das and Dutta (2007) employed

Figure 6.2 Wage Differentials between Dalits and Others Are Much Higher in Salaried Work

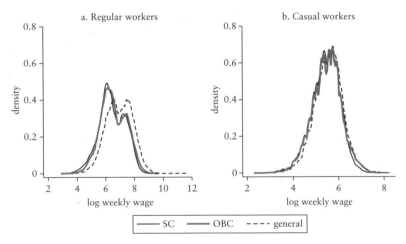

Source: Das and Dutta 2007.

Note: Based on 2004–05 employment and unemployment schedule NSS data. Statistics pertain to men and women between 20 and 65 years of age. SC = scheduled caste; OBC = other backward caste.

the Oaxaca-Blinder decomposition method, which divides the wage gap into two components—one that can be attributed to differences in characteristics (such as education and occupation type) and a second that is explained by differences in returns to characteristics. The second is often taken to be a measure of the extent of discrimination in the labor market, though it could also reflect the effect of unobserved characteristics such as ability or family background. Likewise, it is possible that some of the differences in characteristics have their roots in past discrimination that has led to worse endowments over time. That being the case, a neat decomposition into pure discrimination versus other effects is not possible, but results are indicative. Using 2004–05 NSS data on regular wage workers from both rural and urban areas, Das and Dutta found that nearly 60 percent of the wage gap between scheduled caste and general caste workers is due to the second component. Put differently, the unequal treatment of Dalit regular workers provides an average hourly wage advantage for general caste regular workers of about 36 percent, other things being equal. These findings are consistent with the limited empirical information available on this topic from other studies.[8]

How much does occupational segregation contribute to explaining the wage gap? To examine that question, Das and Dutta (2007) estimated the contribution of occupation type to the endowment and unequal treatment components in the Oaxaca-Blinder decomposition. About one-fifth of the endowment effect was accounted for by caste differentials in occupations. By contrast, they found that unequal treatment within broad occupational categories was not significant.[9] Their results suggest that to the extent that selection into occupations is not random and occupational segregation is indeed present, the effect on wages would operate through this channel.

Das and Dutta (2007) thus propose the notion of "glass walls," in a variation on the idea of "glass ceilings," that prevent occupationally "slotted" castes from leaving their traditional trades or jobs. Castes are clustered around occupations, whether by choice or compulsion, contributing to the unequal labor market outcomes that are evident today. Micro-level studies point to the possibility, especially in rural areas, of small-scale Dalit entrepreneurs being prevented through social pressure and ostracism from moving out of caste-based occupations into self-employment ventures (see, for instance, Venkteswarlu 1990, cited in Thorat 2007). Informal referral systems that mediate access to jobs, or caste-based networks of loans and informal insurance that operate in the absence of well-developed financial markets, are other factors contributing to the persistence of caste-based occupations (Munshi and Rosenzweig 2007).

*Cracks in Glass Walls ... Dalits Are Moving Out of
Agricultural Labor to Relatively Higher Paying, Nonfarm
Casual Work and Into Trade and Self-Employment*

Although the picture of occupational segregation and wage gaps is
bleak, some evidence appears of positive trends. One important
trend, as discussed in chapter 3, is the expansion of the rural nonfarm
sector, which in the decade after 1993–94 grew about four times
as fast as farm employment. With the expansion of the nonfarm
sector, the participation of disadvantaged social groups, including
Dalits, has grown. At the margin, an increasing number of new
workers entering the nonfarm sector are from a scheduled caste or
scheduled tribe background. This is especially the case for casual
nonfarm work, which is also the type of employment that has seen
the fastest growth.

Should the shift among Dalits from agricultural labor to casual
nonfarm labor—and resultant persistence of manual labor as the
main form of employment for Dalits—be viewed as further evidence
of the existence of "glass walls"? We argued in chapter 3 that
whereas casual employment is not a reliable route out of poverty, a
shift away from agricultural labor may not necessarily be distress
driven either. In view of the fact that casual nonfarm employment,
though worth considerably less than regular employment, still pays
considerably better than agriculture (about 45 percent), the shift
from agricultural to casual nonfarm labor is a sign of mobility, albeit
limited.

The importance of new economic opportunities for upward
mobility and social change has also been explored by other recent
research. Deshpande and Palshikar's (2008) study in an urban setting
(Pune) found considerable occupational mobility among Dalits. In
that account, new generations of Dalits have moved to higher-paying
occupations, compared to their forefathers', a degree of net mobility
(upward less downward) exceeding that found for other social groups
in their sample.

Using data from interviews conducted with a sample of 20,000
Dalit households in Uttar Pradesh, Chandrabhan Prasad (cited in
Wax 2008) found that a majority of households send at least one
member to the city. The resulting remittances have led to a change in
spending patterns and in social and political spaces. In 1990, about
88 percent of the families that Prasad interviewed in Gaddopur, a village in Uttar Pradesh, were asked to sit separately during public din-
ners organized by upper castes. In contrast, in 2007, only 30 percent
were asked to sit apart (Wax 2008).[10]

Because aggregate numbers do not capture microtrends, we used qualitative evidence to see whether anything had changed for potential Dalit entrepreneurs. Jodhka (2008) and Jodhka and Gautam (2008), in their field work for this book, uncovered ways in which Dalits have circumvented their environment and gained access to self-employment (box 6.1). Jodhka revisited three Haryana villages after almost 20 years to map changes in the occupational structure and found that with the exception of a small number of those from the scavenging community, Dalit families no longer engaged in traditional caste occupations.

> They go out of the village for work, and many of them have regular employment. Their dependence on local landowners for credit has also declined. They have moved away from the agrarian economy of the village and they rarely, if ever participate in the ritual life of the village. [He goes on to say,] In other words, they no longer see themselves as being a part of the social order of the caste system. This has also given them a sense of independence and political agency. (Jodhka 2008, 27)

Witsoe (2008) found similar evidence in Bihar.

Political Agency, in Addition to Economic Opportunity, Is a Driver of Change

Dalits have benefited from programs of affirmative action (including reservations and land reforms) and caste-based solidarity movements. In their study of four southern Indian states—Andhra Pradesh, Karnataka, Kerala, and Tamil Nadu—Besley, Pande, and Rao (2007) found that reservations of *pradhan* (elected village head) positions in village governments have been successful in enhancing the targeting of government programs in favor of SC (and ST) households.[11] In another study, Rao and Ban (2007) found scheduled castes to be more empowered in villages in Tamil Nadu, perhaps because of a history of solidarity movements in the state, than in villages across the border in Andhra Pradesh, despite their shared language, geography, and land distribution patterns.[12] Their findings show that caste itself adjusts and can be seen as endogenous to economic and political change.

Results found by Dubey et al. (2008) also hint at the importance of political voice. Their results, using a panel dataset for rural India for the period 1993–94 to 2004–05, indicate that SC households registered higher growth in income in villages where scheduled

Box 6.1 Intergenerational Mobility for Dalits Is Visible, Albeit Limited

Ratan Chandra Jatav is among the 321 respondents that Jodhka and Gautam (2008) interviewed for their study on Dalit entrepreneurs in Panipat, Haryana, and Saharanpur, Uttar Pradesh. He is 61 years old and is a famous businessman in Panipat. He owns two gas agencies and one petrol pump and has investments in transport and agricultural land. His total net worth is about Rs 50 million. Ratan Chandra Jatav is a Dalit.

Ratan's father was illiterate. He worked as a sweeper in the local municipality in addition to selling milk. Ratan remembers the discrimination in his early years, starting from school. Very few people bought milk from his family, and those who did kept a distance from him when he went to sell milk in the city. Ratan recounts having to sell all of his wife's jewelry to raise money when he was allotted a gas agency on the recommendation of a Dalit friend.

More than half of the study respondents, owners of small shops, cited lack of social resources as the primary reason for being unable to expand their establishments. They also reported discrimination when starting their businesses, whether in mobilizing financing, finding a space to set up shop, or in the form of hostile competition in the early years. The few who are successful are those who were not as disadvantaged to begin with, for example, those with some initial capital saved from a government job or who had the advantage of higher education.

Why then, do Dalits think of becoming entrepreneurs? The reason is that they see entrepreneurship as a means to move out of their traditional, caste-based occupations. As one respondent concluded, "It is always better to have your own business than to be a slave to others." But most, including Ratan, cannot do away with traditional biases. Ratan wraps up his interview with the following: "Even now when they [non-Dalits] see me in a luxury car, they do not like it."

Source: Jodhka and Gautam 2008.

castes are in the political and economic majority (that is, they are more than 50 percent of the local population and own more than 50 percent of the local land) than when they live in villages dominated by the upper castes. Where upper castes dominate both politically and economically, scheduled castes experience annual per capita growth in real income of 1.9 percent. In contrast, when they themselves are in power, their annual real income per capita growth is 4.5 percent.

Educational Attainment, Especially of Dalit Men, Is Growing Apace with Other Groups'. Improving Access to Education Will Improve Access to All Forms of Nonfarm Employment, But Especially the Better-Paying Regular Jobs

Education, more than labor markets, had a ritual significance[13] in that it was the preserve of upper castes, with an elaborate ideology that excluded particularly Dalits from its pale. Even today, cases such as upper-caste parents refusing to allow Dalit students to sit or eat with their own children are common in some parts of the country (Nambissan 2010).

In higher education, caste-based inequalities show up starkly (figure 6.3). One of the main ritual markers of lower-caste status has traditionally been exclusion from education or matters of the mind.

That condition has begun to change, especially for SC men, whose educational attainment is growing at a pace similar to that of their non–SC and non–ST counterparts. But as in the labor market, gaps are still large. Policies such as reservations have helped but have not reversed the initial disadvantage. Bertrand, Hanna, and Mullainathan (2008) estimated the impact of reservations for lower-caste groups in engineering colleges in India. They found that whereas the marginal lower-caste entrant does benefit from the policy, the gains to his or her earnings from attaining admission are

Figure 6.3 Changes in Postprimary Education by Social Groups and Gender, 1983–2005

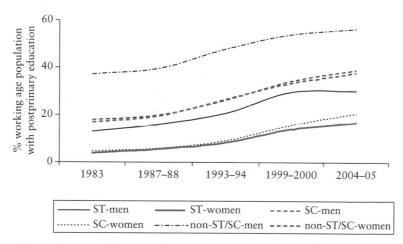

Source: Authors' calculations based on working-age population data from NSS Schedule 10, various rounds.

half those of the marginal upper-caste entrant. The reason is largely that very few lower caste graduates end up being employed in high-skill jobs. Their findings corroborate those of Deshpande and Newman (2007) and Jodhka and Newman (2007) that were referred to earlier, on the difficulties that Dalit students encounter in gaining entry into formal private sector jobs. Considerable anecdotal evidence also exists concerning the discrimination that students from SC communities face in hostels, scholarship grants, and the like.[14]

The Issue of "Caste Mutation" Is a Complex One

Before we hasten to write an "obituary of the caste system" (Srinivas 2003), it is important to add that although signs of change are apparent, because of their poor initial conditions (lack of education and assets, poor access to markets, and so on), Dalits remain disadvantaged relative to other groups. Even in Jodhka's study of Dalit entrepreneurship cited earlier, 58 percent of Dalit households worked as casual labor; only 4 percent were cultivators, and only 5 percent owned land. In contrast, nearly 61 percent of dominant caste and 36 percent of upper-caste households interviewed identified themselves as cultivators. In the Deshpande and Palshikar study, despite sustained upward mobility across generations, 77 percent of the fourth generation of SC families interviewed were stuck at the lower middle class or levels below it, compared to 52 percent of OBCs and 11 percent of upper-caste families. These authors describe the Dalits' inability to break through as "the price they have to pay for the handicap of the starting point" (Deshpande and Palshikar 2008, 66).

Traditional caste-based occupations may also be difficult to leave for economic reasons. Munshi and Rosenzweig (2006) show, for example, that caste networks in Mumbai, organized at the level of the subcaste or *jati*, ensure that members of lower castes send their children (boys) to local-language-speaking schools. The reason is to keep them within the network of the jati, which can help them later in job searches.[15]

There are other examples of caste networks using their ritually ordered positions in responding to new opportunities. Kishwar (2002), for instance, documents how government sweepers in Delhi resisted the efforts of street vendors to self-regulate garbage disposal by asserting their monopoly over cleaning and garbage collection on public land. Leather workers and metal workers similarly have responded to new opportunity by organizing production through caste networks. During fieldwork for this book, we found in Orissa that some women's self-help group federations had decided to purchase milk only from the "gopal" self-help groups, traditionally the cowherd caste.

Thus, changes appear mostly to be cracks in the glass wall, or in some cases attempts to use the walls to advantage. In the aggregate, "It's gone from horrible to bad," says Devesh Kapur, director of the University of Pennsylvania's Center for the Advanced Study of India and collaborator on Prasad's research (described in Wax 2008). "But it's like saying that you have to climb a 10,000-foot mountain and you have climbed 1,000 feet" (Wax 2008).

Exclusion by Tribal Identity

Despite the efforts of the state to address the serious development gaps of tribal groups, widespread discourse is occurring on the manner in which they are being left behind (Maharatna 2005; Xaxa 2001, 2008). In this section, we focus on outcomes that are particularly poor for tribal groups—high poverty and excess mortality among tribal children—and seek to understand their correlates.

Poverty among Adivasis Has Fallen, but Their Discrepancy from the General Population Is Large and Growing

The poverty head-count index for scheduled tribes fell by 31 percent between 1983 and 2004–05, compared to a faster decline of 35 percent among the scheduled castes and an average overall decline for India of 40 percent (table 6.2). Thus, in 2004–05, almost half of the ST population remained in poverty, whereas nationwide the poverty rate had been reduced almost to one-quarter of the population. Scheduled tribes in urban areas fared better than those in rural areas, with a lower poverty rate and steeper reductions since 1983.

The depth and severity of poverty moderated faster than the poverty head-count rate (table 6.3), indicating that improvements were not confined only to those in the vicinity of the poverty line, with the very poor remaining unaffected. However, as with the poverty head-count rate, the depth and severity of poverty are greater among scheduled tribes and have not improved fast enough to close the gap with other social groups.[16] STs are still overrepresented (relative to their overall share in the population) in the bottom 30 percent of the expenditure distribution (see chapter 1). Dubey and Verschoor (2007) arrived at similar findings using income, instead of consumption, as a measure of welfare.[17]

These Findings Need to Be Nuanced by the Highly Unequal Results across States. . .

What is important—and worrying—is that in states with high tribal populations (about 10 percent or more of the total), ST households

Table 6.2 In Terms of Poverty, Scheduled Tribes Are
20 Years Behind the General Population

Social group	% population below the poverty line			% change between 1983 and 2005
	1983	*1993–94*	*2004–05*	
Rural				
ST	63.9	50.2	44.7	–30
SC	59.0	48.2	37.1	–37
Others	40.8	31.2	22.7	–44
All	46.5	36.8	28.1	–40
Urban				
ST	55.3	43.0	34.3	–38
SC	55.8	50.9	40.9	–27
Others	39.9	29.4	22.7	–43
All	42.3	32.8	25.8	–39
Total				
ST	63.3	49.6	43.8	–31
SC	58.4	48.7	37.9	–35
Others	40.5	30.7	22.7	–44
All	45.6	35.8	27.5	–40

Source: Authors' estimates based on Schedule 1.0 of respective NSS rounds and
official poverty lines.

exhibited poverty rates that were higher than in the nation as a
whole in 2004–05 (with the exception of Assam; see table 6.4). The
highest poverty rates recorded for tribal groups were in Orissa.
There the tribal population registered a poverty rate of 75 percent
in 2004–05—an *increase* of about 6 percent from 1993–94 levels.
Tribals in rural areas in Orissa were particularly worse off, with
poverty levels declining by only 13 percent, compared to a decline
of 44 percent for other groups (non–SCs and non–STs) during
1983–2005. Tribals in rural areas in Madhya Pradesh, Maharashtra, Rajasthan, Jharkhand, and Chhattisgarh also recorded far
lower declines in poverty than did other groups.

... And Keeping in Mind Heterogeneity. on Average,
Adivasis in Urban Areas Experienced More Consumption
Growth Than Those in Rural Areas. Within Urban Areas,
Consumption Growth Was Much Greater among the
Better-Off

Figure 6.4 shows the growth incidence curves (GIC) for scheduled
tribes in both rural and urban areas, indicating the growth rate in
expenditures between 1993–94 and 2004–05 at each percentile of

Table 6.3 Depth and Severity of Poverty Have Declined More Slowly among Scheduled Tribes Than Other Social Groups

| Social group | Trends in depth of poverty | | | | Trends in severity of poverty | | | |
	1983	1993–94	2004–05	% change between 1983 and 2005	1983	1993–94	2004–05	% change between 1983 and 2005
Rural								
ST	21.2	12.2	10.7	–50	9.5	4.3	3.7	–61
SC	18.7	11.7	7.5	–60	8.2	4.1	2.2	–73
Others	11.1	6.7	4.1	–63	4.6	2.1	1.1	–76
All	13.6	8.4	5.5	–59	5.8	2.8	1.6	–72
Urban								
ST	17.4	12.4	10.9	–37	7.2	5.0	4.7	–35
SC	16.8	14.1	10.4	–38	7.1	5.6	3.8	–46
Others	11.0	7.2	5.2	–52	4.5	2.6	1.8	–61
All	11.9	8.3	6.2	–48	4.9	3.0	2.2	–56
Total								
ST	20.9	12.2	10.7	–49	9.4	4.3	3.8	–60
SC	18.4	12.2	8.1	–56	8.0	4.3	2.5	–68
Others	11.1	6.8	4.4	–60	4.6	2.3	1.3	–72
All	13.2	8.4	5.7	–57	5.6	2.8	1.8	–68

Source: Authors' staff estimates based on Schedule 1.0 of respective NSS rounds and official poverty lines.

Table 6.4 Trends in Poverty Incidence in States with High
Proportion of Adivasis

percent

State	1983 STs	1983 All	1993–94 STs	1993–94 All	2004–05 STs	2004–05 All
Assam	48.5	41.5	40.9	41.4	12.3	20.5
Gujarat	58.5	33.0	30.9	24.1	33.1	17.0
Madhya Pradesh	71.6	50.4	60.4	41.7	57.5	38.2
Maharashtra	63.1	44.3	53.1	36.8	54.2	30.6
Orissa	86.2	66.3	70.9	48.7	75.2	46.6
Rajasthan	63.0	38.6	44.5	27.5	32.2	21.4
Jharkhand	73.5	59.6	67.7	55.4	53.4	42.1
Chhattisgarh	58.7	50.5	53.1	44.4	53.8	41.0
All India	63.3	45.6	49.6	35.8	43.8	27.5

Source: Authors' estimates based on Schedule 1.0 of respective NSS rounds and
official poverty lines.

Note: States shown had 10 percent or greater Adivasi population in 1983.

the expenditure distribution. In a pattern similar to those for other
social groups, in urban areas, richer STs registered higher expenditure growth than poorer STs. That may perhaps reflect that a few
elite among STs had access to, and benefited from, reserved jobs,
while a significant proportion of the group were manual laborers in
construction projects (box 6.2).

These are patterns based on aggregate national or state-level data.
But scheduled tribes, like scheduled castes, encompass diverse subgroups. Within-group variation and regional variation are central to
an understanding of caste or tribal identity and its impact on welfare. We draw on microstudies and ethnographic accounts to understand that heterogeneity.

Higher Child Mortality among Adivasis Is the Starkest Marker of Deprivation

Table 6.5 shows that the mortality of tribal children starts off on par
with that of other groups but gets rapidly worse in rural areas by the
time the children are five years old.

The continuing pattern of high mortality of tribal children is in
keeping with anecdotal information and data from administrative
records. However, poor registration of births and deaths has led to
frequent haggling over the real numbers. Some studies also report
higher infant mortality rates for tribal groups, whereas others show
a distinct advantage over the nontribal population in the same location (Maharatna 2005).

Figure 6.4 Consumption Growth among Urban Scheduled Tribes Was Highly Skewed, with Bigger Gains near the Top of the Distribution

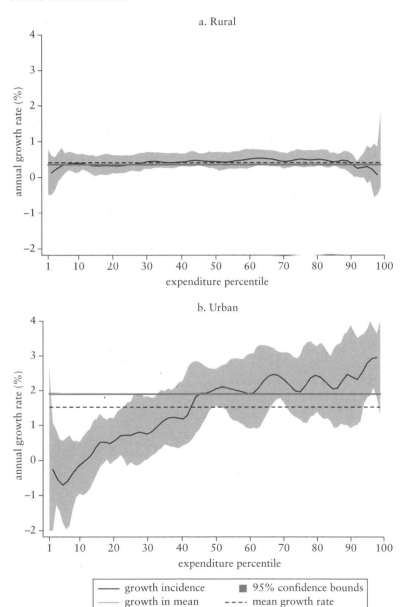

Source: Authors' estimates based on Schedule 1.0 of the respective NSS rounds.
Note: Growth incidence curves show growth in per capita consumption between 1993/94 and 2004/05 at each percentile of the expenditure distribution.

Box 6.2 The Practice of Distress Migration among Adivasis

A survey in 2004 found that nearly 80 percent of Adivasis in rural Maharashtra migrated to cities for four to six months in a year. A majority worked under harsh and hazardous conditions in stone quarries, brick kilns, excavation and construction sites, and salt pans and as casual labor. One report from the salt commissioner's records in the state estimates that nearly 90 percent of all workers employed in salt pans in Thane, Raigad, and Sindhudurg districts are Adivasis.

Most are distress migrants. Some are picked up by contractors from tribal villages as bonded labor in exchange for distress loans to pay for emergencies such as a sudden illness. Lump-sum wages are fixed through an oral agreement *(thar)* between the laborer and contractor and paid at the end of the season after deducting advances. Despite exploitation, the Adivasis prefer the assurance of *thar* to the insecurity of working as daily wage labor. In the latter case, they assemble at fixed spots *(nakas)* in urban centers for work and are often paid less than the mandatory minimum wage. Instances also occur of the contractor disappearing when payment is due. Cases are seldom filed in labor courts, as that requires the tribal laborer to travel back to his original site of work numerous times to pursue the case.

Source: Bulsara and Sreenivasa 2004.

Table 6.5 Mortality of Scheduled Tribe Infants Is on Par with Others but by the Time Infants Are Five Years Old, There Is a Huge Gap

deaths per 1,000 births

Social group	Neonatal	Postneonatal	Infant	Child	Under age 5
Urban					
ST	29.0	14.8	43.8	10.4	53.8
All	28.5	13.0	41.5	10.6	51.7
Rural					
ST	40.9	23.0	63.9	38.3	99.8
All	42.5	19.7	62.2	21.0	82.0
Total					
ST	39.9	22.3	62.1	35.8	95.7
All	39.0	18.0	57.0	18.4	74.3

Source: NFHS 2005–06.

Note: Neonatal = probability of dying in the first month of life; postneonatal = probability of dying after the first month of life, but before the first birthday; infant = probability of dying before the first birthday; child = probability of dying between the first and fifth birthdays; under age 5 = probability of dying before the fifth birthday.

Reasons underlying high mortality rates are also a subject of debate. Maharatna (2005) has documented the more sustainable practices of tribals that historically kept rates of fertility and mortality among them lower than the national average but notes that this began to change as tribals gave up their traditional practices. The pressures that lead to poor health outcomes may differ across states, and the findings therefore need to take into account state- or location-specific factors. Child deaths in tribal areas typically cluster around periods of seasonal stress, such as drought, when household food supplies are low and employment also dries up (as in Rajasthan), or during the monsoon (as in Maharashtra), when access to remote communities is cut off. Public interest lawsuits have been filed on behalf of families that lost their children,[18] and state governments have been repeatedly directed by the courts to take remedial action. The government's response to excess mortality of tribal children is that these losses are not due to malnutrition but that poverty and ignorance are the causes (Khandare 2004). State governments have undoubtedly become more vigilant on this issue than they were before, but solutions are still ad hoc and in response to crises.

It would be wrong, however, to conclude that tribal health outcomes are universally poor. Apart from a large interstate differential in tribal mortality, there is also evidence of wide variation in death rates between different tribal groups (Parasuraman and Rajan 1990). Further, the gap between mortality levels of the tribal and nontribal population (particularly the scheduled castes) is not always to the disadvantage of scheduled tribes. In many cases and areas scheduled castes are more disadvantaged.

Looking at Age-Specific Mortality of Children Brings Out a More Refined Picture

Our analysis shows, first, that a disproportionately high number of child deaths are concentrated among Adivasis, especially in the age group one to five years, and in the states and districts with a high proportion of Adivasis (Das, Kapoor, and Nikitin 2010). Efforts to reduce child morality in the aggregate will need to focus more squarely on lowering mortality among the Adivasis.

Second, we find that the gap in mortality between Adivasi children and others appears after the age of one year (see table 6.6). In fact, before the age of one Adivasi children face odds of dying similar to those of other children—odds that significantly reverse later. This calls for a shift in attention from infant mortality, or overall under-five mortality, to factors that cause a difference between tribal children and the rest between the ages of one and five.

Table 6.6 Scheduled Tribe Children Face Higher Odds of Dying after Age One Than Non–Scheduled Tribe Children

Social group	Neonatal	Postneonatal	Infant	Child	Under age 5
Relative hazard rate (%)					
Non-ST	1.01	0.98	0.99	0.92	0.98
ST	0.96	1.17	1.06	2.25	1.26
Test of significance of difference					
Pr > chi2	0.194	0.174	0.378	0.000	0.000

Source: Das, Kapoor, and Nikitin (2010) based on NFHS 2005–06.
Note: Relative hazard rate compares the relative odds of death in each group. A hazard rate higher than 1 implies odds in favor of death.

Third, our analysis goes contrary to the conventional narrative in which poverty is the primary factor driving differences between mortality outcomes.[19] Instead, we find that tribal status is significant, even after controlling for wealth, if we focus on age-specific child mortality.

The multivariate analyses and governmental claims notwithstanding, it is almost tautological to assert that poverty, not malnutrition, is the cause of excess tribal mortality. The central questions then become the following: Why are tribal households so poor and food insecure? Why do development projects not reach them? Although several factors contribute, Das, Kapoor, and Nikitin (2010) suggest that three lie at the root of tribal deprivation: the tribals' poor physical access to services, their lack of a collective voice, and their removal from their traditional lands and forests.

The Remoteness of Tribal Habitations Creates Problems for Service Delivery and Monitoring

In most states scheduled tribes are physically isolated, concentrated in certain regions and districts and in hilly and forested areas, making it difficult to reach them even in normal circumstances. The lack of all-weather roads can make transportation in emergencies impossible. A deep-rooted cultural chasm and mistrust also exist between the largely nontribal health providers and the tribal residents (Suchitra 2005; see also box 6.3). Several studies also show that tribals may harbor a lingering mistrust of allopathic treatment, even where it is available.[20] Migration of tribals to urban areas during the lean season makes the task of health surveillance even more difficult. Finally, although administrators realize the value of recruiting local residents to many field-level positions, such as the community health worker in the *Anganwadi* (Integrated Child Development Services Center) or the accredited social health activist (ASHA) worker, it is often

Box 6.3 Mistrust Is a Barrier to Adivasi Access to Health Services

"Korku women have to be taught everything about taking care of children .... They don't know how to take care of or feed children. When a child eats dogs and cats eat with him and mother does nothing ...." (Non-Adivasi woman, Dharni block, Amravati district)

"Many times a sick child is taken to the health center and doesn't become better, but dies there. There is no use in taking a child to the health center." (Korku woman, Dharni block, Amravati district, Maharashtra)

Sources: Government of Maharashtra and UNICEF-WIO 1991.

difficult to find tribal women with secondary education who can fill these positions. As a result, the positions either remain vacant or are filled by nontribal, nonresident providers.

A number of very successful initiatives have been undertaken in both the nongovernmental and the public sector to improve access to roads or better health facilities in some tribal areas.[21] However, the best-known interventions have often been small and resource intensive, making the task of scaling-up a challenge. Moreover, such efforts have only been able to influence outcomes marginally, given their restricted reach and small initial base of inputs (or absence thereof), though they are aiming to improve.

Scheduled Tribes Lack a Voice in Decision Making at All Levels

Data from the Reproductive and Child Health Survey II (RCH II) show that in Orissa, districts with the highest proportion of tribals have the worst infant mortality rates. Such districts also have the lowest public spending (not necessarily low allocation) on health, have low institutional capacity at multiple levels, lack priority for health, and are characterized by low articulation of demand (voice) by citizens (World Bank 2006). These findings concur with those of Banerjee and Somanathan (2007) that between 1971 and 1991 fewer education and health facilities were available in parliamentary constituencies with concentrations of scheduled tribes.

It is widely recognized that such disparities are largely related to low voice of tribals and low accountability to them by the ruling elites, many of whom are not tribals (see Guha 2007; Xaxa 2001). Restricted to remote villages, in no state of India, with the exception of the northeastern states, are the Adivasis in majority.[22] They can influence election results in only a few isolated districts where they form the majority. Thus, the concerns of scheduled tribes remain marginal in the national context. A recent Planning Commission report (GoI 2008) places this exclusion at the core of the militant movements against the state that have gathered strength over the last decade in Adivasi areas.

Land and Natural Resources Have a Central Role in Explaining Tribal Poverty

Tribal rights activists have long maintained that poor outcomes are merely symptoms of Adivasi dependence on, and alienation from, land and forests. A large proportion of ST men (44 percent) in rural areas are self-employed farmers. Yet poverty rates among scheduled tribes are the highest among all social groups in rural areas. The reason is largely the low productivity of tribal agriculture, which is mostly rain-fed, hill cultivation undertaken with limited resources. But the relationship of tribals to land extends beyond such subsistence cultivation to their dependence on natural resources for livelihood and food security (Saxena 1999). Plants also provide the basis of traditional tribal medicine, and reduced access to such resources could be a factor contributing to increased child mortality. Over time, economic development has allowed private and state actors to infringe on these traditional mechanisms without establishing alternatives for STs. An example is the case of nontimber forest products, many of which are of high value. The debate, over kendu leaves, for instance, is a heated one, in which tribal rights activists allege that middlemen work to keep the tribals' share of the profits low and cash in on distress sales.

Even as Adivasis are being alienated from their lands and forests, a concomitant change has taken place in their own property and natural resource management systems. Community cultivation is giving way to individual ownership. That has meant a shift away from subsistence (where any surplus is redistributed) to an economy of accumulation, leading to changed needs and aspirations. Given the limited potential of hill agriculture, "stepping out" is being seen as necessary to meet new aspirations (Dorward et al. 2009).

Infrastructure Development Has Led to Displacement and Discontent and Has Played a Part in Tribal Impoverishment

The largest form of alienation from traditional land has taken place through state acquisition of land for development. The 10th Five-Year

Plan notes that between 1951 and 1990, 21.3 million people were displaced, of whom 40 percent, or 8.5 million, were tribal people (Burra 2008; GoI 2001). Tribals have been a large proportion of those displaced—far in excess of their proportion in the population—but other groups have also suffered. Rehabilitation plans have remained difficult to implement, and a recent Planning Commission report suggests that only one-third of all displaced persons have been rehabilitated since independence (GoI 2008). Together these factors have spearheaded massive movements (that include both tribals and nontribals) against the state acquiring lands for development. It is important to note here that tribals do not always oppose state acquisition of land. Conversations held with government officials in states such as Jharkhand suggest that whereas stiff opposition arises to giving Adivasi lands for mining or industrial development, opposition to acquisition of land for road building is limited.[23] The reason is perhaps that the road is perceived as a public good whose benefits are available to the population at large, whereas jobs provided by a mine or industry may be captured and need not go to the Adivasis.[24] The state and the private sector have yet to develop a workable strategy to share benefits from such projects with tribal populations.

Recent Legislation Has Tried to Address Alienation, but Implementation Has Been Problematic

Land reforms have been undertaken since independence, and other legislation has also been enacted to protect tribal land. For instance, laws prevent Adivasi land from being "alienated," but that can be a double-edged sword, in that tribals may not be able to sell their land to nontribals even when they want to. But landgrabbing takes place regardless, for instance, through marriage or through fraud by contractors or lenders as a means to recover debt from tribals. Mander (2002) estimates that nearly 46 percent of land transfers in Jhabua, Madhya Pradesh, in the 1970s were to repay loans. The issue of fake ST certificates has also acquired very sensitive political ramifications.

One of the Most Important Pieces of Legislation in the Last Decade Has Been the Panchayat (Extension to Scheduled Areas) Act

Applicable to Schedule V areas,[25] the Panchayat (Extension to Scheduled Areas) Act (PESA) gives special powers to *gram sabhas* in an effort to enhance the voice of tribal groups in development. In particular, the voice of *gram sabhas* in mining leases and infrastructure development in tribal areas is strengthened. PESA is unique in being in consonance with customary laws, focusing more on tribal, hamlet-based culture than on revenue villages. Several steps have been taken to put PESA into operation. State amendments and rules have been passed, and monitoring is under way. However, it is widely believed that PESA has not been implemented in spirit. Most recently, another act—the Scheduled Tribes and Other Traditional Forest Dwellers (Recognition of Forest Rights) Act, 2006 (known variously in common parlance as the Forest Rights Act or the Tribal Rights Act)—recognizes the preeminent rights of tribals on forest land. Both PESA and the Tribal Rights Act fundamentally question the power relations between Adivasi and non-Adivasi areas and purport to transfer greater power to the former. It is the politics of this power sharing that is at the crux of poor implementation and needs to be taken on squarely at the political level.

Exclusion by Gender

This part of the chapter focuses on aspects of gender inequality in India. In keeping with the feminist discourse in India, we show that key outcomes related to the third Millennium Development Goal (MDG3), on the promotion of gender equality, remain very poor.[26] This is true both temporally—in that progress has been slower than we would have expected at India's levels of GDP growth, and spatially, in that India's progress lags behind that of other countries of its income level and even those below. That is so despite the fact that India spends a larger proportion of its GDP on indicators related to this goal than, for instance, Bangladesh, or even Nepal (see Das 2008). In absolute terms, some numbers stand out more than others, including those relating to maternal health and gender differences in infant mortality and the labor market. Dalit and Adivasi women have been particularly marginalized, despite the fact that the pressures of seclusion and cultural restrictions on mobility are few for them. Gender inequalities are more prevalent among upper-caste Hindus, especially among the poor and the lower middle class. Among the small but fast-growing upper middle class, opportunities seem to have opened up for women, particularly in the professional, business, bureaucratic, and political spaces.

India Has Made Substantial Investments in Human Development but Displays Poor Gender Equality Indicators Compared to Other Countries

Despite its strides in education and health, India fares worse on many outcomes than neighboring Bangladesh and in comparison to some other countries of its income level. The Human Development Index brings that annually to public attention. Female disadvantage, as pointed out earlier, comes through most starkly in the lower survival chances of baby girls compared to boys.[27] This notoriously South Asian pattern is *worsening* only in India, and controversy exists about what may be causing the trend, especially in better-off states. A related fact is that India and, to a lesser extent, Nepal are the only two countries where the survival of infant girls is known to be lower than that of boys (figure 6.5). Mortality rates overall have declined more slowly in India than they have in Nepal and Bangladesh. Finally, the progression of girls to secondary schools is much smaller than in Bangladesh, even though Bangladesh spends a lower proportion of its GDP on education (Das 2008).

At the same time, notable areas of progress are seen. Fertility decline, for instance, frees up women from the cycle of childbearing and child rearing and allows them to enter into other arenas. In India, fertility rates in several states are now below replacement levels and resemble those in developed countries, but rates in other states resemble those in much poorer countries (figure 6.6). The use of contraception is much higher than even a decade ago, and maternal mortality—while at stubbornly high levels across the South Asia region (except Sri Lanka)—is declining more sharply in India than in other countries.

Progress Has Been Highly Uneven, and Dalit and Adivasi Women's Outcomes Are Much Worse Than Those of Other Women

Mothers' dying in childbirth, just as infant and unborn girls' dying by intent or neglect, continues to be the biggest blight on India's performance on major human development indicators. Dalit and Adivasi women fare worse than others. Overall, almost 60 percent of all women and 80 percent of tribal women give birth at home. Only 55 percent of married tribal women aged 15–49 years reported in the 2005 NFHS having ever used contraception. That figure compares to 63 percent of SCs and 62 percent of OBCs and is well below the national average of 65 percent. In comparison to SCs and OBCs, a relatively smaller proportion of ST women report three or more antenatal visits (40 percent, compared to 44 percent for SC women and 48 percent for women from the OBC group) (Das, Kapoor, and Nikitin 2010). Medical practitioners often cite "lack of demand" or "ignorance" as the reasons for poor outcomes for women, and that is visible in the responses shown in

Figure 6.5 Only in India and Nepal Is Infant Mortality of Girls Higher Than That of Boys

number of deaths per 1,000 births

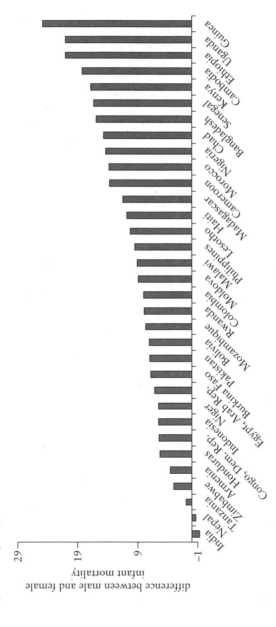

Source: Selected Demographic Health Surveys between 2003 and 2006.

Figure 6.6 Fertility Is Declining, and Many Indian States Resemble More Developed Countries

births per women

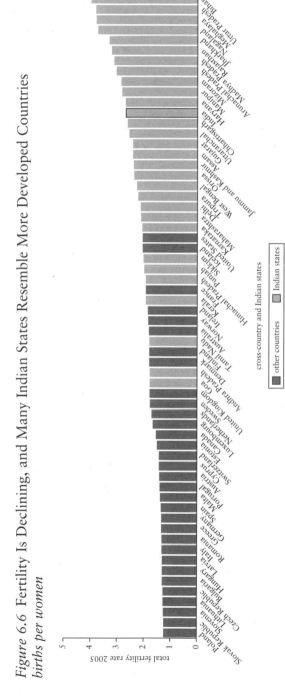

Sources: National Family Health Survey for India and Indian states; EUROSTAT 2008 for European countries; StatCan for Canada; AUSTATS for Australia; and Demographic Health Surveys for selected countries.

Note: Data from 2005 or closest year available.

255

figure 6.7 as well (Khandare 2004). However, low demand for health or nutrition may also be caused by gaps in supply. Although open to modern treatment, tribal women in remote areas find it difficult to reach health facilities because of poor road access. Costs of travel are often weighed against loss of a day's wages. Even when they are able to traverse the distance, the women receive callous treatment. And to what extent is it ethical to raise demand when supply is not assured? These are key questions in the delivery of services.

As in the case of health, Adivasi and Dalit women do worse than others in educational attainment. Postprimary education has improved for everyone who is today of prime working age, but SC and more so ST women have seen increasing divergence between their educational attainment and that of other groups. Non–SC/ST (or upper-caste) men expectedly have the greatest advantage, but over time, SC men, who start from the same base level as upper-caste women, now seem to leave the latter behind ever so slightly (see figure 6.3). This is in keeping with our observations of SC men's growth in employment. Clearly, then, inequalities in access to

Figure 6.7 Reasons for Women's Last Children Not Being Born at a Health Care Facility

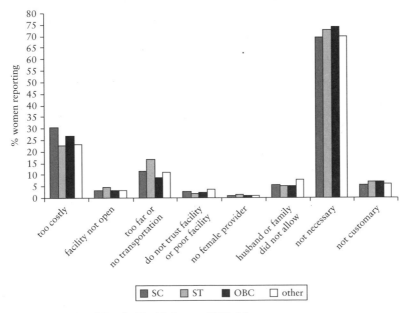

Source: National Family Health Survey 2005–06.

education affect all poor groups, but much more so scheduled caste women and all scheduled tribes.

High Levels of Gender Inequality in the Labor Market Persist, Despite Improvements in Other Areas

Rates of female participation in the labor force in India remain low, with only 40 percent of women employed in full-time work, according to figures from the 2004–05 NSS.[28] Two kinds of explanations have been articulated for this. The first is a demand-for-labor argument, which posits a dearth of well-paying, secure jobs for educated women. Hence educated women, who also belong to the higher socioeconomic strata, prefer to opt out of the labor force rather than accept low-status (manual) jobs. The second, a labor supply argument, rests on cultural mores and the values of status and seclusion in the region, which may prevent higher-status households from allowing women to go out and work or demand jobs.

The two arguments are mutually reinforcing. It is true that women with higher education stay out of the labor force if there is another earning member in the household or because of an income effect. But this explanation is muddied by the fact that so few "appropriate" (regular salaried) jobs are available. In fact, as chapter 3 indicates, regular jobs employ less than 4 percent of rural working women. Women's share in relatively better-paying non-farm activities, too, has declined, from 26 percent in 1983 to 23 percent in 2004–05, relative to men's, despite an expansion witnessed in the sector. If the only options available are in low-status, low-paying manual work, especially in rural areas, households decide to withdraw female labor if they contain another earning member. Because educated women are usually married to educated men and are likely to have some financial resources, instead of accepting poorly paid jobs as casual wage workers, they stay out of the labor force. Not only is it difficult to separate the cultural from the structural, but often the cultural affects the structural, and vice versa.

Although wages rose in the aggregate for all over the last 10 years or so, lower wages for women, as compared to men, are an added disincentive for women to work outside the home. Oaxaca-Blinder decompositions conducted for wages of male and female casual workers in India and Bangladesh found that unobserved factors accounted for over 70 percent of the difference in wages, well above the share of unexplained wage gaps between Dalits and other social groups, for instance (Das 2006; World Bank 2008). Some of these "unobserved" factors may well be discrimination. Thus, gender ideologies can spill over into hiring patterns and exclude women. In any event, the luxury (or ignominy) of work only within the home is mostly for a condition of upper-caste and upper-class women, and poverty is a factor that drives women into the labor market (Das and Desai 2003).

But Indian Women Clearly Aspire to Work Outside Their Homes

Our analysis of 2004–05 NSS data suggests that more than 89 percent of women doing domestic work say that it is from compulsion. One-third of them say that they would accept paid work in addition to their household duties. Clearly, their household responsibilities are paramount, and most say that they would like regular part-time jobs (figure 6.8). Of these, more than 56 percent say the reason is that no other member in the household will take on these duties.

Economic and Social Outcomes for Women Are Underpinned by Low Levels of Security Both Within and Outside the Home

That Indian society is notoriously unsafe for women is well recognized, at least in the feminist literature. Violence begins with selective abortion of unborn girls and extends through the course of life. In the 2005–06 NFHS, 37 percent of Indian women reported ever having experienced spousal violence, and 24 percent had experienced violence in the past year. Interestingly, only 14 percent of women with 12 or more years of schooling reported experiencing violence, compared to 44 percent of uneducated women. We also found statistically significant bivariate associations between violence and women's ability to seek health care for themselves (figure 6.9). Nearly 81 percent of women who have never experienced violence speak of receiving antenatal care, in contrast to only 67 percent of those who have experienced violence. Bivariate analysis also indicates that the children of women who have been subjected to violence are significantly less likely to receive oral rehydration therapy when ill with diarrhea. At the multivariate level, after controlling for wealth quintile, educational level, and other background characteristics, the experience of spousal violence increases the odds of non-live birth by 40 percent, reduces the odds of facility-based delivery by 13 percent, and significantly increases the odds of stunting among children below the age of five.

Domestic violence against women is a marker of extreme inequality in gender relations. Addressing it for its intrinsic importance has great implications for human rights, but it also has an

Figure 6.8 Aspirations of Women Doing Only Domestic Work

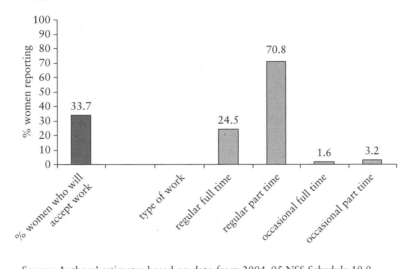

Source: Authors' estimates based on data from 2004–05 NSS Schedule 10.0.

Figure 6.9 Indian Women Who Report Spousal Violence Also Report More Barriers to Health Care

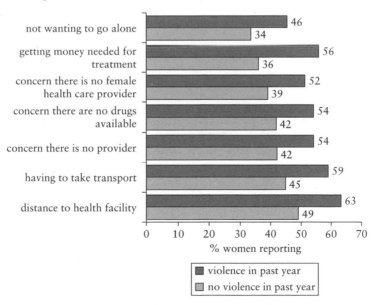

Source: Authors' estimates based on data from 2005–06 NFHS.

instrumental value. Globally, the literature documents worse health and other outcomes among women who have experienced violence.[29] The statistics reported here show that in India, too, violence has a correlation with a range of outcomes for women and their households, particularly for their children. In addition to violence within the family, perceptions by women and their families concerning their safety in public places, as well as fear of sexual harassment (known popularly by the demeaning term "eve teasing"), pose barriers that have not hitherto been measured by national surveys in India.[30] It is likely that violence acts as a barrier to empowerment (for example, impeding access to services and markets), or it may be a result of empowerment, such that women who are more empowered and flout social norms are at greater risk (see World Bank 2008). Whatever the direction of causality, it is reasonable to conclude that domestic violence is associated with poor outcomes for women and their children, the costs of which are too high and too pervasive to ignore.

What can help protect women from violence? That ownership of property, especially of land, matters greatly has long been recognized. A recent study on domestic violence in India found that ownership of land more than any other factor protects women against violence, enhancing their esteem and worth in the household and the community (Panda and Agarwal 2005). Ownership, of course, is not the same as control, but it is a starting point to enhance voice. Although formal property rights in South Asia do not exclude women, and some legislation even emphasizes women's rights of inheritance, cultural pressures often force women to give up their inheritance. The Government of India has also recently put in place legislation that gives married and unmarried women far-reaching legal protection against abuse or "threats of abuse" from their spouses, partners, or other males in the family.[31] An important feature of the Protection of Women from Domestic Violence Act 2005 is its recognition of the abused woman's right to secured housing—a right that is secured by a residence order passed by the court. Despite the landmark changes proposed, little evidence is available to assess the impact of the law.

Several Policies and Programs Are Under Way to Promote Women's Empowerment and Better Gender Outcomes; Both Vision and Implementation Count

Mandatory provisions for reserving seats in local government for women (and scheduled castes and tribes) were introduced in 1992 in the 73rd amendment to the Indian Constitution, as a means of addressing traditional forms of social exclusion at the village level. It is no surprise that reservations have not undone social exclusion in a few short years, nor that elite capture remains a problem. But recent empirical work suggests that reservations are having some impact. In West Bengal, reservations led to increased participation of women in the *gram sabha* in villages with a woman *pradhan* and affected the choice of investments made at the local level (Chattopadhyay and Duflo 2004).

Also, women's development programs and quotas in poverty alleviation have helped women receive the benefits of development programs. For instance, Reserve Bank of India (RBI) guidelines that required public sector banks to lend to women's self-help groups have helped to catalyze such groups across the country by placing the onus equally on banks and state and district administrations. However, reviews of the policy show that women remain significantly deprived of banking services compared to men. Using official data from the RBI, Chavan (2008) found that only 12 percent of individual bank loan accounts belonged to women in 2006, a year when women constituted about half of India's population. Further, for every Rs 100 of bank credit given to a man, a woman received only Rs 15. The disparities among women from different socioeconomic groups in terms of access to banking services also widened. In 2006, Dalit and Adivasi women received only 1.3 percent of the total credit given under the small borrower accounts, compared to 4.8 percent in 1997. Chavan concludes her review by stressing the need for greater financial inclusion of women, "instead of regarding microfinance as the only solution to women's banking" (Chavan 2008, 20).

Countries that have been more successful than India in improving the health and education of women show us that national vision helped shape *all* policies, not just those concerning women. In Organisation for Economic Co-operation and Development (OECD) countries, for instance, tax laws that reward employed women while also encouraging fertility have been central to high levels of women's labor force participation. Sri Lanka showed us decades ago that fixing the health system with a view to lowering mortality rates had a salutatory impact on infant mortality, fertility, and women's status. In Bangladesh, a successful secondary school stipend program, along with growth in women's employment in the garment export industry (which requires basic literacy and numeracy), has meant that girls' enrollment is now higher than boys'. Girls enroll because, in addition to the stipend, their families perceive a return for sending their daughters to primary school. In contrast, the returns to education for girls in India come only at higher levels, after completing high school. For those at lower levels, few "appropriate" regular salaried jobs, such as are offered by the garment export sector in Bangladesh, are available. What each of these initiatives did was first to define an objective of gender equality or women's empowerment, and then to look at which policy needed to be "engendered."

Epilogue

India is not alone in grappling with serious challenges in reaching its most excluded populations. In other countries as well, this challenge is a formidable one. An IADB (2007) report on Latin America states that inclusion

> is not just about changing outcomes, but crucially about chang-
> ing the processes that produce and reproduce exclusionary
> outcomes [and that] in order to make normative changes effec-
> tive, institutions must change the ways in which they operate,
> hire employees, and enforce laws and regulations. This in turn
> materializes as changes in the implementation of programs and
> policies .... (IADB 2007, 14)

The Indian Constitution set the stage for almost unparalleled affirmative action and other forms of positive actions. These have been translated into laws, programs, and procedures. Yet the combination of identity politics, inflexibility of the very systems that seek to promote inclusion, and the attendant poor implementation has resulted in patchy impact, affecting some groups more than others. To state the real challenge is to state a truism—that the implementation of policies and of reforms of institutions is the key to ensuring that growth becomes more equitable.

Notes

1. There are other dimensions of exclusion: religion, age, and disability, to name a few. Chapter 5 examines group differences in consumption and education outcomes by religion.

2. The Hindu hierarchy is said to have evolved from different parts of the body of Brahma—the creator of the universe. Thus, the Brahmans, who originated from the mouth, undertake the most prestigious priestly and teaching occupations. The Kshatriyas (from the arms) are the rulers and warriors; the Vaishyas (from the thighs) are traders and merchants. The Shudras, from the feet, are manual workers and servants of other castes. Below the Shudras and outside the caste system, lowest in the order, the

untouchables engage in the most demeaning and stigmatized occupations (scavenging, for instance, and dealing with bodily waste).

3. Similarly, the scheduled tribes are also referred to as the Adivasis. For purposes of tables and graphs presented in this chapter, we use the terms SC and ST, as these are standard administrative and survey categories. In the text we use the terms Dalits and Adivasis or tribals interchangeably with SCs and STs, respectively.

4. In some respects, such as education, tribes in these states do relatively better. Mizoram, for instance, has the second-highest literacy rate among all states in India, second only to Kerala, according to the 2001 Census of India.

5. See the previous chapter for a more detailed focus on group differences in consumption inequality.

6. Scheduled tribes are less beset by this demarcation because they were traditionally assigned a role outside the pale of the caste system and because for the most part they own some land. They also are more likely to be agriculturists.

7. It is difficult to evaluate precisely the impact of these reservation policies. Borooah, Dubey, and Iyer (2007), for example, found that reservations have increased the representation of SC/STs in the public sector. But they speculate that a policy focusing on improving education or other individual endowments would perhaps have yielded more employment gains. Debate is ongoing about extending reservations to the private sector, but many private sector employers are firmly opposed to the change (Jodhka and Newman 2007).

8. See Banerjee and Knight (1985) and Madeshwaran and Attewell (2007), both focused on urban areas only. The latter study attributes a larger share of the wage gap to worker characteristics. While there are differences in the estimation approach, it is also possible that the role of unequal treatment and caste discrimination is less important in urban India.

9. It is possible that an examination of this question using more disaggregated occupational categories would find some role of unequal treatment within more narrowly defined categories.

10. Migration to cities also provides an escape from the rigidities of the caste system. Caste identities are not as well recognized in urban settings, and new jobs, unlike caste-based, traditional occupations, offer greater flexibility.

11. These results need to be viewed with some caution. Although reservations do encourage some level of equity in access to public goods, the study also found evidence of political capture and private appropriation of public goods.

12. Rao and Ban (2007) used a natural experiment—the 1956 reorganization of Indian states along linguistic lines—to demonstrate that the caste system evolved differently in border villages that otherwise should have

been well matched in their caste structures because of common histories, land distribution, languages, and geographies.

13. On the relationship between education and access to jobs, see chapter 3.

14. See, for instance, the report of the Senthilkumar Solidarity Committee (2008) on the suicide of Senthil, a Dalit research scholar in the University of Hyderabad.

15. Cultural practices and the value attached to traditional occupations passed from one generation to the next could, of course, have very similar effects.

16. See box 1.1, chapter 1 on poverty lines and poverty measures.

17. Using a panel dataset for rural India for the period 1993–94 to 2004–05, Dubey and Verschoor (2007) found that Adivasis are still substantially poorer than upper castes. They earn about half the income the latter do, are more likely to be chronically poor, and are more likely to fall into poverty.

18. See, for instance, *Sheela Barse versus State of Maharashtra*, 1993.

19. Previous analysis seems to indicate that once socioeconomic status is controlled for, the effect of caste or tribal status vanishes in econometric analysis. For instance, our earlier multivariate analysis, using Reproductive and Child Health II survey data, also found that the relationship between infant or child mortality and tribal (or indeed caste) status disappears when we control for wealth quintile and distance to health care (in most cases a private facility) (World Bank 2006). That is corroborated by another recent analysis on child mortality in Orissa, which also found correlation between tribal identity and mortality, controlling for poverty (World Bank 2007).

20. For some tribal groups in the Northeast, for instance, vaccination is a taboo. They believe that blood, once drawn, can be used to put a deadly spell on them. Vaccinating people, therefore, becomes an uphill task.

21. Society for Education, Action and Research in Community Health (SEARCH), in the remote tribal areas of Gadchiroli, Maharashtra, is an international success story in maternal and neonatal health.

22. Even in states such as Jharkhand and Chhattisgarh, which have considerable tribal populations, roughly two-thirds of the population is non-tribal.

23. Dr. Dev Nathan, correspondence dated May 25, 2009.

24. In situations of land conflict, however, roads may have a perverse effect by increasing the value of the land, such that they may increase the risk of Adivasis losing their land.

25. As mentioned earlier, Schedule V of the Indian Constitution identifies special privileges for those areas where the majority of the population belong to scheduled tribes. Schedule VI is different in that it applies special

privileges to tribals who reside in the northeastern states of India. Both Schedules V and VI underscore the area-based approach that the state has followed on addressing tribal issues.

26. The third Millennium Development Goal espouses promotion of gender equality and empowerment of women through targets such as elimination, preferably by 2005, of gender disparities in primary and secondary education and in all levels of education no later than 2015.

27. Northern India, for instance, is known to have a female-to-male sex ratio below 1, and more recently a declining child sex ratio. Complex factors, however, lie behind the declining numbers. Documenting the experiences of families in five districts, one each in five states, John et al. (2009) found that small families are now treated as a veil for not having daughters. Family planning goals are more directly expressed and achieved through planned technological interventions (such as sex determination), thereby leading to lower child sex ratios.

28. This section draws heavily from Das and Desai 2003 and Das 2006, with updates using the 61st round of the NSS.

29. Heise et al. 1994; Morrison, Ellsberg, and Bott 2004. The World Health Organization (WHO 2002) has also conducted detailed estimates of the costs of violence in other areas.

30. See World Bank 2008 for results from Bangladesh.

31. The act has been hailed by feminist groups for its wide definition of domestic violence, covering every possibility of abuse, including all forms of physical, sexual, verbal, emotional, and economic abuse that can harm, cause injury to, or endanger the health, safety, life, limb, or well-being, either mental or physical, of the aggrieved person. Critics claim that the act is draconian and may be misused by women to harass men.

References

Banerjee, A., and R. Somanathan. 2007. "The Political Economy of Public Goods: Some Evidence from India." *Journal of Development Economics* 82 (2): 287–314.

Banerjee, B., and J. B. Knight. 1985. "Caste Discrimination in the Indian Urban Labour Market." *Journal of Development Economics* 17: 277–307.

Bertrand, M., R. Hanna, and S. Mullainathan. 2008. "Affirmative Action in Education: Evidence from Engineering College Admissions in India." Working Paper 13926, National Bureau of Economic Research, Cambridge, MA.

Besley, T., R. Pande, and V. Rao. 2007. "Political Economy of Panchayats in South India." *Economic and Political Weekly* 42 (8): 661–66.

Béteille, A. 1991. *Society and Politics in India: Essays in a Comparative Perspective.* London School of Economics Monographs on Social Anthropology. New Delhi: Oxford University Press.

Borooah, V., A. Dubey, and S. Iyer. 2007. "The Effectiveness of Jobs Reservation: Caste, Religion, and Economic Status in India." *Development and Change* 38: 423–55.

Bulsara, S., and P. Sreenivasa. 2004. "Driven to Bondage and Starvation." *Combat Law* 2 (5). http://www.indiatogether.org/combatlaw/vol2/issue5/bondage.htm.

Burra, N. 2008. "The Political Economy of Tribals in India in the Context of Poverty and Social Exclusion." Paper prepared for the India Poverty and Social Exclusion Report, World Bank, New Delhi.

Chattopadhyay, R., and E. Duflo. 2004. "The Impact of Reservation in the Panchayati Raj: Evidence from a Nationwide Randomized Experiment." *Economic and Political Weekly* 39 (9): 979–86.

Chavan, P. 2008. "Gender Inequality in Banking Services." *Economic and Political Weekly* 43 (47): 18–21.

Das, M. 2006. "Do Traditional Axes of Exclusion Affect Labor Market Outcomes in India?" South Asia Social Development Discussion Paper 3, World Bank, Washington, DC.

———. 2008. "What Money Can't Buy: Getting Implementation Right for MDG3 in South Asia." In *Equality for Women: Where Do We Stand on Millennium Development Goal 3?* ed. M. Buvinić, A. Morrison, A. Ofosu-Amaah, and M. Sjöblom, 261–92. Washington, DC: World Bank.

Das, M., and S. Desai. 2003. "Why Are Educated Women Less Likely to Be Employed in India? Testing Competing Hypotheses." Social Protection Discussion Paper 0313, World Bank, Washington, DC.

Das, M., and P. Dutta. 2007. "Does Caste Matter for Wages in the Indian Labor Market?" Draft paper, World Bank, Washington, DC.

Das, M., G. Hall, S. Kapoor, and D. Nikitin. Forthcoming. "India: The Scheduled Tribes." In *Indigenous Peoples, Poverty and Development*, ed. G. Hall and H. Patrinos. Washington, DC: Cambridge University Press.

Das, M., S. Kapoor, and D. Nikitin. 2010. "A Closer Look at Child Mortality among Adivasis in India." Policy Research Working Paper 5231, World Bank, Washington, DC.

Desai, S., J. Noon, and R. Vanneman. 2008. "Who Gets Good Jobs? The Role of Human, Social, and Cultural Capital." Paper prepared for the India Poverty and Social Exclusion Report, World Bank, New Delhi.

Deshpande, A. 2001. "Caste at Birth? Redefining Disparity in India." *Review of Development Economics* 5 (1): 130–44.

Deshpande, A., and K. Newman. 2007. "Where the Path Leads: The Role of Caste in Post-University Employment Expectations." *Economic and Political Weekly* 42 (41): 4133–40.

Deshpande, R., and S. Palshikar. 2008. "Occupational Mobility: How Much Does Caste Matter?" *Economic and Political Weekly* 43 (44): 61–70.

Dorward, A., S. Anderson, Y. Bernal, F. Vera, J. Rushton, J. Pattison, and R. Raz. 2009. "Hanging In, Stepping Up and Stepping Out: Livelihood Aspirations and Strategies of the Poor." *Development in Practice* 19 (2): 240–47.

Drèze, J., and H. Gazdar. 1997. "Uttar Pradesh: The Burden of Inertia." In *Indian Development: Selected Regional Perspectives,* ed. J. Drèze and A. Sen. New Delhi: Oxford University Press.

Dubey, A., V. Iversen, A. Kalwij, B. Kebede, and A. Verschoor. 2008. "Caste Dominance and Inclusive Growth: Evidence from a Panel Data Set for India." Paper prepared for the India Poverty and Social Exclusion Report, World Bank, New Delhi.

Dubey, A., and A. Verschoor. 2007. "Income Mobility and Poverty Dynamics across Social Groups in India, 1993–2005." Paper presented at the international seminar "Revisiting the Poverty Issue: Measurement, Identification and Eradication," A. N. Sinha Institute, Patna, India, July 20–22.

Dyson, T., and M. Moore. 1983. "On Kinship Structure, Female Autonomy, and Demographic Behavior in India." *Population and Development Review* 9 (1): 35–60.

GoI (Government of India). 2001. *Empowering the Scheduled Tribes: Report of a Steering Committee to Planning Commission.* New Delhi: Planning Commission. http://planningcommission.nic.in/aboutus/committee/strgrp/stg_sts.pdf. Accessed May 2009.

———. 2008. *Development Challenges in Extremist Affected Areas: Report of an Expert Group to Planning Commission.* New Delhi: Planning Commission. http://planningcommission.nic.in/reports/publications/rep_dce.pdf.

Government of Maharashtra and UNICEF-WIO. 1991. *Women and Children in Dharni: A Case Study after Fifteen Years of ICDS.* Mumbai: UNICEF, Western India Office.

Guha, R. 2007. "Adivasis, Naxalites and Indian Democracy." *Economic and Political Weekly* 42 (32): 3305–12.

Heise, L., A. Raikes, C. II. Watts, and A. B. Zwi. 1994. "Violence against Women: A Neglected Public Health Issue in Less-Developed Countries." *Social Science and Medicine* 39 (9): 1165–79.

Hoff, K., and P. Pandey. 2004. "Belief Systems and Durable Inequalities: An Experimental Investigation of Indian Caste." Policy Research Working Paper 3351, World Bank, Washington, DC.

IADB (Inter American Development Bank). 2007. *Outsiders: The Changing Patterns of Exclusion in Latin America and the Caribbean.* Washington, DC: IADB.

Jodhka, S. 2008. "A Forgotten "Revolution": Revisiting Agrarian Change in Haryana." Paper prepared for the India Poverty Assessment, Indian Institute of Dalit Studies, New Delhi.

Jodhka, S., and S. Gautam. 2008. "In Search of a Dalit Entrepreneur: Barriers and Supports in the Life of Self-Employed Scheduled Castes." Paper prepared for the India Poverty Assessment, Indian Institute of Dalit Studies, New Delhi.

Jodhka, S., and K. Newman. 2007. "In the Name of Globalisation: Meritocracy, Productivity and the Hidden Language of Caste." *Economic and Political Weekly* 42 (41): 4125–32.

John, M., R. Kaur, R. Palriwala, and S. Raju. 2009. "Dispensing with Daughters: Technology, Society, Economy in North India." *Economic and Political Weekly* 44 (15): 16–19.

Khandare, L. 2004. *Korku Adivasis in Melghat Region of Maharashtra: A Socio Economic Study*. A course seminar. http://lalitreports.blogspot.com/2004/12/korku-adivasis-in-melghat-region-of.html. Accessed August 2009.

Kijima, Y. 2006. "Caste and Tribe Inequality: Evidence from India, 1983–1999." *Economic Development and Cultural Change* 54 (2): 369–404.

Kishwar, Madhu. 2002. "Working under Constant Threat." *Manushi*, issue 130, May–June.

Madeshwaran, S., and P. Attewell. 2007. "Caste Discrimination in the Indian Urban Labor Market: Evidence from the National Sample Survey." *Economic and Political Weekly* 42 (41): 4146–53.

Maharatna, A. 2005. *Demographic Perspectives on India's Tribes*. New Delhi: Oxford University Press.

Mander. H. 2002. "Tribal Land Alienation in Madhya Pradesh: The Problem and Legislative Remedies." In *Land Reforms in India: Issues of Equity in Rural Madhya Pradesh*, ed. P. Jha. New Delhi: Sage Publications.

Morrison, A., M. Ellsberg, and S. Bott. 2004. "Addressing Gender-Based Violence in Latin American and the Caribbean: A Critical Review of Interventions." Working Paper, World Bank, Washington, DC.

Munshi, K., and M. Rosenzweig. 2006. "Traditional Institutions Meet the Modern World: Caste, Gender and Schooling Choice in a Globalizing Economy." *American Economic Review* 96 (4): 1225–52.

———. 2007. "Why Is Mobility in India So Low? Social Insurance, Inequality, and Growth." International Policy Center Working Paper Series 68, University of Michigan, Ann Arbor.

Nambissan, G. B. 2010. "Exclusion and Discrimination in Schools: Experiences of Dalit Children." In *Blocked by Caste: Economic Discrimination in Modern India,* ed. S. Thorat and K. S. Newman, 253–86. New York: Oxford University Press.

Narayan, D., L. Pritchett, and S. Kapoor. 2009. *Moving Out of Poverty: Success from the Bottom Up.* New York: Palgrave Macmillan; Washington, DC: World Bank.

Panda, P., and B. Agarwal. 2005. "Marital Violence, Human Development and Women's Property Status in India." *World Development* 33 (5): 823–50.

Parasuraman, S., and S. I. Rajan. 1990. "On the Estimation of Vital Rates among the Scheduled Tribes in Western India." In *Demography of Tribal Development,* ed. A. Bose, U. P. Sinha, and R. P. Tyagi. New Delhi: B. R. Publishing Corporation.

Rao, V., and R. Ban. 2007. "The Political Construction of Caste in South India." Draft, World Bank, Washington, DC.

Sainath, P. 2001. "Rajasthan's Drought: Abundance of Food, Scarcity of Vision." *The Hindu,* March 18. http://www.hinduonnet.com/thehindu/2001/03/18/stories/13180611.htm. Accessed April 2009.

Saxena, N. C. 1999. "Forests in Tribal Lives." Government of India Planning Commission. http://planningcommission.nic.in/reports/articles/ncsxna/index.php?repts=ft.htm. Accessed April 2009.

Sen, A. 2000. "Social Exclusion: Concept, Application and Scrutiny." Social Development Papers No. 1, Office of Environment and Social Development, Asian Development Bank, Manila, June.

Senthilkumar Solidarity Committee. 2008. "Caste, Higher Education and Senthil's 'Suicide.'" *Economic and Political Weekly* 43 (33): 10–12.

Silver, H. 1994. "Social Exclusion and Social Solidarity: Three Paradigms." IILS Discussion Papers, No. 69, ILO, Geneva.

Sinha, S. 1958. "Tribal Cultures of Peninsular India as a Dimension of Little Tradition in the Study of Indian Civilization." *Journal of American Folklore* 71: 504–18.

Srinivas, M. N. 1966. *Social Change in Modern India.* New Delhi: Orient Longman.

———. 2003. "An Obituary on Caste as a System." *Economic and Political Weekly* 38 (5): 455–59.

Suchitra, M. 2005. "Remote Adivasis Face Health Care Chasm." *India Together,* July 25. http://www.indiatogether.org/2005/jul/hlt-attappadi.htm. Accessed May 2009.

Thorat, S. 2007. "Economic Exclusion and Poverty: Indian Experience of Remedies against Exclusion." Paper presented at the IFPRI and ADB conference in Manila, August 9–10.

Thorat, S., and P. Attewell. 2007. "The Legacy of Social Exclusion: A Correspondence Study of Job Discrimination in India." *Economic and Political Weekly* 42 (41): 4141–45.

Unni, J. 2001. "Earnings and Education among Ethnic Groups in Rural India." NCAER Working Paper Series 79, National Council of Applied Economic Research, New Delhi.

Walton, Michael. 2007. "Culture Matters for Poverty, but Not because of a Culture of Poverty: Notes on Analytics and Policy." Unpublished paper, Centre for Policy Research, New Delhi; John. F. Kennedy School of Government, Harvard University, Cambridge, MA. http://www.afd.fr/jahia/webdav/site/afd/shared/portails/publications/eudn/eudn2007/walton.pdf.

Wax, E. 2008. "In an Indian Village, Signs of the Loosening Grip of Caste." *Washington Post*, August 31.

Witsoe, J. 2008. "Caste, Public Institutions and Inequality in Bihar." Paper prepared for the India Poverty Assessment, World Bank, Washington, DC.

World Bank. 2006. "Exploratory Analysis of the Health Status of Social Groups from RCH II Data." Work in progress.

———. 2007. *Achieving the MDGs in India's Poor States: Reducing Child Mortality in Orissa*. New Delhi: World Bank.

———. 2008. *Whispers to Voices: Gender and Social Transformation in Bangladesh*. Dhaka: World Bank.

WHO (World Health Organization). 2002. *World Report on Violence and Health*. Geneva: World Health Organization.

Xaxa, V. 2001. "Protective Discrimination: Why Scheduled Tribes Lag behind Scheduled Castes." *Economic and Political Weekly* 36 (29): 2765–72.

———. 2008. *State, Society and Tribes: Issues in Post-Colonial India*. Noida: Pearson Education.